SHARING
HEAVEN'S MUSIC

JAMES EARL MASSEY

SHARING HEAVEN'S MUSIC

The Heart of Christian Preaching

Essays in Honor
of
James Earl Massey

Edited by
Barry L. Callen

ABINGDON PRESS
Nashville

SHARING HEAVEN'S MUSIC

Library of Congress Cataloging-in-Publication Data

Sharing heaven's music: the heart of Christian preaching: essays in honor of James Earl
    Massey/edited by Barry L. Callen
        p.   cm.
    Includes bibliographical references.
    ISBN 0-687-01108-6 (alk. paper)
    1. Preaching. I. Massey, James Earl. II. Callen, Barry L.
    BV4211.2.S49   1995
    251—dc20   95-9007
                                                                                           CIP

95 96 97 98 99 00 01 02 03 04 — 10 9 8 7 6 5 4 3 2 1

CONTENTS

CONTRIBUTORS

Elizabeth R. Achtemeier
Adjunct Professor of Bible and Homiletics, Union Theological Seminary
in Virginia

Ronald J. Allen
Associate Professor of Preaching and New Testament, Christian Theological Seminary

David G. Buttrick
Professor of Homiletics and Liturgics, Vanderbilt University Divinity
School

Barry L. Callen
University Professor of Christian Studies, Anderson University; Editor,
Wesleyan Theological Journal

Donald E. Demaray
Senior Beeson Professor of Biblical Preaching, Asbury Theological Seminary

Michael Duduit
Editor, *Preaching Magazine*; Adjunct Professor of Preaching, Southern
Baptist Theological Seminary

Al Fasol
E. Hermond Westmoreland Professor of Preaching, Southwestern Baptist
Theological Seminary

Justo L. González
Historian and Theologian, former Adjunct Professor of Theology, Columbia Theological Seminary

William L. Lane
Paul T. Walls Professor of Wesleyan and Biblical Studies, Seattle Pacific
University

Thomas G. Long
Francis L. Patton Professor of Preaching and Worship, Princeton Theological Seminary

Henry H. Mitchell
Adjunct Professor of Homiletics, Interdenominational Theological Center (Atlanta)

Calvin S. Morris
Vice President for Academic Services/ Dean, Interdenominational Theological Center, Atlanta

William H. Myers
Professor of New Testament, Ashland Theological Seminary

Frederick W. Norris
Dean E. Walker Professor of Church History and Christian Doctrine, Emmanuel School of Religion

Gail R. O'Day
Almar H. Shatford Associate Professor of Biblical Preaching, Candler School of Theology, Emory University

William E. Pannell
Dean of the Chapel, Professor of Preaching and Evangelism, Fuller Theological Seminary

Robert H. Reardon
President Emeritus, Anderson University

Cheryl J. Sanders
Associate Professor of Christian Ethics, School of Divinity, Howard University

Jicelyn I. Thomas
Elder, United Methodist Church, Ph.D. Student, Vanderbilt University

William H. Willimon
Dean of the Chapel, Professor of Christian Ministry, Divinity School, Duke University

INTRODUCTION

Mﾠore than the twentieth century is coming to an end. According to numerous observers and analysts, so is a whole intellectual and spiritual era in human history. The "modern" age is in definite decay, and what is to follow, the "postmodern," is only now beginning to take shape. The current cultural shift may turn out to be as dramatic as the collapse of the medieval consensus that opened the way for the Protestant Reformation in the sixteenth century. Considerable Protestant-like deconstructing of the modernist (Enlightenment) consensus is now underway. We need, says Justo González, a "metamodern" way of reading Scripture, culture, and the task of preaching. Today is, according to William Willimon, a wonderful time to declare the Christian gospel with conviction!

A Matter of Perspective

The task of Christian proclamation goes on in the midst of all change in cultural perspective. In fact, preaching also is a matter of perspective. On one hand, Christian preaching is rooted in an enduring good news that sheds divine light on all times and subjects. On the other, public applications of the gospel require sensitivity to shifting worldviews so that gospel relevance can be communicated effectively. Those who would preach today, probably more than ever before, are faced with a maze of expectations about exactly what they should be doing in the midst of the community of believers and beyond.

Especially when times are changing so rapidly and fundamentally, wisdom is at a premium. Today proclamation of the Christian gospel is languishing in its public influence. The mainline churches are suffering membership decline as the process of their cultural disestablishment accelerates. The cult of the individual and the curse of consumerism have infected both pulpit and pew. Part of the hope in the coming new time is that some way will be found out of this modern morass. John Cobb, himself exploring one philosophic perspective as a possible way of interpreting Christian hope for the future, poses the key question in a recent book title: "Can Christ become good news again?"[1]

---

1. John B. Cobb, Jr., *Can Christ Become Good News Again?* (St. Louis: Chalice Press, 1991).

Dr. James Earl Massey already has helped the church by pioneering in the business of perspective. Three of his many influential books are *The Responsible Pulpit* (Anderson, Ind.: Warner Press, 1974), *The Sermon in Perspective* (Grand Rapids: Baker Book House, 1976), and *Designing the Sermon* (Nashville: Abingdon Press, 1980).[2] He has explored the sermon and sermonizing from multiple angles. More than publishing homiletic theory, however, for decades he has been a premier preacher of the Christian gospel and a personal model of its transforming potential.

In one sense, Massey has been a deconstructionist, assaulting with penetrating gospel insight some walls that never should have been built. He has crossed racial and denominational lines freely, troubling the security of old and humanly prejudiced paradigms with the sharp edge of the biblical Word (see the Henry Mitchell interview with Massey, 203). A man with sturdy apostolic roots, but not locked mechanically in the past, his has been a truly prophetic voice altering the present by being focused on God's future in the eschatological style explained by Thomas Long. As William Pannell insists is essential, Massey has pursued holiness, practiced ethical relevance, and preached under God's anointing.

Massey has bridged the gulf between faith and learning too often found in the university environment (see William H. Willimon, p. 21). He has broached with gentle courage the reluctant racial barriers in North American society and in the church, as all preachers should be doing (see Ronald J. Allen and Jicelyn I. Thomas, p. 165). He has risen above the entrenched denominational divisions that have both spawned and impeded the ecumenical movement of the twentieth century. Massey has been God's man in changing times. He has both taught and demonstrated that to declare God's good news is to be a servant of biblical meanings as they find application to human needs.

The sermon is to be a structured declaration of the *kerygma*, the divine Word, as Elizabeth Achtemeier explains clearly. According to Gail O'Day, it is to be a creative conversation between biblical text and contemporary preacher. It is a vivid, perceptive, faithful handling of the biblical Word that still can put a hearer's life in perspective and yield essential direction for living in the midst of whatever "postmodern" turns out to mean. Such inspired communication can set contemporary people free—free to be and to become; to act thoughtfully, even prophetically; to share and to serve; to find true community; to participate in the continuing drama of Christ's saving grace.

---

2. A select bibliography of the published works of Dr. Massey is found elsewhere in this volume.

The path pursued by Massey during a lifetime of preaching, pastoring, publishing, and teaching turns out to be that narrow way that Christ opened long ago. This way remains relevant, even into the next stage of human history. Therefore, it is appropriate that, in honor of this exceptional Christian communicator, the most respected and creative Christian homileticians of our generation address themselves to the challenge of what should and can follow the dilemmas of the present transition.

Each chapter of this book was prepared especially for this volume in honor and celebration of the contributions of James Earl Massey, close friend and valued colleague of all the writers. The contributors explore the multicultural hearers of the Word today, the biblical and theological foundations that still define that Word, and the skills required to communicate it effectively in our changing times.

The Metaphor of Music

Volumes like this one often flounder in sentimentality. They wade in the shallow waters of good intentions and feature an array of disconnected material, all in honor of one who is anything but shallow and disconnected. Any such weakness in these pages is the fault of the editor, not the writers. There has been an attempt to overcome the typical failures by setting a theme that draws the several pieces into one coordinated whole, a theme wholly consistent with the person being honored and the subject being addressed. This theme is music.

James Earl Massey, a prince of preachers, also is a concert pianist who received his call to preach while sitting in church memorizing musical scores (see the Mitchell interview). He represents a particular preaching tradition, African American, in which music and the act of preaching are inseparable. He also identifies as his home a particular theological tradition, Wesleyan and Church of God (Anderson, Indiana), in which music has been a central means of making clear and contagious the content and life implications of the gospel of Jesus Christ.[3]

So this volume's title is *Sharing Heaven's Music*. The gospel itself has a cadence, rhythm, and joy that should be music to the world. It's non-Enlightenment dimensions of vision, imagination, and poetic approaches to grasping and sharing truth are especially relevant to postmodern sensibilities. Designing a Christian sermon is an inspired art form as much

---

3. See, e. g., T. Crichton Mitchell, *Charles Wesley: Man with the Dancing Heart* (Kansas City: Beacon Hill Press, 1994); and Robert Adams, "The Hymnody of the Church of God (1885–1980) as a Reflection of That Church's Theological and Cultural Changes" (Ph.D. diss., Southwestern Baptist Theological Seminary, 1980).

as it is a learned skill. Today's multicultural settings, usually discordant, can be transformed by the harmonizing gospel so that diversity becomes a rich melody that witnesses to the God who comes to make all things new and all disciples one.

Christian preachers are to be "God's trombones" (see Cheryl Sanders, p. 151) who help the gospel sing its way into human hearts (see Donald Demaray, p. 109). The people of God are to dance in joy because they hear "the music of God's future being played in the present" (see Thomas Long, p. 191). David Buttrick speaks prophetically of the wonderful mystery of laughing with the gospel (p. 125). May the sheer joy of God's liberating good news be proclaimed anew!

Barry L. Callen

PART · ONE

The Program

PREACHING: PEW RIGHTS AND PROPHECY

William E. Pannell

N ot long ago it seemed as if the powers that defined theological education had concluded that preaching had become obsolete. Such judgment was premature.

The Fall and Rise of Preaching

The church, according to this strand of supposed wisdom, had outgrown the preaching form of communication. Indeed, both the church and the people it was called to serve required something more basic—something that would really speak to their "modern" condition.

The new communication options being offered ranged all the way from the streets to the couch. In the streets were those millions of marching feet propelling bodies against the ramparts of a thousand and one injustices. Words were important during those times, from Berkeley to Boston, but they were not the words used by the church. Action was the proper mode; exegesis was considered obsolete. With the flowering of the therapeutic society, what people really needed—the salvation they craved—was not to be found in the churches.

New prophets had arisen to fill the insatiable need for counseling, and, by the late 1960s, preaching had been eclipsed by this contemporary ministerial "art form." For many, theology had been replaced by psychology. The church, meanwhile, tended to sleep through this dramatic change, in large part because so much of the preaching it was hearing was sleep-inducing.

There were some voices out there trying to correct the situation. The late Karl Menninger was one of them. While lamenting the sad shape many pastors were in personally, Menninger reserved his greatest sadness for pastors whose regard for the preaching task had eroded so far as to render them powerless in the pulpit or in the larger society. "We know," he wrote:

> that the principal leadership in the moral realm should be the clergy's, but they seem to minimize their great traditional and historical opportunity to preach, to prophesy, to speak out. . . . Some clergymen prefer pastoral counseling of individuals to the pulpit function. But the latter is a greater opportunity to both heal *and prevent*. . . . Clergymen have a golden opportunity to prevent some of the accumulated misapprehensions, guilt, aggressive action, and other roots of later mental suffering and mental disease. How? Preach! Tell it like it is. Say it from the pulpit. Cry it from the housetops. What shall we cry? Cry comfort, cry repentance, cry hope. Because recognition of our part in the world's transgression is the only remaining hope.[1]

That was one voice crying in the wilderness of churchly and ecclesiastical fashion. I do not know how it was received in preaching departments across the land, because I had not yet ascended to the halls of academe in the early 1970s. I was still an itinerant evangelist, a preacher, and I had little doubt about the place of preaching in the life of the church and its evangelistic outreach.

I was not alone, of course. By then many people, Christians and non-believers alike, had had their lives changed by the power of the Word *spoken*. By the early 1960s, the country had been powerfully affected by two Baptist preachers, one black and the other white, who had, between them, set the parameters of public discourse in the nation. They were Billy Graham, the evangelist, and Martin Luther King, Jr., the prophet. Together, though on many issues far apart, they shaped the meaning of Christianity in the minds of millions of people worldwide. They did it by preaching. One of them brought massive crowds to numerous outdoor stadiums, while the other added a little marching to his moving rhetoric and helped to change the face of the nation.

America has always listened to preachers. If Page Smith is right when he asserts that the country was conceived by dreams and that those dreams were then spoken into being,[2] those words were not just the words of politicians or statesmen. In a more profound sense, they were

---

1. Karl Menninger, *Whatever Became of Sin?* (New York: Hawthorn Books, 1973), 228.
2. Page Smith, *The Shaping of America* (New York: McGraw-Hill, 1980), xiv.

the Word spoken by preachers and by theologians who could preach. This shaping of a people through preaching was possible because there was an expectancy abroad that when clergy spoke, they spoke God's Word. There was a certain resonance in the culture that responded to this preachment that formed the sounding board for the preacher.

Getting the Hearers into the Act

African Americans were especially "vulnerable" to preaching. The various cultures of Africa were profoundly oral in much of their communication tradition. African slaves in America were sustained by that tradition in both music and speech. Indeed, as preaching developed within the emerging African church on American soil, music and speech blended and formed a new style of communication, a blend of Christian content and African rhythms of speech. This rhythmic quality of preaching often distinguishes black preaching from any other expression in the American preaching tradition. And it is this rhythmic cadence in black preaching that contributes to the "dialogue" that occurs on Sunday morning in the black church setting.

Preaching, to be validated, needs an audience, a people who hear. "How can they hear without someone preaching to them?" (Rom. 10:14 NIV). This is true whether one refers to the broader secular society or that smaller society called church.

I recall a columnist for the *Detroit News* writing about the power of preaching. It was not his usual topic, but he had just returned from a public rally in that racially torn city. The speaker was Martin Luther King, Jr., and the journalist had been profoundly moved. He concluded his column with words to this effect: "I have always thought that the experience of this day was what church should be, and if there was preaching like that in the churches, there would be fewer of us who could stay away."

So the challenge for the preacher is not a simple matter of good homiletics and delivery. It may be that the first consideration should be to the audience. Those who listen are not just there for the preacher. They are part of the act of preaching. They are not simply receptors; they bring to the encounter all the stuff that makes preaching necessary and possible. And many of those listeners know more theology than preachers allow.

I recall a seminarian who approached me about his class in theology. His professor was a world-renowned scholar whose theology was "off the charts" on the liberal side. "What should I do with this man's theology?" the student asked. Not brimming over with style that day, I told him, "Nothing. There is no music to it, and it won't dance. Get the work done, pass the man's class, and then go back to your congregation and they'll save you from that mess." I smiled, of course, but he caught the seriousness of my intention. He knew then that I knew something about his tradition. He was aware that I knew his congregation would not allow him to flounder too long on the shoals of bad theology, because they would talk back. They would help him preach. He could trust them every Sunday morning to make him a better preacher than the one he was on Saturday night.

To raise the question "What's the greatest sermon you ever heard?" is to raise a profound question about how different people at different times and places hear.

I am impressed by Roger Van Harn's insight about the expectations people had when they came to the synagogue and heard the young rabbi Jesus. Van Harn is right when he argues that Jesus' sermon set them on their collective ears that day when he placed Israel's future hopes in the present moment. Funny how a simple word like *now* or *today* can get a preacher run out of town! Van Harn's book, entitled *Pew Rights*, is subtitled "For People Who Listen to Sermons."[3]

Here, then, may be the beckoning frontier for the great tradition of preaching. We may be about to recognize that preaching and listening are inseparable and indispensable, complementary and potentially explosive. What's the best sermon you ever heard? is the flip side of another question, one addressed to the preacher: When was the last time you took a listening audience seriously?

I doubt that any tradition has been in closer sync with its audience than that represented by the black preacher. Sojourner Truth knew what the text meant because she was part of the audience before and during the message. Preaching that takes its shape from within a culture of suffering has a dialogue built within the communication process. It is a call-and-response dynamic that confirms in preaching and hearing that God also has heard, has spoken, and now is prepared to speak—from the pulpit, to and with the people! Thus black preaching begins in the audience; it is given birth within a community with a shared history of yearning to hear the voice of God.

It is because of this association with an oppressed people yearning to hear God's voice that black preaching became the vehicle of hope for oppressed people all over the world. It also became the voice of encouragement to people of goodwill who could be called to action on behalf

---

3. Roger Van Harn, *Pew Rights: For People Who Listen to Sermons* (Grand Rapids: Eerdmans, 1992), 7-9.

of the oppressed. Thus black preaching from the earliest days became, with increasing power, the voice of conscience in a nation of immigrants still yearning to be free.

Preaching and Sacred Anointing

If preaching has the power to stir the conscience of a nation, then it requires preachers whose consciences are clear about the things that stir the heart of God. Effective preaching is the means by which a holy God fastens his gaze upon a sinful humanity and reveals that he knows its failure of character and behavior.

Preaching is, therefore, profoundly ethical in nature. Thus to be a carrier of this insight requires of the preacher a character that is being shaped by the same Word that is being preached. In short, preaching demands that the preacher be a person of integrity. To argue this may sound like a given too obvious to mention. To others, however, it may be an altogether strange assertion. It is made in the light of recent breakdowns among the clergy, including some outstanding preachers—breakdowns suggesting that the connection between character and charisma was lost. Even those who write about the craft of preaching and the necessity for the preacher to address the culture in creative ways give short shrift to the spiritual or character development of the preacher.

This failure to identify holiness in the life of the preacher as a starting point for anointed preaching seems to be a recent development. Any cursory examination of the materials that chronicle the careers of great preachers reveals what a prominent place this emphasis had in their lives. Congregations had come to expect this of their preachers, and often they gloried in this aspect of the ministry more than any other. Even the nonchurched seemed to expect that holiness of life was the *sina qua non* for the occupant of the manse.

Consider, for example, the lectures of Charles Haddon Spurgeon to his students. Commenting on Spurgeon's lifelong emphasis on the proper education for the preaching task, Helmut Thielicke writes: "For the really determinative foundation of the education of preachers was naturally this work on the spiritual man." And on the use of the Scriptures in this process, the German scholar argues that the preacher "must first read it as nourishment for his own soul. For the light which we are to let shine before men is a borrowed light, a mere reflection."[4] If the Scriptures are

---

4. Helmut Thielicke, *Encounter with Spurgeon* (Grand Rapids: Baker Book House, 1975), 10.

the source of the light that is reflected in preaching, it is the Holy Spirit who makes of that light a luminous Presence. Preaching is an encounter with God, and this awesome task requires that the preacher abide in the anointing of God, what Spurgeon called "the sacred anointing."

In this connection, the late Martyn Lloyd-Jones spoke of the difference between a profession and a calling. His text was Romans 1:9 and Paul's sensitive insight about servanthood: "For God is my witness whom I serve with my spirit in the gospel of His Son." Lloyd-Jones argued passionately that a profession is something outside the person, external to the person and thus under the person's control. A calling is internal, subject to the yearnings of the Spirit within, something one cannot walk away from at the end of the day. "You take up your bag, and you put it down when you have done with it. Not so with this. This is something within a man!"[5]

An older generation of saints and preachers referred to this as the "unction," and it is tragic to note that in most traditions where preaching is still part of the worship service, this expectation for preaching is largely missing. So thousands of churchgoers return to their homes impressed with the preaching (sometimes!), but not with the awesome reality of having encountered God.

Preaching is that peculiar encounter that takes place between a preacher and God and between God and a people when the Word is preached in the anointing of the Spirit. When this occurs, the rights of the pew are honored and the will of God is revealed, whether for a congregation or a nation. To God be the glory.

Our times yet yearn for true freedom and anointed preaching. The most recent generation, disillusioned by people, politics, and reform programs that often fall short of their goals, seeks a voice that speaks boldly, meaningfully to the vacuum. They are the audience now yearning to be in dialogue with a voice that brings a word of hope, divine hope.[6] The day of preaching should be today!

---

5. Tony Sargent, *The Sacred Anointing: The Preaching of Dr. Martyn Lloyd-Jones* (Wheaton, Ill.: Crossway Books, 1994), 31.

6. See the next chapter, "Hunger in This Abandoned Generation" by William Willimon, for an explanation of the current Generation X.

HUNGER IN THIS ABANDONED GENERATION

William H. Willimon

When standing up to preach, the preacher must speak to the hungers of people who sit in the pews. Every time James Earl Massey has stood up to break the bread of the gospel, his gentle, dignified words have assured us that important matters were under discussion, that our needs would be taken seriously, and above all that we would be fed. Good preachers know the peculiar hungers of their age and have confidence that the gospel is the Bread of Life for which we hunger.

James Earl Massey has spent most of his life in ministry to students, undergraduates and professional students. Time and again in his own ministry, at Tuskegee and Anderson, James Earl Massey managed to listen to a new generation of students, to hear their questions, their dreams, and then to preach to their hungers. For many of us who now preach on college and university campuses, he has become a model for how the gospel ought to be communicated to the young.

Parable of the Shark

How can one characterize the present age? An Episcopal priest remembered for me the following scene from the movie *Jaws*, which I take to be a metaphor for us.

A marine biologist arrives from Woods Hole. In a desperate attempt to find out what is going awry with the sharks in the area, a local fisherman catches a large shark and brings it into the laboratory. The marine biologist lays the shark up on a table and proceeds to do an autopsy. He slits open the shark's belly and out comes first one fish and then another.

Dozens of fish are extracted from the belly. Then there's a blender, an old license plate, and assorted bits and pieces of this and that. The shark really is an "eating machine," an utterly indiscriminate eating machine. The shark had been consuming everything in sight.

Let this be a parable of modern people. We consume everything indiscriminately—fish, old blenders, license plates. We have deep, vast hungers. We attempt to satisfy them in myriad indiscriminate ways.

The best and the worst of a society often are mirrored by its youth. For instance, the University of Vermont now holds the dubious honor of leading all other colleges and universities in student alcohol and drug abuse, according to a U.S. Department of Education survey. According to the study, 57.7 percent of the university's students under the age of 21 admitted to binge drinking at least once during the two-week period prior to the survey, compared to the national average of 47.5 percent. Furthermore, 40.6 percent binged at least twice during the same two-week period, compared to 33 percent for the country as a whole. Among those 21 and older, 49 percent binged during the survey period, compared to 35 percent for the nation.

On average, the university's students consume 6.5 drinks a week, compared to 5.3 drinks nationally for students attending four-year colleges. A recent survey found that students at colleges with fewer than 2,500 students consume an average of 6.9 drinks a week, while students at larger institutions, with more than 20,000 students, report 4.3 drinks per week on average. The big, impersonal university, therefore, is no sufficient explanation for alcohol abuse. Behind these statistics, then, is some sort of void that is being fed by the widespread alcohol abuse on college and university campuses.

One particularly troubling disclosure in the University of Vermont study was the fact that 37.1 percent of Vermont's students drove once a year while intoxicated or under the influence, while 9.4 percent admitted to doing so six to nine times a year. Eighteen percent of University of Vermont students acknowledged taking sexual advantage of somebody else as a result of drinking. Not surprisingly, the University of Vermont is ranked the third "best" party school in the nation by *Playboy*. Alcohol was a contributing factor in the deaths of four of the university's students in five years.

Unfortunately, the University of Vermont is not an exception, unless it is this school's exceptional willingness to expose its students' alcohol abuse patterns to public scrutiny. In 1994 a commission convened by the Center on Addiction and Substance Abuse at Columbia University, with Joseph Califano, Jr., as chair, issued a rather alarming report titled "Rethinking Rites of Passage: Substance Abuse on America's Campuses."

It noted that now one in three college students drinks primarily to get drunk. In a curious perversion of the Women's Movement, the number of women who reported drinking to get drunk more than tripled between 1977 and 1993, a rate now equal to that of men. According to the U.S. Surgeon General, our country's college students drink nearly four billion cans of beer and enough wine and liquor to bring the annual consumption of alcoholic beverages up to 34 gallons a person. The Califano report noted that college students spend $5.5 billion a year on alcohol, more than on all other beverages—and their books—combined. The average student spends $446 on alcohol per year, far exceeding the per capita expenditure for the college library.

Not surprisingly, the beer industry targets young adults as its best hope for increasing sales. Thus NCAA basketball telecasts are heavily sponsored by beer companies. On campus, when we speak of "TV revenues" from intercollegiate athletics, we mean "beer revenue." One rarely sees anyone my age in a beer commercial. Beer consumption has been declining among adult Americans each year for the past decade, except for one group of adults—college aged students, many of whom are under the legal drinking age. It is sad that our students, who ought to be among the nation's most thoughtful young adults, are so easily manipulated by sophisticated Madison Avenue gurus.

For youth off campus, the picture is equally disturbing. The rate of violent crimes committed by youth in the United States rose by 25 percent during the 1980s. The teenage suicide rate has tripled over the past three decades. Suicide is the second leading cause of death of 15 to 19 year olds. A Gallup Poll found that 15 percent of American teenagers have seriously considered suicide and that 6 percent have actually tried it. Over 70 percent of teenage suicides involve the frequent use of alcohol or drugs.[1] The image of our nation's best and brightest mindlessly consuming large amounts of alcohol is not an attractive one, yet it is an image that accurately portrays an important aspect of today's young adults. The omnivorous shark is us.

Spiritually Unconnected

How can one characterize today's generation of young adults? I have sometimes called today's twenty-something crowd "The Abandoned Generation."[2] Today's young adults have the dubious distinction of

---

1. Thomas H. Naylor, Magdalena R. Naylor, and William H. Willimon, *The Search for Meaning* (Nashville: Abingdon Press, 1994).
2. William H. Willimon, "Reaching and Teaching the Abandoned Generation," *The Christian Century*, October 20, 1993, 187-90.

being our nation's most aborted generation. After scores of interviews with them, Susan Littwin called them "The Postponed Generation,"[3] those children of the children of the 1960s who were raised by parents so uncertain of their own values that they dared not attempt to pass them on to their young. Recently, *The Wallstreet Journal*, in an article on the shrunken futures of today's recent college graduates, called them "The Damned Generation." Not too flattering a collection of labels for today's novice adults.

I know of no better observer of this generation than one of its own, Vancouver novelist Douglas Coupland, a young writer whose novel *Generation X* provides one of the more popular ways of characterizing young adults today.[4] In Coupland's most recent novel, *Life After God*, we see a series of snapshots of a generation wandering, the first generation, says Coupland, raised by parents who no longer even took the trouble not to believe in God.

> I have never really felt like I was "from" anywhere; home to me . . . is a shared electronic dream of cartoon memories, half-hour sitcoms and national tragedies. I have always prided myself on my lack of accent—my lack of any discernible regional flavor. I used to think mine was a Pacific Northwest accent, from where I grew up, but then I realized my accent was simply the accent of nowhere—the accent of a person who has no fixed home in their mind.[5]

Here is a generation, many of whom have never had enough sense of place, roots, or identity to consider themselves lost. "Lost" implies that one was once somewhere, that once there was a home. Speaking with some of his young adult friends, a character in *Life After God* exudes cynicism as he declares, "I know you guys think my life is some big joke— that it's going nowhere. But I'm happy. And it's not like I'm lost or anything. We're all too . . . middle class to ever be lost. Lost means you had faith or something to begin with and the middle class never really had any of that. So we can never be lost. And you tell me, Scout—what is it we end up being, then—what exactly is it we end up being then—instead of being lost?"[6]

---

3. Susan Littwin, *The Postponed Generation: Why America's Grown-Up Kids Are Growing Up Later* (New York: Morrow and Co., 1986).

4. Douglas Coupland, *Generation X: Tales of An Accelerated Culture* (New York: St. Martin's Press, 1991).

5. Douglas Coupland, *Life After God* (New York: Pocket Books, 1994), 174.

6. Ibid., 305.

At times, James Earl Massey's preaching to young adults has meant helping those from narrow and limited backgrounds to grow out of their provincialism and to expand their intellectual horizons through the gospel. At other times, in days of stormy student protest, Massey has quietly but firmly asserted the revolutionary quality of the message of Jesus. What ought to be our message in the present age, this age of young people who live, if Douglas Coupland has it right, with "no fixed home in their mind"? Here is the way Chicago's Allan Bloom puts the problem:

> The souls of young people are in a condition like that of the first men in the state of nature—spiritually unclad, unconnected, isolated, with no inherited or unconditional connection with anything or anyone. They can be anything they want to be, but they have no particular reason to want to be anything in particular.[7]

A Countercultural Adventure

I believe that communication of the gospel to this generation of young adults requires a rethinking of the task of our preaching. In speaking to "The Abandoned Generation," we are not calling them back to something they have previously known but have now forgotten; we are not attempting to open them up from a closed-minded provincialism of their childhood years; we are not doing cautious Christian nurture of youth who, having been raised in a basically Christian culture, now need a little spiritual nudge to cultivate the best that is within them. We are taking people to places they have never been, calling them to become part of a countercultural adventure called discipleship, assaulting them with a weird way of configuring the world called the gospel, adopting them, giving them a new home called church.

My last congregation met next to the synagogue in Greenville, South Carolina. The rabbi and I often had coffee on Mondays. Over coffee one Monday, I noted to the rabbi my surprise that our church was experiencing an influx of young adults, particularly single young adults of college age and just beyond. In my previous congregations, this had been the most difficult age group to reach, thus my surprise to discover these young people returning to the church.

The rabbi replied, "Hardly a week goes by that we don't have some twenty-something person show up at the synagogue saying, 'I want to be

---

7. Allan Bloom, *The Closing of the American Mind* (New York: Simon and Schuster, 1987), 290.

a Jew again. My parents were only nominally Jewish, but I want to be Jewish for real.' "

"What is this?" I asked. "Is this part of the Reagan years, some new conservative trend?"

The rabbi said, "I think they're looking for their parents. We've got a generation who have been so inadequately parented that they are desperate for parents, roots, and identity. I think they're looking for their parents."

And that is what I have found to be one of the most appealing aspects of this generation of young adults—appealing, at least, to a preacher like me or James Earl Massey. These young people are willing to listen, amazingly willing to sit still and to focus if we are bold enough to speak. For what could a preacher ask but that? My student generation of the 1960s was unable to hear words spoken by anyone over thirty. Our parents had lied to us. They did not tell us the truth about Vietnam; they failed to be straight with us about civil rights. We had to discover these truths for ourselves. If our parents had been wrong on such important issues, was there any reason to listen to them on any other major matter?

Thus we in the 1960s saw ourselves as inaugurating the "Age of Aquarius." Everything was so fresh and new that we had to make up the rules as we went along, and without instruction from those who had gone before because they had taken so many wrong turns. During my sophomore year of college, Joseph Fletcher published *Situation Ethics.*[8] Faced with such fresh, new moral dilemmas like lust, we assumed that we must jettison the wisdom of the past and think for ourselves, do our own thing. And we did.

But now, what of our children? In her book *Campus Life,* Helen Lefkowitz Horowitz, in chronicling the development of undergraduate culture on American colleges and universities since the end of the eighteenth century, concludes with a hopeful observation. The children of the rebels of the 1960s were now entering college. She predicted that they would bring with them to campus "an assertive independence" and "heightened consciences." She foresaw that there would be a new brand of college rebel, a student who wants to learn, who believes in academic accomplishment, but who is free of the mindless grade-chasing that characterized many of the students she observed in the 1980s. She predicted that these children, new rebels who were children of the old rebels of the 1960s, would work for positive change and would soon be "transcending the tired plots of the past to create new scenarios."[9]

---

8. Joseph Fletcher, *Situation Ethics: The New Morality* (Philadelphia: The Westminster Press, 1966).

9. Helen Lefkowitz Horowitz, *Campus Life* (New York: A. A. Knopf, 1987).

Horowitz's dreams were dashed by Susan Littwin who, in her 1986 book *The Postponed Generation*, showed clearly that the children of my student generation were anything but committed students and earnest campus activists. The children of the children of the 1960s, rather than committed, were characterized more by their mindless consumerism, their binge drinking on campus, and their political cynicism and disengagement.

In my opinion, in many of today's young adults we are seeing the results of our parenting—or lack of it. Our major educational project was breaking free of our parents and their traditions and communities. As parents have always done, we naturally assumed that our children would have the same project. We were surprised to discover what nearly every generation of parents before us has discovered: Our children did not want the same world that we wanted; they did not come from the same place from which we came. We wanted to break free; our children had little need to break free (having been raised by us). Our children yearned more for roots than for freedom.

The differences in perception between generations accounts for the vast differences between generations. David Buttrick has recently made a good case for the argument that those of us who are called to preach had better get in our heads a good understanding of how the world looks to those to whom we speak.[10] When comparing today's adults to today's young adults, I characterize the differences in generational perception this way: When my generation thinks "space exploration," we think of heroic John Glenn going up against the Russians, or perhaps the "One Giant Leap for Mankind" on the moon. Last year, when Harvard's Arthur Levine asked young adults on twenty-eight campuses to name the social or political event that best characterized their generation's view of the world, the one most often mentioned was a schoolteacher being blown up in the *Challenger*.[11]

Here is another example of a difference in perception that leads to a difference in hearing in this generation: Divorce was invented by my generation sometime in the early 1970s. Up until that time, this country's divorce rate was characterized by amazing stability and lack of growth. Divorce was often depicted in the 1970s as the natural outgrowth of a generation come of age. Unwilling to be trapped in drab, bourgeois mar-

---

10. David Buttrick, "Who Is Listening?" in Gail R. O'Day and Thomas G. Long, eds., *Listening to the Word: Studies in Honor of Fred B. Craddock* (Nashville: Abingdon Press, 1993), 189-206.

11. Arthur Levine, "The Making of a Generation," *Change* (September/October 1993): 8-14.

riages, we would put that behind us, venture forth, be liberated, free, on our own. As a campus minister in the nineties, working with undergraduates, I quickly learned that this generation of students has a distinctly different impression of divorce. Divorce is something that happened to them when they were twelve. Divorce looks different from the bottom looking up.

Having left our children nowhere to stand, we produced a generation of young adults desperate for somewhere to be, the "abandoned generation" eagerly listening for a word that might help to overcome their crisis of identity, a crisis characterized by their designation as Generation X.

Douglas Coupland claims that this generation's "life was charmed but without politics or religion. It was the life of the children of the children of the pioneers—life after God—a life of earthly salvation on the edge of heaven."

Then the narrator catches himself in midsentence and doubt creeps in, not the conventional doubt of the person who once had faith but now has none, but the new doubt of the once proud, self-sufficient, liberated, and autonomous modern person who has the nagging doubt that maybe, just maybe, there is something beyond this alleged earthly paradise, something which we know now only through gnawing, but ill-expressed hunger:

> Perhaps this is the finest thing to which we may aspire, the life of peace, the blurring between dream life and real life—and yet I find myself speaking these words with a sense of doubt. I think there was a trade-off somewhere along the line. I think the price we paid for our golden life was an inability to fully believe in love; instead we feigned an irony that scorched everything it touched. And I wonder if this irony is the price we paid for the loss of God. But then I must remind myself that we are living creatures—we have religious impulses—we must—and yet into what cracks do these impulses flow in a world without religion? It is something I think about every day. Sometimes I think it is the only thing I should be thinking about.[12]

A Time to Speak

This ambivalence about disbelief, this pervasive cynicism matched by a yearning to believe in anything if given half a chance to believe in something is what most impresses me, as a preacher, about this generation of young adults. They will listen because today's "abandoned gener-

---

12. Coupland, *Life After God*, 273-74.

ation" brings a new curiosity and openness to the gospel. Leaders of the church, therefore, might need to revise some of their conventional wisdom about the imperviousness of young adult hearts to the gospel. Thomas Long says it well:

> There is a growing recognition that it is not enough for the community of faith to wait around for the "boomers" to drift back. . . . Conventional wisdom holds that there are three broad phases in religious commitment: There is childhood, a pliable and receptive age when religious instruction can and should be given; there is mature adulthood, when people, given the right incentives, can be persuaded to take on the responsibilities of institutional church life. In between childhood and adulthood, there is the vast wasteland of adolescence and young adulthood, a time when most people wander, or run away from their religious roots. The most that a community of faith can do in this middle period is to wait patiently, to leave people alone in their season of rebellion, smiling with the knowledge that, by the time these rebels arrive at their thirties, they will probably be back in the pews and may well be heading up the Christian education committee. This conventional wisdom is wrong.[13]

Long feels that the contemporary church must take the religious wanderings of Generation X with new seriousness. The time is ripe for new strategies of evangelization and Christian education of a generation who, having been left to their own devices, religiously speaking, now needs to be addressed by the church.

This leads to a few concluding observations about preaching to the hungers of the abandoned generation.

1. I find in today's young adults a new respect for tradition matched with a growing cynicism about modernity. When I first became a pastor (1972), many couples whom I married wanted to write their own wedding services. It has now been a decade since any couple has asked me for that privilege. Having seen so many marriages dissolve, today's young adults seem grateful for any wisdom the past may have to offer as they make their unions.

We are living in a world now to be described as "postmodern." The modern world, characterized by unbounded faith in science and technology, confidence in objectivity and universal values, is over. The younger generation knew this before the rest of us. Therefore, we need not continue to apologize because the Bible is an ancient, culturally conditioned book. The postmodern person knows that all of us are culturally conditioned.

---

13. Thomas G. Long, "Beavis and Butt-Head Get Saved," *Theology Today* (July 1994): 199-203.

The modern point of view is just that—a point of view. The modern world is not a fixed fact to which Christians must somehow struggle to adapt ourselves and our message. The modern world is a point of view, a moment in the long history of humanity, a moment that may be ending. Science no longer holds its once privileged place in intellectual discourse. Therefore, those of us who work on Sundays out of a premodern book, the Bible, will be pleased to find a generation of postmoderns more open to biblical insights, less prejudiced against all things that occurred before Francis Bacon, more willing to consider the claims of biblical faith, less prone to judge all truth, all insight, and every statement on the basis of what has happened personally to us.

2. This shift of perspective means that those of us who have expended a great deal of theological energy translating biblical faith into the thought patterns of the modern world, accommodating our truth claims to what modernity deemed permissible, may find ourselves in difficult circumstances when it comes to communicating with today's young adults. After a number of decades of reducing the Christian faith to something that nine out of ten intelligent, average, sensitive modern Americans can affirm, we may now need to rediscover how wonderfully weird is the Christian faith!

I find in today's young adults (say, in comparison with middle-aged professors in university departments of religion) a marvelous, open-minded curiosity about the weird, particularly the religiously weird. Rather than accommodating ourselves to what we believe to be the limits of modern, positivistic people, we ought exuberantly to explore the weird, the surprising, and the shocking within biblical faith. In their cynicism about merely political solutions to what ails us, today's young adults tend to exhibit a keen perception that what is needed to heal us is something beyond the political, more than the economic, something of the spirit.

I remember the young Lutheran pastor in an inner-city Philadelphia congregation who told me about a Bible study she recently was leading with a group of young adults. She said that she began the study very defensively, saying, "Now, in Acts we are going to read about miracles; there will be angels. But we will not be sidetracked by such concerns. We will be seeking the deeper meaning of miracles, what these ancient authors were trying to convey by these primitive means."

A few weeks into the study, however, she felt she needed to say, "If you have had a vision, if God has appeared to you personally, if you know someone who has experienced a miracle—keep it to yourself. We don't have time to go into all that." These were not modern people. They were postmodern.

Not bothered by visions, claims of the miraculous, they were open, willing, eager to discuss such claims.

3. Not all of the hungers of today's young adults are worth meeting. In *The Brothers Karamazov*, Dostoyevsky has the Grand Inquisitor declare that, in the future, science will banish sin, evil, and freedom, reducing all human beings to nothing but "a race of hungry men." The vocation of the church is not simply to "meet people's needs" or "to satisfy their hungers." In a consumeristic society, where my desires are quickly elevated to the level of need and then my alleged needs are further elevated to the level of rights, it is risky to talk about meeting people's needs. My desires are virtually limitless, and woe be unto the person who goes out to meet my needs! Two church sociologists declare in a recent study, "All the evidence suggests that the boomer's relation to the church is fundamentally different from that of previous generations—that is, . . . more 'voluntaristic,' consumer-oriented, and captive to the subjective, expressive dimensions of cultural individualism."[14]

Any of us, at whatever age we come to faith in Christ, must be schooled in wanting the right things in the right way. The gospel is not merely the offer of food; the gospel is also a debate about which hungers are worth having. The preaching of the church is one way in which I am schooled in how to be hungry in the right sort of way.

As an outsider, from what I could observe of young adults' response to the Presbyterian Church's (USA) attempt to reach out nonjudgmentally, liberally, permissively to its young adults in its sexuality study of a few years back, this generation of young adults has the good sense to know when it is being patronized.[15] Many young adults, having been victimized by the sexual revolution, created, not by themselves, but rather by their parents, were not flattered that the church seemed so eager to adapt itself to what it perceived to be their sexual attitudes. Promiscuity is often a problem for many members of the abandoned generation. In a society that elevates personal freedom and autonomy to godlike status, there is going to be much loneliness.

The church is in the love business, but not in the way this culture speaks about love. In the church, one finds life by losing it, and one receives by giving. The goal of preaching is not to meet people's hungers, but to meet those hungers in the name of Jesus.

14. David A. Roozen and Kirk C. Hadaway, *Church and Denominational Growth: What Does (or Does Not) Cause Growth or Decline* (Nashville: Abingdon Press, 1993).

15. See *Keeping Body and Soul Together: Sexuality, Spirituality, and Social Justice,* 1991. The majority report of the General Assembly Special Committee on Human Sexuality, Presbyterian Church (USA).

4. We live in a marvelous time for Christian preaching. Watch James Earl Massey in the pulpit of Duke Chapel, and you will see how much a man over sixty has to say to young adults one third his age.[16] Because they value integrity, honesty, and the courage of anyone who stands up to speak in a time when so many seem so hesitant to take a stand on anything, they are able to hear. The wonder of one human being's daring to stand and tell what he or she has seen and heard has not diminished over the ages. Indeed, that wonder may now be more wondrous than ever in a generation nurtured on TV and sixty-second sound bites, media hype, and the vacuous promises of a consumptive culture.

Mainline, liberal Protestantism has been unable to retain its young. The departure of young adults from the churches that nurtured them (none too well, it would appear) is one of the more dramatic and depressing aspects of the American religious scene in the past two decades. My colleague C. Eric Lincoln has documented a similar dramatic exodus of young adults from black churches.[17]

In regard to members of the abandoned generation, the stakes are high for the church. If we lose this generation, the American church will find itself in a vastly different situation in the future. Indeed, Roozen and Hadaway declare, "The future of the black church in the city is really dependent in the long term on the black church's ability to involve the less educated, younger adults who currently have little disposition—and possible disdain—for the church."[18] The North American church may look at this situation and either despair or see the present situation as a marvelous evangelistic opportunity in which the fields are ready for harvest.

Many of the hungers of this generation are hungers for which the gospel of Jesus Christ is the Bread of Life. God grant us the grace to break that bread with renewed confidence in our time, even as James Earl Massey has done in his.

---

16. See, e.g., James Earl Massey's sermon "Songs in the Night," in James W. Cox, ed., *Best Sermons I* (San Francisco: Harper & Row, 1988), 348-55.

17. C. Eric Lincoln, *The Black Church in the African American Experience.* (Durham, N.C.: Duke University Press, 1990).

18. Roozen and Hadaway, *Church and Denominational Growth*, 154.

CHAPTER THREE

DISENTANGLING THE CALL TO PREACH: CERTAINTY, AMBIGUITY, MYSTERY

William H. Myers

G|ardner C. Taylor, one of the premier preachers of our time and beloved especially by African American preachers, highlights a most significant aspect of the call to preach. It comes in his oral articulation about his own call.

> I wanted to be a criminal lawyer. But in the Spring of my senior year in college, I had a traumatic experience with an automobile accident. I was chauffeur for the college president, and there was an accident on the highway driving his car. Three men, White, cut across me in an old Model T Ford. One was killed on the spot, one other died later. That experience—and this was a rural Louisiana highway in 1937—the only people who gathered were Whites. Now, I did not associate this directly with my call, with any call. But I would guess that this was the culmination of some disquiet that had been going on in me for some time. Within the next week or two, I went into the president's office and, I suppose to his surprise, told him that I felt called to the ministry. . . . But this accident brought it to the fore. . . . The call grew out of this. I would not want to say that that was the cause of it. I would not want to say that I would have surrendered to this without it. I can't disentangle these things. . . . I just don't know.[1]

---

1. William H. Myers, *The Irresistible Urge to Preach: A Collection of African American "Call" Stories* (Atlanta: Aaron Press, 1992), 328-39.

A Place for Mystery

Whereas some people who have had similar cataclysmic experiences speak with absolute certainty about their call, Taylor manifests a critical-restraint that retains the tension between certainty and ambiguity. Such restraint opens the door for the hearer and reader to catch a glimpse of the mystery referred to as the "call to preach."

Perhaps this is why Taylor, who knew that as a scholar I would be critically examining this phenomenon, made this request when our interview was completed: "Doc, don't analyze the call too much, less it loses its mystery." In order to fully appreciate the call, one must make a determined effort to maintain the balance between certainty and ambiguity so that mystery has a place as well. Appeal only to objectivism or subjectivism as the only way of knowing leads us down the wrong knowledge path and leaves no room for mystery.

The call is first and foremost a story—an oral accounting—about a human-divine encounter. It is the narrator's retrospective attempt to articulate a divine mission—a call to ministry. It is an attempt to reconstruct the chronological account of what happened. The call is equally a narrative. It is a narrative structured with one main purpose: to persuade the hearer of the veracity of the story. Hence, call stories and call narratives are not necessarily the same.

Narrative theorists make a distinction between "story" (the signified, the content, the "what") and the "narrative" (the signifier, the discourse/structure, the "how"). If the story is what happened, then the narrative is how one tells what happened. In this regard, even things like story time and narrative time are different. While it might have taken a person four years in story time to receive a degree, it can be narrated in one second of narrative time ("I received my B.S. at Harvard"). An individual's attempt to articulate a call is also an act of retrospective interpretation. Hence, the call is also hermeneutics.[2]

However, if we are to fully understand and pass on our knowledge about this phenomenon, we must critically and carefully attempt to disentangle as many aspects of the call as we can. The more we know about it in its parts, the better we may be able to understand it as a whole. Otherwise, we will be left with the consequences of myriad unsubstantiated subjective conclusions, and with all "doing what is right in their own eyes."

The task is important because we are confronting those who wish to

---

2. William H. Myers, *God's Yes Was Louder Than My No: Rethinking the African American Call to Ministry* (Grand Rapids: Eerdmans, 1994), parts I, II, IV, and VI.

take on the awesome task of proclaiming a word from God. Paul put it best in his letter to the Romans: "But how are they to call on one in whom they have not believed? And how are they to believe in one of whom they have never heard? And how are they to hear without someone to proclaim him? And how are they to proclaim him unless they are sent?" (Rom. 10:14-15*a*). Without a calling, there can be no preaching.

This chapter briefly addresses three major concerns that become entangled as a result of articulated calls and, more basically, the construct known as the "call to preach." These concerns can be formulated as questions: How is one called? What is one called to do? Who can be called? Obviously these are not the only concerns raised by this construct; however, they are of sufficient importance that the contemporary church needs to consider them anew.

The Entangled Call Experience: How Is One Called?

People who claim to have had a divine encounter that led them to articulate and accept a call from God are not relegated to the African American religious community. Scripture records numerous call narratives that emphasize a divine encounter as a key element of the call. The calls of Abraham, Moses, Samuel, Amos, Hosea, Isaiah, Jeremiah, Gideon, and Paul are but a few.

The encounter often creates a sense of *mysterium tremendum et fascinans* ("fascination with inexpressible mystery") in the recipient. The call, therefore, "appears as a disruptive experience for which there has been no obvious preparation. The call marks the initial interruption of God in the life of the individual."[3]

Whether it is Moses' burning bush, Gideon's angel, Isaiah's majestic temple vision, Samuel hearing his name called, Ezekiel feeling a spirit entering him, or Paul seeing the risen Christ, many of these people articulate calls that are phenomenologically laden. Most often this part of the experience is so overwhelming that it tends to dominate all other aspects of the call.

A number of matters become entangled for both the narrator and the recipient of calls that have a cataclysmic element. This is especially true as one attempts to wrestle with the question "How is one called?" Is one called only by God or does the church call as well? Is there only one type of call—namely, cataclysmic? Is the knowledge of the one called so certain so that it eliminates all ambiguity?

Habel's form-critical analysis of Old Testament call narratives suggests

---

3. N. Habel, "The Form and Significance of the Call Narratives," *Zeitschrift für die alttestamentliche Wissenschaft* 77 (1965): 298.

that they can be observed in six parts: the divine confrontation, the introductory word, the commission, the objection, the reassurance, and the sign.[4] Baird found this same structure in the aspects of Paul's call that appears in Galatians.[5] As helpful as these analyses are, they create a major problem for our understanding of call by overemphasizing the divine aspect to the exclusion of the human. It entangles the call of God and the call of the church, the personal (inner) call and the congregational (outer) call in such a way that underplays their interdependence. This is not a new matter. The place and proper relationship of God and the church have been debated for centuries.

The second problem is similar to the first; in fact, they are linked by the way Scripture creates tension. The careful reader will observe that different people are called in different ways to different ministries. However, the more cataclysmic stories (e.g., Moses, Isaiah, Jeremiah, Paul) are given greater literary prominence and the divine receives more emphasis than those of others who are called (e.g., Timothy, Titus, Junia). In fact, one gets the point that the former are people who have been called even when the Hebrew and Greek terms for "call" are not used.

Furthermore, Paul adds to the difficulty when he argues that God gives gifted people to the church to function in certain capacities and that the Holy Spirit distributes gifts to people in order that they might fill different specialized ministries (Rom. 12:3-8; 1 Cor. 12:3-8; Eph. 4:1-16). Moreover, Scripture heightens the tension when it spotlights certain people who have been called out for ministry and go through a ritual, laying on of hands, that is very similar to what we call ordination, a ritual set aside for certain restricted ministries.[6]

My own research among contemporary African American preachers illustrates one effect of this entanglement. Many people who articulated calls that did not contain cataclysmic elements were aware of calls that do, and to some extent felt the need to acknowledge that and defend their call as legitimate as well. As Joseph L. Roberts juxtaposed his own call to some others, he questioned both the emphasis and the interpretation of these cataclysmic calls:

---

4. Ibid., 297-323.
5. William Baird, "Visions, Revelation, and Ministry: Reflections on 2 Cor. 12:1-5 and Gal. 1:11-17," *Journal of Biblical Literature* 104 (Dec. 1985): 651-62.
6. The relevant passages are Acts 6:1-6; 13:1-3; 14:23; 1 Tim. 4:14; 5:22; and 2 Tim. 1:6. See a most penetrating analysis of the biblical basis for this ritual in R. Alan Culpepper, "The Biblical Basis for Ordination," *Review and Expositor* 78 (Fall 1981): 471-84. Cf. Eduard Schweizer, "The Nature of Ministry in Reformed Understanding: New Testament Dimensions," *Horizons in Biblical Theology* 9 (June 1987): 41-63, who argues against the necessity of ordination today.

[My call] is not, therefore, something that I can date in terms of a Tuesday at one o'clock when anything happened but, rather, something that I think was rather gradual. And not to sound defensive, but I believe when people stop lying most of them will admit that it was a gradual thing that they were nudged to and not a catastrophic, one-day piece that suddenly came and hit them like a bolt of lightning out of the air.[7]

Finally, knowledge about certainty and ambiguity gets entangled, especially in call experiences that contain a cataclysmic element. The overwhelming aspect of the event leaves one with some knowledge— for example, when it happened ("In the year King Uzziah died . . . "); what one saw ("I saw the Lord . . . "); what one said ("Woe is me! I am lost . . . Here am I; send me!"); and what one heard ("Whom shall I send, and who will go for us?" Isa. 6:1-9).

Similarly, in the New Testament Paul claims in his letters some knowledge about his own call. He knows that God set him apart before birth and called him to be an apostle, that his mission was to proclaim Jesus among the Gentiles, and that he saw the resurrected Christ. Often, however, the cataclysmic nature of these calls and their narration may suggest a certainty broader and clearer than it actually was when it happened and less ambiguity than really existed. Closer examination reveals that there is far more ambiguity than the retrospective narrations suggest on the surface and the narrator chooses to admit without critical interrogation.

The Entangled Call Commission: What Is One Called to Do?

The call narrative of Paul highlights better than any other one of the great tensions about the call commission. In response to this transcendent event that we refer to as Paul's call experience, Paul's response in the form of a question unveils a central concern that few have addressed adequately: "What am I to do, Lord?" (Acts 22:10).

Here again Scripture, especially as seen in call narratives, engenders more tension. Whether it is Moses (Exod. 3:10) who is sent to speak to Pharaoh, Isaiah (6:9) or Ezekiel (2:3) who are sent to speak to the people of Israel, or Jeremiah (1:5) who is appointed a prophet to the nation, there is the question of what one is called to do and for what period of time. The total parameters of the commission in terms of the breadth and depth of its function and duration are not totally clear at the time of the

---

7. Myers, *The Irresistible Urge to Preach*, 309.

call. The one called has many questions about the nature of the commission long after the experience occurs.

One of the more unfortunate effects of being familiar with Scripture is that we often think we know more about the whole story than we do, and thus we read these narratives not with critical inquiry but with additional knowledge. We know, for example, that most if not all of these biblical characters, at least in the narrative, functioned in the same roles for the duration of their lives. This is true whether they are referred to by labels such as prophet, priest, apostle, or some other title. Moreover, some of them used these labels as titles, thereby conveying their self-understanding of the call. We observe this especially with Paul's rhetoric to the Corinthians: "Am I not an apostle? Have I not seen Jesus our Lord?" (1 Cor. 9:1).

The difficulties that these redactional and retrospective hermeneutical accounts create for us on this side of Scripture are enormous. The first problem is not unlike one we exposed earlier: What is the role of the church in the commission? One danger coming with cataclysmic call experiences is drawing the conclusion that the commission is clear because it came from the divine. Moreover, if one overly emphasizes certain retrospective self-understandings (e.g., I was called to be an apostle to the Gentiles), it might appear that the divine aspect of the encounter is all that is necessary.

Another problem emerges as the one called begins to articulate a retrospective understanding of the call. In his polemical rhetoric to the Galatians, Paul connects his call experience with his self-understanding of his commission: "But when God, who had set me apart before I was born and called me through his grace, was pleased to reveal his Son to me, so that I might [*preach*] him among the Gentiles" (Gal. 1:15-16). Here again Scripture gets in its own way. Has Paul, the charismatic apostle who affirms a variety of calls to ministry, reduced his own call to ministry to a "call to preach"?

Whether that was his intent, in many parts of the contemporary church that is what has happened. The unfortunate result is that *call* has become a technical term in many places to refer to the ordained clergy; moreover, its basic manifestation is to be seen in the act of preaching. We need to ask anew, however, what we mean by a call to ministry over against a call to preach and how this understanding helps us to better respond to the question "What specifically is one called to do?"

A clearer understanding of the first problem (overstated certainty) and the second problem (reductionism of the call) will help us with the third: the shape of the call throughout one's life. Once again we encounter the tension created by literary artistry in Scripture. Without doubt we observe a host of people who appear to have functioned in only one ministerial capacity throughout their lives. Of course, Paul did not help matters when he announced, "For the gifts and the calling of God are irrevocable" (Rom. 11:29). In many parts of the church today this means that the one called serves in one ministerial capacity for life. Sometimes that role is described in nothing more than the ambiguous construct, called to preach. The consequences of such an interpretation are mindboggling. Some people stay far too long in one role and become overly frustrated and burned out. Others remain beyond their physical capacity to serve effectively. Still others never utilize all of their gifts and talent. Worst of all, some are never given a chance to begin.

The Entangled Call Gift: Who Can Be Called?

In addition to the call, Paul claims that the gifts of God are irrevocable as well. The linking of the call with gifts and the amount of emphasis Paul places on gifts in his letters create another set of problems for our understanding of call. If gifts are necessary for those who are called, what gifts are we talking about and, most important, who can receive them? In simpler terms, who can be called? Moreover, since it is God who distributes these gifts, are they self-sufficient? Is anything else needed? More directly, to what extent is education necessary for those called and gifted in order for them to serve effectively?

The tension is as great, if not greater, in this entanglement as those previously discussed. Here again, Scripture compounds the problem. The first concern is more of a gender battle than anything else. In many parts of the church persons believe that women cannot be called, at least to certain roles. Scripture becomes the battleground where proponents and opponents come fully armed to do battle. The conflict is self-evident as this same authoritative canon is appealed to for support by both sides.

Some of the *loci classicus* appealed to by opponents are 1 Corinthians 11:2-16; 14:34-35; 1 Timothy 2:8-15; 3:1-13; and the grouping known as the Haustafeln (Col. 3:18–4:1; Eph. 5:21–6:9; 1 Pet. 2:18–3:7). These passages 1—along with others, about the maleness of Jesus and the disciples he chose, the lack of females in leadership roles, the fact that a woman cannot be the husband of one wife, the mandate that women be submissive to men, to name a few—are used to challenge the extent to which women can be called. In spite of any Pauline interpolation or Deutero-Pauline theories, opponents argue that these passages are still a part of Scripture and, therefore, are authoritative.

Proponents of women's right to be called to any role appeal to a different set of Scriptures. The most dominant passage is Galatians 3:28-29 (others include Matt. 28:1-10; John 20:1-18; Rom. 16:1-16). Proponents argue that, contrary to their opponents, passages such as these and others show women as disciples and in leadership positions, and that God never intended for women to be unequal to men in any ministerial role.

The second problem is just as troublesome. Is education necessary for those called to speak on behalf of God? Again, parts of the church feel that only the divine part of the call encounter is necessary. God distributes the irrevocable gifts, and the Spirit controls the specificity of ministry and the effects. Thus nothing else is needed. Once again Scripture is invoked.

"Now when they saw the boldness of Peter and John and realized that they were *uneducated* and ordinary men, they were amazed and recognized them as companions of Jesus" (Acts 4:13, italics added).[8] "As for you, the anointing that you received from him abides in you, and so you *do not need anyone to teach you*. But as his anointing teaches you about all things, and is true and is not a lie" (1 John 2:27, italics added). "But the Advocate, the Holy Spirit, whom the Father will send in my name, *will teach you everything*, and remind you of all that I have said to you" (John 14:26, italics added). Texts such as these are interpreted and used once again to diminish the importance of the human encounter in favor of the divine, arguing that all one needs to be effective in ministry is to know Jesus and to be anointed. After all, the divine will "teach you everything" you need to know.

Two of the problems created by the gift entanglement (who can be called and what training is necessary) are enormous. Ministers and ministries are effected because gifted people are denied access to ministry. Similarly, unequipped people are sent out into the community of believers to wreak havoc on a host of unsuspecting people because of a lack of appropriate training necessary to perform certain ministerial roles. Some problems go unresolved in our communities because the appropriately gifted and trained persons are never sent out to minister. A very large part of these problems can be attributed to some traditional understandings of call and interpretations of Scripture—better, misunderstandings and misinterpretations that need to be revisited.

---

8. Some translations exacerbate the problem. The King James Version, which is sacrosanct in a very large part of the church, reads, "they were unlearned and ignorant men."

Disentangling the Call Experience

Protestantism has debated how the call to ministry should be understood and constituted, generally emphasizing different aspects of the call in varying denominational histories.[9] For example, Luther believed that God with the church calls ministers. In his concept of the "priesthood of all believers," he emphasized the importance of spiritual gifts as the basis of ministry—and for the entire congregation, not just pastors. Calvin added to the debate by distinguishing between the inner (personal) and outer (congregational) call of ministers. He argued for a decisive role of the congregation in the call of a minister.

Since that time, interdenominational and intradenominational distinctions have emerged regarding the relative importance of the inner and outer calls in validating ministry. Certain groups have added their own insights to this debate. For example, the Puritans and Pietists emphasized the experiential aspect of the call, the latter focusing especially on the role of the Holy Spirit in the call.

The emphasis that the Pietists placed on the Holy Spirit can also be observed in the Methodists' emphasis on the Holy Spirit in holiness. As a result, they emphasize the importance of "fruits" as the major proof of whether an individual has been called. Baptists also have emphasized the importance of the experiential dimension of the call. Although Methodists and Baptists have stressed the importance of the inner call, they also have recognized the importance of the outer call. Thus, in their acknowledgment of the role that each plays, they are similar to Calvin. Congregationalists and Presbyterians have also leaned toward Calvin in their acknowledgment of the importance of the inner and outer calls. In addition, they emphasize the importance of formal education.

It is undeniable that the inner call, the divine dimension, is a prevalent part of the call; however, it is but one aspect of the understanding of call. Although it is true that God calls, it is also true that one is called by a congregation of believers. At some point all people who have been called went to a community of believers for clarity and, most important, sanctioning.[10] Therefore, we must argue that the church's call is as important as the divine call. Hence, the church has the right, indeed the responsibility, to test any purported call from God.

This tension is reminiscent of what we see in the life and writings of Paul to selected congregations of believers, but perhaps also in his self-

---

9. For a detailed documentation of examples that follow, see Myers, *God's Yes Was Louder Than My No*, 195-214.

10. Ibid., 54-60.

understanding of call. In the actual call experience where he encounters the divine, he is sent to a community of believers in Damascus to gain further clarity about his call. The response to Paul's question about what he is called to do is: "Get up and go to Damascus; there you will be told everything that has been assigned to you to do" (Acts 22:10). Later, he is brought to Antioch by Barnabas, and both of them are set apart by the church and the divine to be sent out on a mission (Acts 13:1-3).[11] More-over, Paul knows "apostles of the churches" (2 Cor. 8:23), to which he doesn't seem to object.

The greatest tension, however, can be observed in Paul's letter to the Galatians. He makes what at first glance appears to be two irreconcilable arguments. Initially, he seems to argue that he neither sought nor needed the church's sanctioning of his call (1:11-24). But then he acknowledges that he sought it, needed it, and received it (2:1-2). Interestingly, both assertions are attributed to revelations from God. Scholars have empha-sized various aspects of the tension that appears in this letter and have resolved it in a variety of ways, some attributing it to the polemical rhetoric of the letter, while others emphasize the differences between Paul's account and Luke's.

For our purposes, it is noteworthy to emphasize and resolve the conflict of Paul's self-understanding of his call. What we have here, among other things, are interpretations and reinterpretations of Paul's call experience. Whereas at one given moment he says that the call is only of God, at other times he is made painfully aware of the fact that congregations of believ-ers are a part of the process. He may grudgingly yield to the latter, but yield he does. In so doing he both gives and acknowledges the church's right to test not only the content of his message, but also the call of God itself. The answer to the question "How is one called?" is "By God and the church." We must not allow retrospective interpretations or reinter-pretations of call experiences, whether biblical or extra-biblical, whether descriptive or polemical, to keep us from maintaining this balance. The very lives of many—physically, emotionally, and spiritually—inside and outside the church, depend on the church's sounding the trumpet against charlatans, lunatics, and misfits claiming only a divine call.

Another aspect of the call experience that needs disentangling is types of call. Because cataclysmic calls are so unusual in the experiences of most people, they tend to get more attention. Again, the Scripture helps to create more tension in this regard because of the space given to those

---

11. See "the seven" in Acts 6 for a similar mutual responsibility between the church and the divine.

who had such experiences. Hence, we don't get as much emphasis on the calls of Timothy, Titus, Epaphroditus, Stephen, Lydia, Junia, and others. However, their presence as well as their commitment to ministry causes us to consider the possibility of other types of call experiences. Moreover, our personal awareness of a variety of call experiences in our different communities of faith causes us to suspect that there is more than one type of call experience.

My own research of call experiences among black churches across denominational lines reveals three different types of call. They are: Type A—Cataclysmic/Reluctant; Type B—Noncataclysmic/Reluctant; and Type C—Noncataclysmic/Nonreluctant.[12]

Type A persons connect to their call some momentous events, open to being interpreted as natural or supernatural. Ocular, aural, and sensory phenomena (such as visions, dreams, and signs) are a part of this type, but they do not necessarily occur with every individual. The crucial moment of this call occurs in the call experience stage. In addition, persons of this type are reluctant individuals who resist the call for a variety of reasons. Finally, a sense of relief, joy, and peace emerges as they surrender to the call. Although the community of faith plays an important role in the sanctioning of the call, for these individuals it appears to be a secondary role in relation to the cataclysmic event, at least in tracing the locus of the call. More than any other type, this call has the most similarities to the biblical call narrative of Paul.

Type B contains no cataclysmic moments that are crucial turning points. This type of call unfolds gradually. However, like Type A, these persons are reluctant as well. The sanctioning of the community is much more important for this type. The locus of the call is equally traced to the sanctioning of the church and the divine.

Type C contains no cataclysmic moment. Unlike both A and B, there is no reluctance in these persons; they were always willing to be called. In this sense, Type C is a different kind of awareness from the sudden or gradual one found in both reluctant types. These individuals view the call as their destiny, something that they were born, "groomed," and "nurtured" to do. Their call is gradual. As to their consciousness, however, they assert that they have always known. Although there are some in Types A and B who assert that they always knew, Type C is distinguished by the fact that these persons assert that they always saw the call as their destiny, never wanted any other vocation in life, and did not resist it when the time came. Certain aspects of the biblical calls of Isaiah and Timothy are observable in this type.

---

12. Myers, *God's Yes Was Louder Than My No*, 15-115.

Is there only one type of call—namely, cataclysmic? No. There are at least three identifiable types.

The final matter that needs disentangling is the tension between certainty and ambiguity in call narratives. As discussed earlier, persons who have been called leave the hearer with the impression that there is little doubt when it comes to their call. But how true is this assertion? There is as much uncertainty, lack of understanding, and ambiguity in Paul's call experience as there is certainty.

Paul's call is sudden and cataclysmic; it includes voices and lights from heaven. There is not enough light in this transcendent event, however, to make all things clear for Paul. On two later occasions when Paul needs to give an apologia for his apostleship, he retrospectively reinterprets this experience with such great certainty as to eliminate all ambiguity about what he knew. Paul's unambiguous assertion to the Galatians is that God revealed his Son, Jesus Christ, to Paul (1:11-17). "Have I not seen Jesus our Lord?" is Paul's rhetorical question that demands an affirmative response from the Corinthians (1 Cor. 9:1). However, Paul's very ambiguous response to all the voices and lights is filled with darkness: "Who are you, Lord?" (Acts 9:5).

On another occasion (Acts 22:6-16) when Paul is depicted as telling his story in a different context, it is evident that ambiguity existed. In all of his subsequent letters, Paul speaks retrospectively about the certainty of his call as well as his mission. The fact that God has set him apart before he was born and called him to proclaim Jesus among the Gentiles is one way he defines his call (Gal. 1:15). "Paul, called to be an apostle of Christ Jesus" is another way (e.g., 1 Cor. 1:1; cf. Rom. 1:1; 2 Cor. 1:1). However, Paul's question "What am I to do, Lord?" coupled with the question "Who are you, Lord?" makes it clear that Paul didn't know initially what his mission was or who he was asking to respond to the questions.

More confusion abounds in this telling of the story because Paul asserts that even those with him cannot corroborate his experience. In this instance only he hears the voice, although he claims that the witnesses saw the light. This account is even more confusing because the earlier account (Acts 9:1-22) says just the opposite—the witnesses did hear the voice, but they saw no one, and there is no mention of whether they saw the light.

In the final account (Acts 26:12-25), which is yet another occasion, the ambiguity continues. In the first two instances, Paul is depicted as the one falling to the ground, whereas on this occasion everybody falls to the ground. Moreover, in this instance he asserts that he knows more about the specificity of his call and mission. The attempt of some to explain the differences in Luke's three accounts as compared to Paul's letters by Lukan literary inadequacies fails to have any appreciation for Luke's assertion in the prologue of the two-volume work that he had carefully investigated and reported his facts.[13] Moreover, it fails to take into account the fact that this same certainty-ambiguity tension exists in Paul's letters. In fact, Galatians is the very letter that is held up as a model of an authentic Pauline epistle.

This degree of clarity and certainty versus lack of clarity and ambiguity is evident in extra-biblical call narratives as well. Many persons who have been called assert that they have always known without doubt that they were called to preach. Like Paul, some even claim to know that they were called from birth.[14] However, as with Paul, this is a retrospective interpretation of a past experience, an experience that at critical moments in the past usually was filled with doubt and ambiguity. In fact, doubt, reluctance, uncertainty, and ambiguity are common occurrences experienced by most persons called by God.

Let us return to Gardner Taylor's story, which opened this chapter. The ambiguity in his experience and its relationship to Taylor's call are arresting. First, there appears to be both an internal and an external struggle over the direction of Taylor's vocational choice. He is set against becoming a preacher, an "antipathy" arising "out of some . . . family members' attitudes," although his father is a rather well-known pastor whom Taylor admires. Therefore, he decides to become a criminal lawyer. Before he can launch out on this vocational choice, however, a traumatic accident occurs, and it becomes the stimulus for his acknowledgment of his call.

Although Taylor did not "associate this directly" with his call at the time, he does interpret it as "the culmination of some disquiet that had been going on in me for some time." The ambiguity about this experience and its relationship to Taylor's call are self-evident. Taylor did not associate it with the call at the time, but does connect it now as the culmination of an internal struggle.

Some people who have been called, as well as some narratives, leave the hearer or reader with the impression that knowledge of the call is complete, clear, and certain, without a hint of doubt or ambiguity. The great value in a call narrative like Taylor's is his maintenance of the ten-

---

13. See Ernst Haenchen, *The Acts of the Apostles: A Commentary* (Philadelphia: Westminster Press, 1971), who at various points refers to Luke as untrustworthy, a distorter whose work is flawed and historically suspect.
14. See Myers, *The Irresistible Urge to Preach.*

sion between certainty and ambiguity by acknowledging what was clear versus what was unclear.

> I just don't know. More than what I've said, I just don't know. I know I wasn't comfortable, I was going to the University of Michigan Law School, but I wasn't comfortable. I guess something was going on inside of me.[15]

We would do well not to diminish or overemphasize the place of certainty or ambiguity in the call experience. Perhaps pushing toward one end or the other is similar to asking whether the call is by God or the church. Most important, maintaining the balance between certainty and ambiguity allows mystery to enter the equation. Stagg asks: "How do we really distinguish between the general calling common to us all and the special calling which comes to only some? The mystery cannot be completely dispelled."[16] Where uncertainty and mystery exist, faith is possible. Where absolute certainty exists, who needs faith?

Disentangling the Call Commission

Although one may emerge from the call experience with a degree of certainty about the call, this does not mean that what one has been called to do is clear. Hence, there is a need for us to disentangle the call commission.

The first matter is the place of the church in the commissioning process. We established earlier how the church was involved in the call experience, especially in sanctioning the call of God to biblical and extrabiblical individuals. Here, however, we are interested in the extent to which the church should be involved in answering the question "What is one called to do?"

A return to Paul's call sheds some light. The response to Paul's question about what he was called to do is "Get up and go to Damascus; there you will be told everything that has been assigned to you to do" (Acts 22:10). Hence, although the initial commission comes from the divine, the one called is sent to the community of believers in order to gain greater clarity on the specific nature of the commission.

This passage makes it self-evident that the church is involved in helping people who have been called to work out the details. Paul suggests elsewhere that people are given to the church for the common good

---

15. Myers, *The Irresistible Urge to Preach*, 329.
16. Frank Stagg, "Understanding Call to Ministry," in *Formation for Christian Ministry*, eds. Anne Davis and Wade Rowatt, Jr. (Louisville: Review and Expositor), 32.

(1 Cor. 12:1-31) and the equipping and perfecting of the saints (Eph. 4:12). Since this is the place where one should expect to find others who have had similar experiences as well as others who know something about the called person's abilities, talents, and gifts, it would appear to be the best place to go.

Again, my research illustrates that people who received a call from God, regardless of how phenomenologically laden the experience was, turned to the community of believers for greater clarity. Most people went to pastors or other ministers for help. This would suggest that they sought people who knew something about this type of experience, could help them gain greater clarity about their own call, and would help them negotiate the rites-of-passage process existing in their community of faith.

In order to gain greater clarity on this matter, we need to address another issue: the distinction between the construct "call to preach" and a "call to ministry." In his call narrative, Mack Carter offers this opinion:

> First of all, I think the whole issue of the call has been misunderstood. . . . In a broad sense, in the New Testament there is no such thing as "the call to preach" as we have articulated. Everybody is called to preach in the New Testament sense. . . . When I'm called to salvation, I'm also called to preach in the sense of spreading the word. . . . I was saved in 1953 and I was called to preach in the New Testament sense in 1953; but I received a special anointing in 1966 to be a pastor-teacher, upon which I later would go on and receive training for the gift that God had given me in this particular area.[17]

In addition to Carter's insight, we need to offer the insight of Renita Weems:

> But see, one of the things about asking about your calling you still haven't asked is "Called to what?" You know, you are assuming that it's preaching. And I think that one of the things that especially women bring to this new movement of the ministry is that we are reinterpreting what it means to be in the ministry. We are reinterpreting ministry. . . . I think that our presence in the ministry forces the church, forces us, forces our colleagues to have to rethink ministry, rethink gifts, rethink the notion that in the black church only the preaching ministry is the ordained ministry in our churches.[18]

In far too many of our churches today the concept of a "call" has been reduced to "the call to preach." Instead of questioning people who claim to have a call about what they are doing, too often the expected response,

17. Myers, *The Irresistible Urge to Preach*, 72-73.
18. Ibid., 342.

and given response, is a call to preach. If Carter is correct in his assertion that "we confuse preaching with sermonizing" and that everyone in a New Testament sense is called to preach, then we certainly need to rethink our use of this very reductionistic phrase.

A few New Testament examples may help. In some denominations deacons are not allowed to preach because they haven't been "called to preach." It is ironic, then, that the communities holding this position usually claim that the seven in Acts 6 are the first deacons. It is irrefutable that at least two of the seven, Philip and Stephen, are described as preaching in Acts 7 and 8. Furthermore, when the scattering of the church takes place (Acts 8:1-4), Luke records that all went about proclaiming the word (i.e., preaching), except the apostles. These texts, not to speak of numerous others, require us to clarify what we mean by "called to preach" as well as why we have restricted the task in our traditions in a manner not found in the New Testament.

While it is true that Paul refers to himself on occasion as one called to preach (e.g., 1 Cor. 1:17; Gal. 1:15), his most favored self-description is one called to be an apostle to preach the gospel (e.g., Rom. 1:1; 1 Cor. 1:1; Gal. 1:1). Hence, the task of preaching was but a description of one function he fulfilled as an apostle. In his calling as an apostle, he functioned not only as a preacher, but also as a shepherd, a teacher, and a church planter.

Carter's distinction between his call to preach, which he believes everyone receives, and the call to be a pastor-teacher, which further distinguishes between the functions of those called to preach, is arresting. It is precisely at this point that Weems's insight broadens even further that of Carter's. Weems wants us to rethink and reinterpret not just our understanding of the call to preach, but also our understanding of the call to ministry. She argues that the variety of gifts present among those entering the ministry in our time, especially the gifts of women, should be cause enough for us to rethink our understanding of the call to ministry.

Carter's shift from call to preach as the defining term of his call to pastor-teacher is a concrete shift in ministry. Weems's notion that we need to rethink ministry, rethink gifts, and rethink the ordained ministry is striking. Both of these individuals shift the emphasis where it needs to be, on concrete aspects of ministry, not just an elusive call to preach.

Shouldn't the times, cultural conditions and circumstances, and the new faces that are making themselves available and the different kind of gifts they bring to the table cause us to think about what God may be doing in our time? Shouldn't this make us rethink our understanding of call as a call to ministry? Shouldn't we inquire whether this call to ministry is a call to serve in the church, the academy, or some parachurch organization, serving youth, the elderly, drug addicts, abused women, people with AIDS, or in some other way we have yet to envision? Shouldn't we determine what training people are prepared to undergo to fulfill concrete ministries such as those just mentioned?

Gifts, skills, desire, commitment, and fitness for specific ministry can be tested, and individuals can be prepared for the challenge. This is possible only to the extent that we help people to concretize what they have been called to do.

Finally, we must disentangle the perception of what shape the call must take throughout one's life. Prevalent in many churches is the idea that one can never retire from a call to preach. In Paul's words, the call is irrevocable. What an unfortunate misreading of the text. First, although Paul is assuredly addressing the text to Israel, it can be extended to Gentiles. In this context, however, it has more to do with the graces of election. Second, with Kasemann we accept that the gifts and call of God are interwoven.[19] In addition, in this context it is the faithfulness of God that is emphasized.

One of the most unfortunate consequences of not understanding call as a process that may continue to unfold differently throughout one's life is getting frozen into one aspect of ministry, sometimes merely one function, even when the individual would like to do something different. This evolves from misunderstanding the call, ministry, and retirement. When one sees the call to ministry as a process that continues throughout one's life, then one can continuously move on (i.e., retire) from one understanding of ministerial function to another, especially when one has the gifts and desire to do so. Any narrower understanding of ministry may keep one in a state of total ambiguity for life.

The call may unfold in a multiplicity of different ways (e.g., layperson, clergy, pastor, professor, ecclesiastical administrator, college or seminary president, author, or retired volunteer) throughout the lifetime of the one called. This may be due to new opportunities that did not exist earlier because of traditions at the time (e.g., gender), inadequacies of the one called (e.g., lack of experience, education, maturity), new revelations, or a different self-understanding of call and mission. As all of these new understandings break forth, both in the individual and in religious communities, the circular, almost spiral, nature of the call as a series of rites of passage continues to evolve as a ritualizing process.[20]

---

19. Ernst Kasemann, *Commentary on Romans,* trans. and ed. Geoffrey W. Bromiley (Grand Rapids: Eerdmans, 1980), 316. "God does not give gifts without calling and vice versa."

20. See Myers, *God's Yes Was Louder Than My No,* 119-31, for a discussion of the call as a rite of passage and a ritualizing process.

Disentangling the Call Gifts

Few issues divide the contemporary church more than the role of women in ministry, especially in certain leadership positions in the church. The issue of who can be called forces us to deal with who can receive the appropriate gifts commensurate with certain calls. One of the most overlooked aspects of opponents of women in selected ministerial roles is the fact that nowhere in the New Testament are gifts distributed on the basis of gender. Moreover, since God, according to Paul, makes the unilateral decision about who receives what gifts for the common good of all, we must consider anew how anyone manifesting certain gifts would be denied a role or function in the body of Christ on the basis of gender.

We observed earlier how Scripture, especially when it is inappropriately interpreted, creates some of the tension on this issue. It is beyond the scope of this chapter to revisit those exegetical battlegrounds; the literature from both sides of the debate is legion.[21] Since we are limiting ourselves to the disentanglement of the call and its relationship to gifts, two points will suffice.

The first point we draw from Weems in her narrative quoted earlier. She argues that the variety of gifts present among those entering the ministry in our time, especially the gifts of women, should be cause enough for us to rethink our understanding of call to ministry. She refers specifically to second-career people, like teachers and nurses. Furthermore, she asserts that strong abilities in preaching and pastoring are not enough reason to relegate these individuals to roles that satisfy the way we have understood call.

This is a crucial insight. How can we argue that God is sovereign, in control of the distribution of gifts necessary for effective ministry, then deny an entire group of people access to certain roles strictly on the basis of gender? How much ministry is being denied to the larger community when we deny people whom God has gifted in new and exciting ways? Can God do a new work among us if we are not open to it?

The second point is that we need another way of discussing this issue

---

21. For an introductory source that lays out four views (traditional, male leadership, plural ministry, and egalitarian), see Bonnidell Clouse and Robert G. Clouse, eds., *Women in Ministry: Four Views* (Downers Grove, Ill.: InterVarsity Press, 1989). For critical presentations from the perspective of opponents, see James B. Hurley, *Man and Woman in Biblical Perspective* (Grand Rapids: Zondervan, 1981). From the perspective of proponents, see Elisabeth Schüssler Fiorenza, *In Memory of Her: A Feminist Theological Reconstruction of Christian Origins* (New York: Crossroad, 1987), and Aida B. Spencer, *Beyond the Curse: Women Called to Ministry* (Peabody, Mass.: Hendrickson, 1985).

---

that might disentangle it. The difficulty with the issue of women's role in ministry is that, like many others, it is adversely determined in the name of God and Scripture. Who wants to be against God and Scripture? For the most part, this debate takes Scripture as the appropriate starting point. The articles and books that have made exegesis of critical passages the battleground for settling this issue are vast indeed.

However, perhaps another hermeneutical point of departure will be helpful. Something is evident in all accounts of a call from God, both biblical and extrabiblical, male and female. People ultimately accepted a call to ministry because they became convinced of its authenticity. They believed in a process that began as a divine-human encounter and continued as a human-human encounter among a community of believers.

What is intriguing about this process is that Scripture is not usually invoked until the process is nearly complete—that is, ordination. Scripture is not the starting point for assessing the authenticity of the call. What the individual has to say about self-authenticating aspects of the existential encounter with the divine, what the corporate body has to say about its experiential encounter with the one called, as well as how it assesses the person's story—these together make up the point of departure. Indeed, each of these components is central to confirmation and ordination, and without them the process is truncated.

The structural and content similarities of males and females who have received a call are instructive.[22] A very large part of the church has utilized call narratives for centuries as key evidence in the process of legitimization. Such is also the case in Scripture, especially as regards Paul's call. If call narratives have served as the starting point and as key data for confirmation of men, then why not for women as well? If one factor, like gender, can negate the value of call narratives, why not other factors, like lack of seminary training? Does not the negation of call narratives on the basis of gender alone undermine the value of call narratives in the church for all? Shall we go back into the annals of history and expunge all calls that relied on a call narrative as legitimizing evidence of a call? Whose shall we start with? How about Paul?

Training for Ministry

Who can be called also forces us to deal with the issue of training for ministry. To what extent is education a necessary component of a call to ministry? We observed earlier how the tension in Scripture, especially

---

22. Myers, *God's Yes Was Louder Than My No*, 15-66, 133-91, 227-32.

certain translations and much misinterpretation, exacerbates the problem. Misguided is the emphasis usually given to the Acts 4:13 passage about how ignorant and uneducated the disciples were. The normal term for "ignorant," in the sense of "not to know" does not appear in this passage. Luke says that these are uneducated laymen. Since the former is a *hapaxlegomenon* (appears only here) in the New Testament, we must inquire further into its meaning. The force of the passage with these two terms together would be better rendered to say that the disciples are common, unskilled laymen who lack rabbinic training.[23] Unlike Paul, who had sat at the feet of Gamaliel, earning the equivalent of his Master of Divinity, these men had no theological training.

However, this overlooks the other observation that is in the text. It was recognized that they had been with Jesus. This juxtaposition highlights the type of training they had received and from whom they had received it. Jesus knew and taught, although he lacked rabbinical training. Hence, although his disciples had not been to the formal training schools and were not exposed to the teaching of the recognized rabbis, their training from Jesus stood them well.[24] We might ask then, how many years in seminary would be equivalent to spending three years with Jesus.

However, unlike the disciples, we do not have the opportunity to spend years of training under the tutelage of Jesus; he is no longer here. Although he said he would send the Holy Spirit, we are also told that we are given teachers for our training. Why give the church gifted teachers who have been trained if we need no one other than the Spirit to teach us?

We cannot overlook the tension created by the Johannine Scriptures. Scripture affirms that God has given the community of believers teachers for the edification of the body; it also affirms the enlightening work of the Spirit. The tension is observed in the Johannine Gospel and epistle.[25] John asserts that the readers do not need anyone to teach them, but he is teaching them with the epistle.

---

23. For a helpful discussion on this text, see F. F. Bruce, *The Acts of the Apostles: Greek Text with Introduction and Commentary*, 3rd ed. (Grand Rapids: Eerdmans, 1990), 152-53.

24. Schweizer, "The Nature of Ministry," 41-63, says that there are two biblical models for ministry: the rabbinic and the prophetic. The former required training for legitimization; the latter did not. Schweizer, however, does not deny the importance of education today for those going into ministry.

25. For a helpful discussion of John 14:25, see Raymond E. Brown, *The Gospel According to John XIII-XXI: A New Translation with Introduction and Commentary*, in *The Anchor Bible*, eds. William F. Albright and David N. Freedman (Garden City, N.Y.: Doubleday, 1970), 650-53; and similarly *The Epistles of John* (Garden City, N.Y.: Doubleday, 1982) 374-76 for the 1 John 2:27 passage.

Just as we cannot separate the calling from the gifts, so also we cannot separate what one is called to do from the training necessary to do it. There is an urgent need for us to rethink the interpretation of call and the education necessary to carry it out in our churches. Carter draws attention to the issue of training when he makes a distinction between his "call to preach," which he believes everyone is called to do, and his call ("special anointing") to pastor. He connects his specific calling to the need for specific training to perform his ministry. Weems's emphasis on the special training that some second-career people bring to the call emphasizes how God may be trying to prepare the church to address new areas of ministry unheard of heretofore.

Hence, when someone says that he or she has been called, the church should not only ask what that person has been called to do, but what training is necessary to perform that particular ministry. Moreover, the church must be prepared to assist all those called to receive the type of training, academic and ministerial, necessary for them to perform well in their area of calling. The more specific our understanding of the call, the more specific should be our demands for training. Certainly, one whom God calls and gifts to be a pastor, and whom the church calls to be pastor, needs a different kind of training from that of a minister of music or a counselor.

One final point will connect the three aspects of gifts: gender and training in relation to who can be called. Never in the history of the church have so many women attended seminary, articulating their calls to ministry. They are surviving and doing well in seminary, often with little support from family, churches, denominations, or friends. In many parts of the church, we have a long history of accepting, supporting, and giving the benefit of the doubt to men in ministry who have shown far fewer gifts, little or no interest in accepting the rigors of academic preparation, and much less commitment than these women. What makes it so difficult for us to give the benefit of the doubt to women?

Consider a biblical basis for extending the benefit of the doubt in matters like these. Paul argues this way about some people who claim the call of God:

> Some proclaim Christ from envy and rivalry, but others from goodwill. These proclaim Christ out of love, knowing that I have been put here for the defense of the gospel; the others proclaim Christ out of selfish ambition, not sincerely but intending to increase my suffering in my imprisonment. What does it matter? Just this, that Christ is proclaimed in every way, whether out of false motives or true; and in that I rejoice. Yes, and I will continue to rejoice. (Phil. 1:15-18)

When the apostles were brought before the council for preaching in the name of Jesus after being ordered to stop, Gamaliel, a Pharisee and teacher of the law (and Paul's teacher) and highly regarded by all the people, spoke indirectly on their behalf: "So in the present case, I tell you, keep away from these men and let them alone; because if this plan or this undertaking is of human origin, it will fail; but if it is of God, you will not be able to overthrow them—in that case you may even be found fighting against God!" (Acts 5:38-39).

Call Narratives: Summary

It is ironic and chilling that, while we may think we are in step with Scripture, we discover that we are completely out of step with God and may be "found opposing God." Is withholding the benefit of the doubt worth the risk of being on a team opposing God?

Call narratives are retrospective hermeneutical stories constructed to persuade the hearer that God has chosen the one called to be a spokesperson for God. As such they are valuable material for the church to weigh in the rites of passage process of sanctioning these people. However, this weighing should not be done without raising some critical questions and considering carefully the answers to those questions.

How is one called? What is one called to do? Who can be called? The conclusion drawn here is that one is called by God and the church. People are called to a variety of ministries that the church must help them to concretize while resisting the temptation to reduce the call to the elusive construct known as a "call to preach." Finally, the call is not determined by gender, but by commitment and preparedness that is manifested by gifts and nurtured by training.

PART · TWO

Basic Chords

CANONS OF SERMON CONSTRUCTION

Elizabeth R. Achtemeier

E|very preacher has his or her own way of constructing a sermon, and no one can claim to have the perfect method. A solid, clear, and simple but profound proclamation of the gospel may be achieved by any one of a number of different methodologies. One has only to study the various structures of some of the great sermons of the past to realize the truth of this statement.

Nevertheless, there are some canons—some basic rules—of sermon construction that, if followed, can at least prevent the preacher from egregious distortion of the sermon's frame, and that, if obeyed, can at least ensure that the organization of the sermon has not been a detriment to the gospel.

Getting Inside the Text

Constructing the sermon is, however, very much a secondary enterprise. Before any preacher puts together a sermon, there is the first and most important step of exegesis of and meditation on the biblical text. No structure, no matter how well planned, can compensate for the failure to get inside the chosen biblical passage for the day. Either we preachers preach the Bible's message, through which there speaks the voice of the living God, or we might as well give up our pulpits and sell insurance. We have no authority, no worthwhile opinion, no special insight into the ways of God and the world apart from the Word of God. That Word comes to us from outside of ourselves, from the Scriptures, and we are its servants. We cannot create it out of our own hearts and minds, much less out of our own experience.

So the first, absolutely necessary step in sermon construction is to get inside the biblical text—not, let it immediately be said, by turning to a commentary, but by the preacher's analysis of the text's own structure and content. What are the primary emphases in the text? What are its repetitions, its imperatives, its questions, its parallelisms? What are its key words? What phrases go with what others? If it is poetry, how is it divided into strophes? Are there inclusios in the text? What is its genre and has that genre been altered in some significant way? What is the historical context of the text? And how does the text fit into its present literary context?

Most important of all, what does the text say about God? What is God doing in the text? What does the passage say about God's character, actions, and desires? In light of what is being said about God, what are the implications for human beings and the world? Probably the one characteristic that separates good and great preachers from poor and mediocre ones is that the former preach mostly about God, while the latter preach largely about human beings and their sins and follies. A twelve-year-old can tell us what is wrong with us and our world; it takes a real preacher to tell what God is doing about it.

Thus, from the biblical text, the preacher must first of all get inside, discern, and understand the message to be preached for the day. Each major point of the sermon will come from this message, resulting in a truly biblical sermon. If the preacher achieves nothing else, the biblical basis of the sermon will guarantee that it will not be a total loss.

Sermon construction is an art, however, and once having uncovered the major points of the biblical text, the way the preacher then utilizes them in the construction of the sermon determines in large measure whether the biblical message is effectively communicated to the congregation. The sermon's structure can be decisive for whether the congregation hears, or refuses to hear, or indeed is unable to do so.

Filling Out the Sermon's Content

The voice that speaks through the chosen text is that of the living God, and our God is one who, amazingly and mercifully, has stooped down from his majesty to enter into conversation with human beings. Thus the preacher does not want to ignore such conversation.

Conversation One

First, God has entered into conversation with his people Israel and with the New Testament church. That is, the chosen text is set in the context of the entire canon. The preacher, therefore, wants first to inquire into what the rest of the canon has made of the text. How, using a good Reformation principle, has Scripture interpreted Scripture?

There are numerous helps to aid the preacher in answering this question. Among them is a center-column, cross-reference Bible. In that center column are listed the biblical passages where the same text is found elsewhere in the canon, where its key words have been utilized in other passages, or where similar ideas may be found in other texts. These cross-references are invaluable for aiding the preacher to expand on the points of the text.

For example, Malachi 5:4 tells us that, before God brings final judgment on the world in the form of the Day of the Lord, God will send Elijah to preach repentance and "to turn the hearts" of the people. The cross-references listed for this verse in the RSV (the best English translation) are Matthew 11:4; 17:11; Mark 9:11-13; and Luke 1:17. All of these refer to John the Baptist. In Mark 9:13 Jesus says, "But I tell you that Elijah has come"! John the Baptist has been our prior warning, and we are called to repentance before the judgment comes! Utilizing the cross-references, the preacher who is preaching from Malachi 5:4 has been guided to the canon's indispensable new understanding of the Malachi promise.

In addition, a biblical concordance and a biblical dictionary, such as *Harper's Dictionary of the Bible,* are valuable tools to aid the preacher in understanding the text in the context of the canon. Texts have key words. For example, we read in Isaiah 40:5, "And the glory of the LORD will be revealed,/ and all mankind together will see it" (NIV). But what is the meaning of "the glory of the Lord"? How does the canon understand the terms? A study of passages containing the word *glory,* listed in a concordance, can help furnish the answer. The article on *glory* in a Bible dictionary can explain the word, and thus aid the preacher to explain to the congregation what is meant by the term.

A concordance and a Bible dictionary also are useful for uncovering the meaning of traditional motifs that are found in the chosen text. For example, suppose the preacher has chosen Isaiah 45:18-19 as the passage for the day. Central to that text is the word *chaos.* But the motif of "chaos," with its characteristics of disorder, darkness, evil, and death, runs through the Scriptures from beginning to end. It is a traditional motif that, if understood, can lend the most profound meaning to the chosen Isaiah text. The study of such traditional motifs brings depth to a sermon not ordinarily heard from the pulpit.

Conversation Two

There is a second conversation to which God has condescended through the Word of Scripture, however, and that is his speaking through the text to the congregation gathered on Sunday morning. As Paul Scherer once remarked, "God did not stop speaking when his book went to press." God did not speak only to his people in biblical times. Rather, through his Word, he continues to speak to his people in our time: "Where two or three are gathered in my name, I am there among them" (Matt. 18:20). God makes this promise true through his biblical Word.

The preacher is the meeting point, therefore, between that speaking of God through the biblical text and the gathered congregation. The preacher hears the text, listens to the text, and absorbs it not for himself or herself, but on behalf of the congregation. The preacher stands in the shoes of the people, as it were, and hears the biblical text as they hear it.

As the preacher engages in such "priestly listening" (as Leander Keck calls it), the text raises questions about itself that represent the questions of the congregation: Can what is stated here possibly be true? If it is true, then what kind of world do we live in? What if the message of this text were not true? What would that imply about God and us and our world? Do I really believe what this text says? Does our society believe it, or does it believe something else instead? Does this text mirror my life with God? Do I identify with persons in this text? Does this Word from God connect with my inner feelings and thoughts? What should I believe and do in response to this passage? What must I do to be saved?

The preacher, by struggling with such questions on behalf of the people, becomes the wrestling ring where the Word of God engages the church. From this struggle emerge manifold thoughts and answers that may be necessary to include in the sermon.

Out of such conversations of God, through the text, with the canon and with the congregation, the preacher is furnished with abundant thoughts that can be used to fill out the sermon's content.

Making Crucial Choices

Now the preacher is faced with some crucial choices. What will be the principal subject of the sermon? A plenitude of material has been assembled. From it, probably several sermons may be constructed. But the preacher wants to focus on one subject and use only the material connected with it. She or he, therefore, needs to set aside all material that is not pertinent, saving it for other Sundays or for the time three years hence when the same text recurs in the lectionary.

Making such choices sounds easy, but we preachers have a way of treasuring every thought that has entered our heads and of being reluctant to lay aside any theological "gem" we think we have dug up. Surely, we think, our people would like to hear that precious thought too! Thus our sermons sometimes become a chest full of mixed "jewels," some worthless, some valuable, but few belonging together in the same collection.

Sermons must be logical. They must hold together as unified pieces, centered around one principal subject. They need to introduce a subject, illumine it, and then bring it to a close. They have to lead the congregation through a centered experience of thought and feeling to a satisfactory conclusion. They cannot wander from one place to another, with no clue on the congregation's part as to where on earth they are being led.

Thus, having gathered together a plethora of possible materials on the basis of the biblical text, the preacher then extracts from that mass a list of points to be included in the sermon. They need not be in order initially, but they should be centered around a principal subject.

Always, as the art of sermon construction proceeds, the preacher needs to be a self-critic. Thus the preacher should ask several probing questions. First, are these points all taken from the biblical text, or from the canon's and congregation's responses to it? That is, will the message of the Word of God be preached by this sermon, or is it something I have dreamed up myself? If the latter is the case, then the preacher should throw it out and start over.

Second, do these points that I have listed concur with the apostolic faith of the church? This is a new question to be considered, one that rises out of the tradition in which we stand. We preachers are not reading the Bible and proclaiming its message for the first time in the history of the church. We stand in a long line of tradition that has so read and so proclaimed for 2,000 years. Out of that reading and proclamation there has been formed the *sensus fidelium*—the orthodox faith of the Christian church, which has found its expression in the great councils and creeds of Christianity.

The preacher, therefore, needs to ask, Does what I am going to preach accord, for example, with the faith found in the Nicene or Apostles' creeds? Is my understanding of God or of Christ or of the Holy Spirit consonant with these creedal expressions? If the answer is no, then the preacher can be sure that a wrong direction has been taken, and he or she needs to backtrack and rethink the theology involved in the sermon. The great creeds of the church are summaries of the theology of the Scriptures. If the preacher is contradicting them, she or he has not understood the Scriptures.

Outlining the Sermon

Having assembled a list of the various points, centered around one subject, the preacher has now reached one of the more important canons of sermon construction. Outline the sermon before you write!

In saying that, I immediately put myself at odds with some of the leading homileticians in this country who have written to advise that sermons should never initially be outlined. Their reasons for such advice are cogent. Outlining sermons produces static sermons, they argue. Worst of all, outlining often produces sermons that have nothing to do with the biblical text—and such sermons have been legion in the decades just past.

For an example of such a nonbiblical sermon, suppose a preacher takes as the text "He was despised and rejected by others," from the Servant Song (Isa. 53:3). The question of the sermon is then framed to be, "Why do we reject Jesus?" But the answer given comes not from Second Isaiah, but from the preacher's own speculations. Point 1: We reject Jesus because he is so familiar. Point 2: We reject Jesus because he is hard to understand. Point 3: We reject Jesus because he demands so much of us. Surely my colleagues are correct in wanting to do away with such nonbiblical sermons forever!

In defense of outlining, however, is the argument from the press of time. Far too many preachers sit down at their desks, with a good sermon "idea" in mind, and begin typing out the manuscript on the basis of that initial idea. They type furiously for two or three pages, and then they get stuck. The "idea" has been exhausted, but what should fill the other four or five pages of the sermon is unknown, because the sermon has not been thought through to the end, and the preacher has no idea where it is going or what its conclusion should be. The result is that the preacher starts all over again, or perhaps spends countless hours trying to make a whole out of what has been just an initial, if not a half-baked, idea. Preachers do not have that kind of extra time! Only the most skilled can follow such a methodology.

My view is that, if the exegetical and meditative procedures discussed above are followed, the preacher is almost automatically led to preach from the biblical text, and the result is a sermon that is far from static, but that rather proclaims the dynamics of the biblical passage. At least in my thirty-four years of teaching homiletics, I have found this always to be the case.

Outlining the sermon before writing it out in full manuscript form not only saves time but it also has several other advantages. It can enable the preacher to organize the sermon in a logical sequence so that the congregation is led through a reasonable experience of thought and feeling. If the outline is full—and it should be, with major and minor points all written in—it can immediately show the preacher whether he or she is repeating a thought. It makes clear in the preacher's mind the conclusion toward which the whole sermon is driving and helps the preacher to formulate the desired response to the sermon. It gives some indication of where illustrative material is needed in each section. And, if the outline is well done, it frees the preacher to shape and form language to its fullest power when composing the full manuscript.

When outlining the sermon, probably the preacher will first want to set down the major points and subpoints of the body of the sermon. Such a priority will ensure that the principal subject of the sermon is clear in the preacher's mind. Obviously, there need not be just three points. There may be five or four or just two. Then the preacher ponders the best way to get into the body by means of the introduction, and he or she plans the most effective way to conclude, to drive home the point of the sermon and to call forth the desired response from the congregation.

Once again, several choices have to be made. Should the introduction begin with the situation of the congregation or with that of the biblical text? Either alternative may be employed. Will the historical context of the text need to be explained, given the average congregation's ignorance of the content of Scripture? Does the structure of the text immediately suggest an outline for the sermon? Some biblical texts lay themselves out in a logical progression that almost dictates the outline of the sermon; others demand rearrangement of the progression of thought and experience. Does the text have a leading motif that might serve as a recurring refrain throughout the sermon? What does the biblical text do, and how can that function be duplicated in the sermon?

Above all, the preacher wants to consider how the sermon may move constantly back and forth between the content of the text and the life of the congregation. This is one of the more crucial questions to be answered in the process of sermon construction. No major point should ever be made in a sermon and brought to a closure without at the same time treating the life of the congregation. Speaking from the Bible should always, at the same time, be speaking about our present life. God, speaking through the Scriptures, addresses not only the life of Israel and of the church in the past, but he also addresses us through that history in the present. Good biblical sermons, then, involve a constant movement back and forth between the Bible's text and the experience and thought of the gathered people.

This means that one of the forms of sermons that always should be avoided is that of the "plain-form." Such a form has the following outline: (1) the situation of Israel or of the New Testament church; (2) the solution of the text to that situation; (3) our analogous situation; (4) the solution of the text for our situation. The whole first half of such a sermon involves persons other than the congregation and, indeed, persons who lived centuries ago. As one churchgoer remarked about such a sermon, "I get so tired of being talked to as if I were a Corinthian." The result is that the congregation becomes convinced during the first minutes of the sermon that it has nothing to do with them, and they stop listening and turn off their minds and hearts—or perhaps fall asleep. The listening people must be involved from the first in the experience of the sermon—an experience prompted by the biblical text—and that involvement must continue throughout the sermon, with a constant movement back and forth between biblical Word and the congregation.

There are manifold types of sermon forms, and, for the sake of variety, the preacher may want to utilize a number of them. For example, one of the most common these days is the narrative form, popularized by Eugene Lowry, in which the sermon takes on the structure of a good novel or short story. A problem is introduced at the beginning to arouse a tension in the listeners. The sermon then moves through a "plot" to a conclusion that resolves the tension. Variety in the pulpit, however, is not the main goal of preaching. Rather, the aim is to communicate the message of the biblical text, and the content of the text is what should dictate the form chosen. Content determines form; form should not determine content—not when we are dealing with the Word of God.

Writing the Sermon

All sermons should be written out in full manuscript form, whether the preacher later preaches from memory or from notes, from an outline or from a manuscript. No one of these methods is better than another, despite the unjustified pride that some homileticians take in having no notes before them in the pulpit. Some of the greatest preachers of the past generation always had manuscripts before them. The fully written manuscript allows the preacher to shape and hone the language of the sermon to its sharpest and most powerful edge. It prevents the preacher from saying something unplanned that he or she wishes afterward had not been said. It guards the preacher from repetition and allows the sermon to drive forward to a climax and conclusion. And it frees the preacher to enter into worship with the congregation rather than being distracted by thinking about what is going to be preached.

Writing the Introduction

There are several "canons" for writing the introduction to a sermon, which the preacher should always keep in mind. First, the introduction should express the principal subject of the sermon—a canon that seems so obvious and yet is so often ignored! It sometimes happens that the preacher has a good story or a telling incident that he or she is eager to share with the congregation. So it is used as the sermon's introduction. Then, to the congregation's confusion, the body of the sermon goes off in an entirely different direction, and the people in the pews never are quite certain what the sermon is all about.

Second, introductions should awaken immediately the congregation's interest by informing them that the sermon will have something to do with their lives. Even when the introduction begins with the content of the biblical text, immediately a problem should be posed or a question raised or an analogy drawn that shows that this text concerns the listening people.

Third, the most common error of sermon introductions is that they are too long. Some preachers spend two pages introducing what they are going to talk about, whereas proper introductions are, at most, about three-quarters of a double-spaced page. Introductions should present the principal subject, arouse interest, and then move smoothly into the first point of the sermon's body. "Get on with it!"—that is the canon for sermon openings.

Writing the Body of the Sermon

Words are preachers' tools, and few more effective tools have been granted to us than the English language. With its rhythms, its cadences, its rich vocabulary, its flexibility, its sounds, the English language, when properly used, can sustain an embattled nation (as it did for England in the Second World War), or inspire a people to dream of equality (as it did at the 1963 March on Washington, D.C.), or convey a lover's heart (as *Sonnets from the Portuguese* testify). Indeed, when properly used, the English language can open our ears and hearts to listen for the voice of the living God.

Preachers, therefore, are to be masters of words, and the preacher who will not work with words to improve his or her language skills and strive always to convey at least something of the treasures of the riches of Christ is like the carpenter who will not sharpen saw and chisel but instead uses only an ax. We Christians have a glorious God, and the language we use to tell about God should at least strive to mirror something of that incomparable glory.

The language that is employed to write out the body of a sermon, however, should be as clear and simple and pictorial as possible. Human beings live by images—by pictures created in their minds. If we hear the words *chocolate sundae,* we make a mental image. If we hear the word *mother,* our hearts become involved. In writing our sermons, therefore, one need always to ask oneself: What do my people see when I say this? If I say the word *grace* or *salvation* or *justification* or *sin*—all those big theological terms—do my people have any mental image of what I mean? Or do all of those terms need to be put in other pictures so the realities lying behind the terms are grasped by the congregation? Speak pictures in the people's hearts, pictures prompted by the Scriptures—that is the canon for writing the body of the sermon.

Illustrating the Sermon

It sometimes is the case that a preacher's language is so vivid and so pictorial that no illustrative material is needed in the sermon. The images created by the preacher's language furnish their own illumination of what is being said. But most preachers need to use illustrative material in the body of the sermon in order to make concrete and vivid the message being preached, and in order for the congregation to identify with it. There are some canons for the use of illustrations that every preacher should heed.

The most common error preachers make in the use of illustrations is to make them too long. Very often preachers recount a long story in the middle of a sermon, but stories have their own points, which frequently have nothing to do with the biblical text. They have their own rhythms, which can interrupt the rhythm of the sermon. They are easily identified with, so that the congregation lives into the story rather than into the biblical text. The results are that the lengthy story brings the forward movement of the sermon to a halt, and the congregation is lost in the lesson of the story and not in the scriptural message.

In similar fashion, preachers often quote long poems or stanzas of hymns. But if good poetry is quoted, whether from hymn or verse, the average congregation member cannot absorb more than two or three lines read orally. Bad poetry, which is trite and didactic or sentimental, should be omitted altogether. And rarely is it necessary to quote more than two or three lines of a hymn for the congregation to grasp the illustrative point being made.

Illustrations should not be piled on top of one another. There are preaching traditions in which the sermon consists entirely of one little moral story after another. The congregation then is supposed to extract some "eternal truth" from such a hodgepodge. But inspirational stories are no substitute for the proclamation of the biblical message, and it is with the latter that the preacher is entrusted.

The primary function of illustrations is to illumine and make concrete the message being delivered, but if they are skillfully used, they can also function as a change of pace in the sermon. The preacher may proceed in a narrative fashion for several minutes, at which point an illumining illustration is inserted, which not only clarifies, but also breaks the rhythm of the narrative and serves to increase attention to what is being said.

Writing the Conclusion

Conclusions are intended to sum up and drive home the principal point of the sermon. As George Buttrick used to say, "Here is where you nail 'em to the pew." They should be brief, they should come soon enough, and they should form the climax of the sermon.

The most frequent error committed in sermonic conclusions is suddenly to introduce a new scriptural quotation or a new thought that has not been treated previously in the body of the sermon. This gives the impression that the preacher is starting all over again with another sermon, or it distracts from the point of the message that has been delivered. If the preacher wants to quote Scripture in the conclusion, then she or he should return to the chosen text. That text forms the center upon which the whole sermon has been concentrated, and it must not be abandoned at the end.

Further, conclusions should be put in positive and not negative form. At the close of a sermon, we want the congregation to affirm the gospel, to answer "Yeah!" as it were. We do not want people left hanging, wondering how to respond, or even left with a question. The conclusion should point them in the right direction and nudge them along the way, so that the desired response is forthcoming in their thought and action. Biblical preaching pictures for a congregation what the Christian life looks like. A good conclusion to a biblical sermon prompts a start on the path of that life.

What's at Stake

Such are some of the elements of preaching that must be considered in the construction of biblical sermons. Some of them are hard and fast canons that never should be neglected; some are of lesser importance; but all can contribute to the construction of sermons faithful to the Word of God.

Faithful preaching is not an easy task—no one ever said it would be. It takes study and thought, prayer and meditation, writing and self-criticism, and just plain hard work. Sometimes the words flow onto the page, as if the Holy Spirit were dictating them. Sometimes they come slowly, wrenched out one by one in the most agonizing struggle.

But, after all, the purpose of preaching is so to frame human words that God may use them to create new persons in Jesus Christ. We preachers are dealing with new birth when we preach our sermons, and birth frequently is painful and even bloody. But the aim is eternal life for our people, whom we love. Their eternal life or death may depend on whether God can use what we say on any given Sunday. Since that is what is at stake, let us get on with the task!

BIBLE AND SERMON: THE CONVERSATION BETWEEN TEXT AND PREACHER

Gail R. O'Day

In this essay I use the metaphor of "conversation" to describe the interaction between preacher and biblical text in the preparation of a sermon.[1] I choose this metaphor because it captures the dynamic dimension of interpretive work, evoking a variety of voices that are present in the preacher's study as he or she explores the biblical text.

Unfortunately, more often than most teachers of preaching and Bible are willing to admit, this conversation ends almost as soon as it begins for many preachers, because the conversation too quickly becomes one between antagonists rather than allies.[2] The stillborn nature of this conversation results in part from the way preaching is taught and understood, and in part from the way biblical interpretation (exegesis) is taught and understood.

For example, when preaching is understood as the transmission of an idea or lesson to the congregation, then exegesis is a largely irrelevant act for the preacher. Once the idea or lesson is gleaned from the biblical text, the text can be (and often is) abandoned. When exegesis is understood strictly as reconstructing the past of a biblical text and its original meanings, then it is hard for the preacher to take seriously how an "ancient" text can speak to the modern world. We therefore need to revisit how we

---

1. I do not use "conversation" with the full ontological weight of Gadamer (see Hans-Georg Gadamer, *Truth and Method* [New York: Seabury Press, 1975]) and Gadamerian hermeneutics (e.g., David Tracy, *The Analogical Imagination* [New York: Crossroad, 1981]), but as a heuristic device.

2. See Walter Brueggemann, "The Preacher, the Text, and the People," *Theology Today* 47 (1990), 237-47.

understand both biblical interpretation and preaching in order to revital-
ize the conversation between them.

Biblical Interpretation: Discovering the Voices of the Text

Traditional historical-critical exegesis tends to accentuate the gap
between what a text said and what a text says, by focusing on the past of
the biblical text and on the world behind the text.[3] When the past of the
text is exclusively emphasized, and especially when that emphasis falls
on the sources and editorial processes that led to the composition of a
canonical biblical text, it is very difficult for the preacher to identify what
that particular history has to offer contemporary believers.

One result of the traditional historical-critical approach to the past,
then, has been to isolate questions of biblical history and culture from
questions of contemporary appropriation of the biblical text, an isolation
that has flattened the conversation that can be conducted between the
text and the preacher. This is unfortunate, because without an informed
awareness of the historical, cultural, and social factors that surround
both the stories related in biblical texts and the social environment in
which those texts were written, any contemporary appropriation of a
biblical text risks becoming a docetic appropriation of the text. That is,
the preacher risks separating the biblical text from the concrete struggles
of faith to which it speaks.

This isolating focus on the past is balanced, or perhaps answered,
within biblical studies by the move toward what is now known as literary criticism.[4] In literary criticism, the focus is on the present of the text
and on the world of the text. That is, literary-critical biblical study
focuses on the rhetorical dimension of the biblical text, on how the text
says what it says.[5] It pays attention to the world that each text creates
and emphasizes the role of the reader in entering that world. Literary
criticism recognizes the inseparable unity of form and content, and proceeds from the foundational assumption that no biblical books are purely

---

3. See, for example, the classic statement of this perspective in Krister Stendahl,
"Biblical Theology," *Interpreter's Dictionary of the Bible,* vol. 1 (Nashville: Abingdon Press, 1962), 418-32.

4. For a general overview to this approach to Scripture, see the two books in
the Guides to Biblical Scholarship Series published by Fortress Press: William A.
Beardslee, *What Is Literary Criticism?* (Philadelphia, 1970); and Phyllis Trible,
Rhetorical Criticism: Context, Method, and the Book of Jonah (Minneapolis, 1994).

5. See Gail R. O'Day, *Revelation in the Fourth Gospel* (Philadelphia: Fortress
Press, 1986).

historical (or ethical) documents, but all are also literary compositions, some with elaborate rhetorical and formal features.

Two cautions, however, need to be raised about literary criticism and biblical interpretation. First, literary criticism—and literary critics—cannot afford to be either ignorant or disdainful of the fruits of historical criticism. Literary criticism depends on much of the work of historical criticism to do its own interpretive work with integrity, even when that dependence is unacknowledged. It is not an either/or interpretive situation, either historical or literary criticism.

One of the central contributions of literary criticism has been to draw the interpreter's attention to the narrative world of the text.[6] Yet this narrative world is created by drawing on images and assumptions from the author's culture. For example, it is possible to read Jesus' parables in isolation, as independent stories in their own right. But these stories as story are even more compelling if the interpreter knows something about agricultural practices in first-century Palestine, about how day laborers normally got paid, about proper decorum for fathers and sons in the ancient Mediterranean world.[7] Historical criticism can be an ally to literary criticism because it gives the interpreter additional tools to open up the metaphors and images of the Bible.

Second, there is a tendency in much contemporary literary-critical biblical studies for literary-critical method to occupy the center of scholarly conversations, rather than the texts themselves. We are in danger of becoming skilled in interpretive method rather than skilled in interpretation. This is a danger for any scholarly method, but literary criticism now seems particularly prone to this danger. Note the following quotation from the novel *How to Make an American Quilt*:

> Literature was my next love. Until I became loosely acquainted with critical theory, which struck me as a kind of intellectualism for its own sake. It always seems that one has to choose literature or critical theory, that one cannot have both.[8]

The choice may not be quite as stark as this novel's character articulates, but the character's words do contain a note of caution for the interpreter.

---

6. The seminal example of this approach is Amos Wilder, *Early Christian Rhetoric: The Language of the Gospel*, 2nd ed. (Cambridge, Mass.: Harvard University Press, 1971).

7. See, for example, John Donahue, *The Gospel in Parable* (Philadelphia: Fortress Press, 1988).

8. Whitney Otto, *How to Make an American Quilt* (New York: Villard, 1991), 3.

Any interpretive method that loves itself more than it loves the text it is intended to interpret will lead to the same stillborn conversation that tends to happen in traditional historical-critical exegesis.

Because the reader plays such a primary role in literary-critical methods, this approach to biblical interpretation allows and indeed encourages the interpreter to engage in playful conversation with the biblical text. How language is used and images are constructed, the effect of those images on the reader, the inseparability of form and content—these concerns all point to the reader's own engagement with the biblical text. As a result of this emphasis on the present of the text and the interaction between text and reader, literary criticism can be seen as a method of immediacy. The gap between meant and means is closed through the emphasis on what the text means in the reading of the text.

Biblical Preaching: An Exercise in Textual Imagination

We have thus far identified two voices that are present in the conversation between the preacher and the text: the voice of traditional exegetical disciplines that can be understood as focusing on the past of the biblical text and the world behind the text, and the voice of literary criticism that focuses on the present of the biblical text and the world of the text. I would like to propose a third voice in the conversation, the voice of biblical preaching that focuses on the future of the biblical text and the world in front of the text.

To speak of the future of the text is to inquire into how and where the world of the text intersects in generative ways with the worlds of those who attempt to live their lives in and through the biblical texts. While it is true that the work of literary criticism on the present of the text can spill over into a consideration of the future of the text, the biblical text's future is the primary domain of biblical preaching.

This discussion of the worlds of the text as they pertain to biblical preaching should suggest that by "biblical preaching" I do not mean the type of preaching often identified as "expository preaching." The goal of biblical preaching is not to explain the ideas of a text. Rather, the goal of biblical preaching is to invite the listener into the world of the text, so that he or she can discover what new possibilities for life become available if one allows one's life to be shaped by this particular text.

This requires a shift in the way preaching is understood. At the heart of the Christian faith is the Word:

> Then God said, "Let there be light . . . "
> And God said, "Let there be a dome . . . "

And God said, "Let the waters . . . "
And God said, "Let there be lights in the dome of the sky . . . "
And God said, "Let the waters bring forth swarms of living
   creatures . . . "
And God said, "Let the earth bring forth living creatures of
   every kind . . . "
Then God said, "Let us make humankind in our image,
   according to our likeness . . . "
And it was so. (Gen. 1:1-31)

In the beginning was the Word, and the Word was with God,
   and the Word was God. (John 1:1)

Long ago God spoke to our ancestors in many and various ways by the
prophets, but in these last days he has spoken to us by a Son, whom he
appointed heir of all things, through whom he also created the worlds.
(Heb. 1:1-2)

These texts remind us that the Christian community is a people of faith
who claim the centrality of words, who acknowledge the power and
presence of the Word of God through words. It is the task of the preacher
to attend carefully to the words of faith and to allow one's preaching to
be shaped by the invitation offered by the biblical texts to embrace a
world of evangelical possibility. It is in this embrace of evangelical possibility that the future of the text is discovered. This understanding of the
relationship between biblical text and preaching is in marked contrast to
the way the voice of the biblical text is frequently constrained by an
understanding of preaching as essentially dogmatic or moral exhortation.

The phrase "in many and various ways" in Hebrews 1:1 is especially
important for biblical preaching. It is this variety of ways of speaking that
biblical preaching, with its attentiveness to form, content, and imagination,
can reintroduce into the conversation between text and preacher. The
preacher can use words, as the biblical authors used words, to reform,
reshape, and renew people's imaginations about the shape of life with God
and with one another. It is, therefore, possible to think of preaching as an
exercise in imagination, and of biblical preaching in particular as an exercise
in textual imagination.

Joseph Sittler has powerfully articulated the role of the imagination, of
the reconceptualization of what is possible, in preaching:

In a sense, that's what a sermon is for: to hang the holy possible in front of
the mind of the listeners and lead them to that wonderful moment when

they say, "If it were true it would do." To pass from that to belief is the work of the Holy Spirit, not of the preacher or the teacher.[9]

The sermon opens up the possibility of new ways of thinking and being, and by so doing opens up the possibility of new lives and new worlds. The words the preacher uses to lead and shape these fresh possibilities, this new reality, are crucial. The task of biblical preaching is to find a way to stay inside the world of the text while, at the same time, revealing the futures of that text and that world, because those futures constitute the present for the listener.

The Bible itself provides the preacher with a wealth of examples of the conversation among the past, present, and future voices of traditions that constitute the proclamation of the good news of God for new and changing communities of faith. This essay will briefly examine two of these examples: (1) the book of Deuteronomy and (2) Paul's use of tradition in 1 Corinthians 15:1-11.

Deuteronomy as a Model of Biblical Preaching

Two scholarly hypotheses provide the background for the interpretation of Deuteronomy as biblical preaching. First, Old Testament scholars have long recognized that the designation of Deuteronomy as a "law code" is inadequate as a description of both the content and the function of this concluding book of the Pentateuch. While Deuteronomy does contain legal ordinances, the presentation of these laws in Deuteronomy "is something unique in the legal literature of the Old Testament."[10] Unlike the presentation of the legal code in the Book of the Covenant (Exod. 20:22–23:33), for example, the legal material in Deuteronomy is not formulated as the words of God to Moses, but as the speeches of Moses to the people of Israel. Its very genre thus indicates that Deuteronomy is an interpretation of the law, not merely a recital of the law.

Second, the narrative setting of Deuteronomy, the words of Moses spoken to the people on the plains of Moab at the end of their wilderness wanderings and immediately prior to their entering the promised land and Moses' death, is a literary device, not an indication of the actual origins of the book of Deuteronomy. It is clear from internal references that Deuteronomy comes from a much later period in Israel's history and that

---

9. Joseph Sittler, *Gravity and Grace* (Minneapolis: Augsburg, 1986), 63.

10. Gerhard von Rad, "Ancient Word and Living Word: The Preaching of Deuteronomy and Our Preaching," *Interpretation* 15 (1961): 3.

the received, canonical text of Deuteronomy went through several stages of composition. Most of Deuteronomy derives from the late monarchical period (eighth century B.C.E.), and those traditions probably served as the basis of King Josiah's reforms in 621 B.C.E. (2 Kings 22–23). Additional material was added to these traditions as a result of those reforms, and the final revisions of the book of Deuteronomy were probably completed in the Exile (Deut. 4 and 30).[11]

These two hypotheses provide the background for understanding Deuteronomy as biblical preaching because they help to identify the theological and pastoral intent of this book. Deuteronomy was not written for a people about to enter the promised land, but for a people who had long lived in the land and had grown complacent about this gift from God and their relationship and responsibilities to God and to one another in the land. Yet Deuteronomy chooses to speak to that later audience through the lens of that earlier story. That is, instead of speaking directly to the conditions that governed life in the eighth and seventh centuries, the author(s) of Deuteronomy invited Israel to see itself as the people on the plains of Moab.

It is quite possible to interpret Deuteronomy's handling of traditions as "preaching." Indeed, one of the most commonly held scholarly conclusions about Deuteronomy is that it is essentially a sermon, or collection of sermons, on the Mosaic laws and traditions.[12] Gerhard von Rad identifies the purpose of Deuteronomy this way: "The task which these preachers set themselves is clear. They are concerned to make the old cultic and legal traditions relevant for their time."[13]

The hermeneutical work of Martin Noth on Deuteronomy provides the most assistance in understanding Deuteronomy as biblical preaching. In one of Noth's seminal articles, he speaks of Deuteronomy as engaged in the "re-presentation" of tradition.[14] That is, the authors of Deuteronomy take what belongs to the past (i.e., the Sinai and Moab traditions) and give it new life by bringing it into the present of a new audience. The

---

11. For discussion of the composition history of Deuteronomy, see, e.g., Richard Nelson, "Deuteronomy," *Harper Bible Commentary*, ed. James L. Mays (New York: Harper & Row, 1988), 209-11.

12. This view of Deuteronomy is argued most clearly and persuasively by Gerhard von Rad. He speaks of Deuteronomy as "law preached" (*Studies in Deuteronomy* [London: SCM Press, 1953], 16). See also his *Old Testament Theology*, vol. 1, trans. G. M. Stalker (New York: Harper, 1962), 220-31.

13. Gerhard von Rad, *Deuteronomy*, Old Testament Library (Philadelphia: Westminster Press, 1966), 23.

14. Martin Noth, "The 'Re-Presentation' of the Old Testament in Proclamation," *Interpretation* 15 (1961): 50-60.

traditions are reformulated "in such a way as to make Israel hear the Law as if it were for the very first time."[15] Deuteronomy is thus a classic example of the convergence of past, present, and future that constitutes the preacher's conversation with the text.

This conversation among past, present, and future can be illustrated with two texts. Moses introduces the Decalogue in Deuteronomy 5:2-3 with the words, "The LORD our God made a covenant with us at Horeb. Not with our ancestors did the LORD make this covenant, but with us, who are all of us here alive today." This is not a historical slip on Moses' part—he has not forgotten the making of the covenant at Sinai a generation before (Exodus 20–24), nor is he arguing for the superiority of the Horeb covenant.[16] Rather, the authors of Deuteronomy place the "representation" of tradition in the mouth of Moses himself, thus giving Mosaic sanction to their own interpretive work.

Moses asks his listeners to cross the gap between past and present. They are not members of the Sinai generation (that generation is already deceased), yet he claims for this new generation the present moment of the covenant, explicitly declaring it a covenant made with "all of us here alive today." It is a brilliant literary and pastoral move; just as the audience of Deuteronomy is intended to understand itself as if it were present on the plains of Moab, so also the audience within Deuteronomy is asked to imagine itself as if it were the immediate generation with whom the covenant was made.

The second text also asks the listening audience, both inside and outside of the story, to understand the "old" story as their own story, and hence a "new" story. Deuteronomy 26:5-11 is one of the foundational creedal statements of Israel's religious identity.[17] In this text, Israel confesses its faith in God and affirms its relationship with God in the form of a story, the recital of the events of the exodus. What is remarkable about this text is not the story it relates, for that story is the foundational narrative of the Pentateuch, but the way it tells the story. The story begins as historical recital, as a story about someone else. "A wandering Aramean was my ancestor; he went down into Egypt and lived there as an alien" (v. 5). But very quickly it becomes "our" story: "When the Egyptians treated us harshly and afflicted us . . . we cried to the LORD, the God of our ancestors; the LORD heard our voice and saw our affliction. . . . The LORD brought us out of Egypt . . . and he brought us into this place and gave us this land" (vv. 6-9).

---

15. Ibid., 55.
16. Ibid.
17. See von Rad, *Old Testament Theology*, vol. 1, 121-22.

As at Deuteronomy 5:2-3, even within the narrative construct of the book of Deuteronomy, this first-person plural pronoun is striking because the generation on the plains of Moab is not the generation that struggled under Pharaoh. Yet within the broader framework of Deuteronomy, the first-person plural is even more striking, because Israelites more than seven centuries removed from the events of the exodus are asked to see that story as part of their story, are asked to claim those events of the past as the constituting events of their present lives.

What does it mean to ask later generations of Israelites, of believers who affirm their faith in the God of the exodus, to see their present lives as an extension of the exodus story, to read their present as a part of the future of those traditions? For the authors of Deuteronomy, it was a bold preaching move, because the audience to which they proclaimed the presence and promises of God no longer stood on the edge between promise and fulfillment, standing at the River Jordan looking at what might be and what could be, but was not yet. Instead, they preached to a generation that had long lived in the land, that understood the land as their due, not as a gift, and for whom the struggles of faith that had brought them to their present situation were at best a distant memory, reenacted when the cultic festivals required it, but no longer the defining reality at the core of their lives with God and one another.

To invite their audience to stand on the banks of the Jordan, listening to Moses on the plains of Moab, was to invite them to enter that world and to discover what fresh possibilities for life that world had to offer their situation. It was to invite the listeners to examine how and where the world of the Mosaic traditions intersects with their own world. It was to invite the listeners to reshape their lives according to the shape of that "old" story. The book of Deuteronomy is a powerful example of an exercise in textual imagination that intends to uncover the future of the text in the present lives of the community of faith.

First Corinthians 15:1-11 as a Model of Biblical Preaching

First Corinthians 15 comes near the end of a letter that provides a revealing look at Paul's pastoral style. The concerns that Paul addresses in most of this letter are quite practical—divisions among the members of the community (1 Cor. 1–4), questions of marriage and sexuality (1 Cor. 5; 7), lawsuits against community members (1 Cor. 6), relationships between Christians and non-Christians (1 Cor. 8–10), problems in worship (1 Cor. 12–14), and the collection for the poor (1 Cor. 16). Yet Paul does not settle for giving the Corinthians "practical" advice.

Instead, he attempts to help the Corinthians place their community problems in a theological and christological framework. The centerpiece of the discussion of relationships between Christians and non-Christians, for example, is Paul's reflection on the meaning of Christian responsibility to the gospel (1 Cor. 9), and the centerpiece of the discussion of problems in worship is the hymn to love (1 Cor. 13). Paul does not separate the practical and pastoral from the theological, but instead demonstrates that it is in practical and pastoral crises that theology needs to be its strongest.

In 1 Corinthians 15 Paul is no longer addressing one particular issue in the life of the Corinthian community, but instead addresses a theological problem that has implications for all aspects of the community's life. The subject of this chapter is the resurrection, of both Jesus and the believer, and its significance for Christian faith and life. Throughout 1 Corinthians 15 Paul confronts the variety of views the Corinthians seem to hold about the resurrection, and he shows how such beliefs move the community away from the core of the gospel of Jesus' death and resurrection.

First Corinthians 15:1-11 is the introduction to this theologically rich chapter, and these verses provide the preacher with another example of "biblical preaching."[18] Paul engages the Corinthians' contemporary disagreements about the resurrection by bringing their conversations back to their beginnings in the proclamation of the good news of Jesus. First Corinthians 15:1-11 consists of a recital of the Jesus tradition (vv. 3-8), framed by two units that make the contemporary dimensions of the conversation explicit. In verses 1-2, Paul points to the Corinthians' experience of the tradition; in verses 9-11, he points to his own.

Verses 1-2 provide the key to understanding Paul's use of tradition to speak to the Corinthians' present experience. These two verses are one long, complex sentence in the Greek text (and are correctly punctuated that way in the NRSV). They focus on the personal and communal claim that the proclamation of the gospel makes on those who hear and receive it. The complex syntax, in which each phrase is intrinsically connected to the one that follows, points to the inseparability of proclaimer, community, and proclamation that is at the heart of Paul's message in 1 Corinthians 15:1-11.

These two verses also have a concentrated use of personal pronouns. Paul speaks of himself three times in verses 1-2: "now I would remind

---

18. For a general overview of Paul as preacher, see David Bartlett, "Texts Shaping Sermons," in *Listening to the Word: Essays in Honor of Fred B. Craddock*, ed. Gail R. O'Day and Thomas G. Long (Nashville: Abingdon Press, 1993), 157-60.

you"; "of the good news that I proclaimed to you"; "the message that I proclaimed to you." Each of his self-references describes his identity and vocation as the proclaimer of the good news. Paul's authority as apostle to this community does not derive from anything intrinsic to Paul himself, but from what he does and the word that he makes available to them. Moreover, Paul's self-identity is inseparable from the relationship of his work to the community of faith. His proclamation of the good news is important because he proclaimed it "to you," not simply because Paul proclaimed it. Paul's words about his own role as gospel proclaimer point to the intersection of present community experience and the foundational "news" of the Christian faith.

What is even more noteworthy about verses 1-2, however, is the number of times Paul refers to the Corinthians themselves. He addresses them directly eight times in these two verses. This concentration of the second-person plural pronoun points to Paul's central emphasis: This tradition is part of who "you" are, and "you" cannot contemplate "your" present or future lives independently of the good news of Jesus. The pivot of the second-person plural references (e.g., "which you in turn received," "in which you also stand," "through which you are also being saved") is the "if" clause in verse 2, "if you hold firmly to the message that I proclaimed to you." The Corinthians' experience of the salvation that the gospel of Jesus Christ offers them depends on their continuing reception of the gospel. If they remove themselves from the good news, they remove themselves from its offer of salvation. It is a remarkable pastoral move, through which Paul invests the reception of the gospel message with as much theological significance as the proclamation of the gospel message.

The theological significance of the reception of the gospel message is further underscored in Paul's opening words in verse 3. The language that he uses is that of tradition, "I handed on . . . what I in turn had received." As the proclaimer of the good news, Paul understands himself to be one in a series of witnesses to the good news, a witness that began when he received the message himself.

Verses 3-5 are the oldest written testimony to the death and resurrection of Jesus.[19] Paul uses this early creedal formulation to remind the Corinthians of their identity as recipients of the gospel. The creed consists of two parallel parts, one that focuses on the death (vv. 3*b*-4*a*) and a second that focuses on the resurrection (vv. 4*b*-5). Each part contains a

---

19. Hans Conzelmann, "On the Analysis of the Confessional Formula in 1 Cor. 15:3-5," *Interpretation* 20 (1966): 15-25.

main verb ("died," v. 3*b*; "was raised," v. 4*b*) and a secondary verb that corroborates the action of the main verb ("was buried," v. 4*a*; "appeared," v. 5). In addition, each part of the creed contains the phrase "in accordance with the scriptures." The references to Scripture are general and do not cite particular verses, because the phrase is intended to show that the death and resurrection of Jesus were in accordance with God's plan for salvation as contained in Scripture, not to engage in looking for proof texts. In these verses, then, Paul reminds the Corinthians of the core tradition, the central good news that informs their life as Christians.

Verses 6-7 expand the core tradition by expanding the list of appearances. This expansion serves several purposes. First, it introduces the notion of the openness of the experience of the gospel. The encounter with the risen Jesus was not limited to Cephas and the twelve, but was available to a multitude of believers. Second, this openness allows for Paul's introduction of his own experience (v. 8). Paul understands his own experience of the risen Jesus as of a piece with the appearances recounted in the creed.[20]

Verses 9-11 return the focus to the contemporary setting. By including his own story in the recital of the core story of the faith, Paul shows that the stories and events of the past do indeed open up to present experiences of faith. The stories of the past contain the seeds of their own future. As verse 9 makes clear, Paul was the least likely candidate for an experience of the risen Jesus, yet the grace of God opened the death and resurrection of Jesus to Paul, so that his story does indeed belong to the gospel story (v. 10). It is not arrogance that leads Paul to include his own story in the recital of the gospel tradition, but a deep faith in the power of that tradition to remake lives. This faith lies behind his final reminder to the Corinthians in verse 11: It does not matter from whom one received the gospel; what matters is that the gospel has been proclaimed and believed. And, as Paul's own experience recounted for the Corinthians in verses 8-10 demonstrates, when one understands one's own experience in continuity with the stories of the tradition, one's life is opened up to previously unimagined present and future possibilities of life with God.

First Corinthians 15:1-11 is thus an analogous text to Deuteronomy 26:5-11 in that both involve a recital of the foundational story of the faith of the community. In the case of 1 Corinthians 15, this story is that of the death and resurrection of Jesus. What is significant about 1 Corinthians

---

20. In the larger argument about the resurrection in 1 Corinthians 15, v. 6 serves another function by introducing the deaths of some believers (cf. 1 Cor. 15:12, 19, 29).

15 as a model of biblical preaching is the way in which Paul moves back and forth between the tradition he recites and the community's experience of that tradition. As with the use of tradition in Deuteronomy, the tradition of Jesus' death and resurrection does not remain lodged in the past as historical artifact, but is presented with an eye toward its significance for the present lives of the Corinthian believers. Paul thus models the conversation among past, present, and future that is the preacher's conversation.

The Conversation of Biblical Preaching

Deuteronomy and 1 Corinthians 15 are biblical examples that help the preacher see the promise of the conversation in which the biblical traditions and contemporary experience speak to each other. The authors of Deuteronomy and Paul knew that the faith community ultimately learns who it is by the words that it speaks, by the language through which it tells its faith.

The words of the disciples on the road to Emmaus evoke the possibilities of the conversation among past, present, and future that can occur around the biblical texts.

> They said to each other, "Were not our hearts burning within us while he was talking to us on the road, while he was opening the scriptures to us?" (Luke 24:32)

The challenge for the preacher is to open up this conversation in his or her own preaching, so that the members of the congregation can imagine their lives transformed and renewed by the possibilities of the biblical texts.

PREACHING AND EXEGESIS IN THE FIRST CENTURY: HEBREWS

William L. Lane

I first met James Earl Massey in Nashville in May 1990. We had gathered with eight other specialists in Old Testament, New Testament, and Homiletics at the invitation of The United Methodist Publishing House and Abingdon Press to constitute an editorial board for a major new venture, *The New Interpreter's Bible*. In the course of informal conversation, shared meals, and editorial board deliberations, I recognized immediately that Massey was a brother whose wisdom, friendship, and collegiality I wanted to enjoy.

In 1986, Dean Massey delivered the Newell Lectures in Biblical Studies at Anderson University. He chose as his topic "The Letter to the Hebrews: Current Understandings and Use" and devoted himself to developing the rich resources for preaching in this important document.[1] Whenever Massey approaches the biblical text, the deep love that he has for Scripture and for preaching is transparently clear. These qualities have been the hallmark of a distinguished career as an interpreter and proclaimer of the Word of God.

Defining the Genre of Hebrews

In the Greek manuscript tradition of the New Testament, Hebrews appears exclusively in association with the letters of Paul. The oldest copy of this document is provided by a collection of Pauline letters, the

---

1. These resources soon will be seen in the forthcoming Massey volume, *Preaching from Hebrews: Homiletical and Hermeneutical Helps* (Grand Rapids: Zondervan).

Chester Beatty Papyrus (P46), which dates from the beginning of the third century. Within this collection it bears the superscription "To the Hebrews" in the same way that a letter of Paul's is identified as "To the Romans" or "To the Corinthians." In this early manuscript, Hebrews is placed after Romans and before 1 Corinthians. In several of the later uncial codices, it is positioned after the letters to the churches (i.e., after 2 Thessalonians and before 1 Timothy). The association of Hebrews with the letters of the New Testament encourages a reader to regard this work as a letter. Thus it is conventional to refer to the "Letter to the Hebrews."

Hebrews, however, does not exhibit the form of an ancient letter. The document lacks the conventional prescript of a letter and has none of the characteristic features of ordinary letters from this general period.[2] The opening lines fail to identify the writer or the group addressed. They contain neither a prayer for grace and peace nor an expression of thanksgiving or blessing. Hebrews begins with a majestic sentence celebrating the transcendent dignity of God's Son through whom God has spoken his final word (Heb. 1:1-4). These first lines are without doubt a real introduction that would not tolerate any prescript preceding them. The opening statement is confessional in character and compels attention. It engages an auditor or reader immediately. Hebrews begins like a sermon.

The accuracy of this impression is confirmed by the writer. In brief personal remarks appended to the end of the document (13:22-24), the writer describes Hebrews as a "word of exhortation": "I appeal to you, brothers and sisters, to bear with my word of exhortation, for I have written to you briefly" (13:22). This descriptive phrase recalls the form of the invitation extended to Paul and Barnabas by synagogue officials in Antioch of Pisidia following the public reading from the Law and the Prophets on a sabbath evening: "Brothers, if you have any word of exhortation for the people, give it" (Acts 13:15). Paul responded by addressing the assembly in a homily or edifying discourse (Acts 13:16-41).

The expression "word of exhortation" appears to have been an idiomatic, fixed designation for a sermon in Jewish-Hellenistic and early Christian circles. Similar language occurs in a Palestinian setting in 2 Maccabees 15:8-11: Judah the Maccabee "exhorted his troops . . . encouraging them from the law and the prophets. . . . He armed each of them . . . with the inspiration of brave words." When the writer of Hebrews appeals to the members of the assembly to listen willingly to

---

2. W. G. Doty, *Letters in Primitive Christianity* (Philadelphia: Fortress, 1973), 21-47.

the offered "word of exhortation," the customary idiom for a sermon is used. The descriptive phrase is appropriate to a homily in written form.[3] The classic study of the Jewish-Hellenistic and early Christian homily form in the period close to the first Christian century is the investigation of Hartwig Thyen, *Der Stil des jüdisch-hellenistichen Homilie* (1955). Thyen seeks to demonstrate that a number of Jewish and early Christian writings in Greek from this general period reflect the style and influence of a Jewish-Hellenistic homily. For each of several primary sources he sought to trace the influence of popular preaching in Hellenism, the homiletical use of the biblical text, and the variety of ways in which paraenetic tradition was treated. Thyen classified Hebrews as a skillfully crafted paraenetic homily in the Jewish-Hellenistic synagogue tradition.[4] In fact, Hebrews is "the sole example of a completely preserved homily from this period."[5]

Thyen's volume marked an important advance in establishing the literary genre of Hebrews and provided a foundation for more recent studies of the form of Hebrews. In 1984, Lawrence Wills published his research on a common form of the Jewish-Hellenistic and early Christian oral sermon, which can be reconstructed in a precise way.[6] Appealing to Acts 13:16-41 as a paradigmatic homily, Wills discerned a firmly entrenched pattern of argumentation that appears to reflect the typical synagogue hortatory homily. On the basis of Acts 13:15, he tentatively applied the designation "word of exhortation" to this formal type.

The pattern, according to Wills, consists of three formal elements: (1) authoritative exampla, in the form of biblical quotations, examples from the past or present, or reasoned exposition; (2) a conclusion inferred from the preceding examples, developing their relevance for the audience; and (3) a final exhortation. Wills demonstrates that this oral form was flexible and could be developed in a variety of ways. It could stand alone, as in the case of Acts 13:16-41, or be extended in a cyclical fashion as the

---

3. See W. L. Lane, "Hebrews: A Sermon in Search of a Setting," *Southwestern Journal of Theology* 28 (1985): 13-15.

4. Hartwig Thyen, *Der Stil der jüdisch-hellenistischen Homilie* (Göttingen: Vandenhoeck & Ruprecht, 1955), 7-39, 69-74, 85-110.

5. Ibid., 106. For a summary of Thyen's argument in English, with a mildly critical evaluation, see J. Swetnam, "On the Literary Genre of the 'Epistle' to the Hebrews," *Novum Testamentum* 11 (1969): 261-69; and W. L. Lane, *Hebrews 1-8*, Word Biblical Commentary 47A (Dallas: Word, 1991), lxx-lxxi, with bibliography. For a more recent investigation of synagogue preaching in the Diaspora, see W. R. Stegner, "The Ancient Jewish Synagogue Homily," in *Greco-Roman Literature and the New Testament*, ed. D. E. Aune (Atlanta: Scholars Press, 1988), 51-69.

6. L. Wills, "The Form of the Sermon in Hellenistic Judaism and Early Christianity," *Harvard Theological Review* 77 (1984): 277-99.

pattern is repeated in a longer sermon (e.g., Heb. 1:5–4:16; 8:1–12:28). Wills argues that the writer of Hebrews followed a modified form of this latter pattern in creating a very complex sermonic text.[7]

In an article published in response in 1988, C. C. Black II stressed the remarkable coherence of the sermon form identified by Wills with the conventions of classical rhetoric.[8] Black freely illustrated his argument with reference to Hebrews, which he categorized as an early Christian sermon exhibiting highly nuanced and sophisticated forms of proof.[9] He discerned in Hebrews an "epideictic attempt to stimulate belief in the present."[10]

In 1990, Harry Attridge published his approach to the "word of exhortation" form.[11] Basing his proposal on an inductive analysis of the formal features of Hebrews, Attridge suggests that the "homily" or "word of exhortation" form is a sub-genre within the genre of paraenetic literature for which it is appropriate to use the modern terms *homily* and *sermon*. The technical literary designation for this sub-genre is "word of exhortation" (Heb. 13:22) or "paraclesis." Attridge proposes that the setting for the emergence of this homiletical form was the synagogue in the social world of major urban centers in the Greco-Roman period. Paraclesis is "the newly minted rhetorical form that actualizes traditional Scripture for a community in a nontraditional environment."[12] The writer of Hebrews adapted this form in order to confirm the values and commitments of a Christian group exposed to social ostracism and alienation in their own environment.[13]

The research of L. Wills, C. C. Black II, and H. W. Attridge on the form of Hebrews has done much to vindicate and refine the recognition of Hebrews as a written sermon or homily. Hebrews brings us into direct contact with first-century Christian preaching.

Recognizing the oral, sermonic character of Hebrews permits important features of the style and structure to receive the attention they deserve. The writer skillfully conveys the impression of presence with the gathered community and of actually delivering the sermon in that setting. Until the postscript (13:22-25), the preacher carefully avoids any

---

7. Ibid., 280-83.

8. C. C. Black II, "The Rhetorical Form of the Hellenistic Jewish and Early Christian Sermon: A Response to Lawrence Wills," *Harvard Theological Review* 81 (1988): 1-18.

9. Ibid., 13.

10. Ibid., 5.

11. H. W. Attridge, "Paraenesis in a Homily (*logos parakleseos*): The Possible Location of, and Socialization in the Epistle to the Hebrews," *Semeia* 50 (1990): 211-26.

12. Ibid., 217.

13. Ibid., 219-23.

reference to actions like writing or reading that would tend to underscore the distance that separates the preacher from the group addressed. Stressed instead are the actions of speaking and listening, which are appropriate to persons in conversation or to the event of preaching. The writer (preacher) identifies with the audience in a direct way (2:5; 5:11; 6:9; 8:1; 9:5; 11:32), assuming a conversational tone in order to diminish the sense of geographical distance that separated preacher from audience and made writing necessary. Although written, Hebrews was conceived by its author as speech. By referring to speaking and listening, the writer is able to establish a sense of presence with the audience.

The writer was clearly a gifted preacher. Hebrews is characterized by a skillful use of alliteration, of oratorical imperatives, of euphonic phrases, of unusual word order calculated to arouse the attention, and of literary devices designed to enhance rhetorical effectiveness. The alternation between exposition and exhortation characteristic of the literary structure of Hebrews provides an effective vehicle for oral impact. Hebrews was prepared for oral delivery to a specific community.

The character of Hebrews as sermonic discourse invites an interpreter or reader to be sensitive to the abrupt shifts between orality and textuality. There is an important difference between oral preaching and written discourse. The dynamic between communicator and audience is distinct in each case. The writer expressly declares in 13:22 that his "word of exhortation" has been reduced to writing. As such, it has become frozen, with a life of its own quite independent of the audience for whom it was written. But it is clear that that was not its original intention. It is equally clear that the writer would have preferred to have spoken directly and immediately with those addressed (13:19, 23). In the realm of oral speech, the speaker and the auditors are sustained in relationship within a world of sound. Although forced by geographical distance and a sense of pastoral urgency to reduce this homily to writing, the writer never loses sight of the power of oral impact.

Hebrews is a sermon prepared to be read aloud to a group of auditors who will receive its message, not primarily through reading and leisured reflection, but aurally. Reading the document aloud entails oral performance, providing oral clues to those who listen to the public reading of the sermon. This complex reality emphasizes the importance of rhetorical form and the subtleties of expression in this homily. In point of fact, aural considerations, in the event of communication, often prove to be the decisive ones.[14]

---

14. For recent approaches to the rhetorical and discourse analyses of Hebrews, see Lane *Hebrews 1–8*, lxxv-lxxxiv.

Preaching and Exegesis in Hebrews

The pastor responsible for this homily we call Hebrews had the highest regard for Scripture. He not only acknowledged the authority of the words of the biblical text, but also clearly appropriated the text to address a church at risk through accepted modes of interpretation. The biblical text was regarded as the living word of God. The concern was to bring the text into the experience of the group addressed.

Within the limits of this chapter no more can be done than to offer a brief examination of two of the ways in which the author of Hebrews made use of the biblical text to strengthen and reinforce the convictions of a discouraged group of Christian men and women. Yet even this cursory examination will illustrate important aspects of early Christian exegesis in the service of preaching in the first century.[15]

The writer of Hebrews is fond of stringing biblical quotations together with minimal comment. In 1:5-13, for example, a chain of biblical quotations is compiled to demonstrate the superiority of the Son of God over the angels.[16] Each of the texts cited is interpreted from a christological perspective. The preacher draws the quotations together in order to expound and confirm what has already been confessed concerning the exalted Son in the opening lines of the sermon. The result is the following synthetic parallelism between the confessional statements concerning the Son of God in 1:2b-3c and the string of quotations in 1:5-13:

1: 2*b*-3*c*	1:5-13
A. Appointment as royal heir (v. 2*b*)	A. Appointment as royal Son and heir (vv. 5-9)
B. Mediator of the creation (v. 2*c*)	B. Mediator of the creation (v. 10)
C. Eternal nature and preexistent glory (v. 3*a-b*)	C. Unchanging eternal nature (vv. 11-12)
D. Exaltation to God's right hand (v. 3*c*)	D. Exaltation to God's right hand (v. 13)

15. For a more comprehensive treatment of the importance and appropriation of the biblical text in Hebrews, see ibid., cxii-cxxxv.

16. See J. W. Thompson, "The Structure and Purpose of the Catena in Heb. 1:5-13," *Catholic Biblical Quarterly* 38 (1976): 352-63; R. Koops, "Chains of Contrast in Hebrews 1," *The Bible Translator* 34 (1983): 220-25; J. P. Meier, "Structure and Theology in Hebrews 1, 1-14," *Biblica* 66 (1985): 168-89.

The purpose of the collection of biblical texts is to document the superiority of the Son overo the angels in a manner that reinforces the community's confession of his transcendent dignity.

The seven citations have been arranged in three groups, each of which draws an antithetical comparison between the Son and the angels. The first group (vv. 5-6) consists of three quotations. The first two provide evidence for Jesus' sonship (Ps. 2:7; 2 Sam. 7:14), and the third (Deut. 32:43) asserts his superiority in rank to the angels. With the second group (vv. 7-12) the preacher moves from assertion to argument. He brings together one quotation concerning the angels (Ps. 104:4) and two that refer to the Son (Pss. 45:6-7; 102:25-27) to substantiate the conclusion that the Son is superior by documenting from Scripture his eternal, unchangeable nature and his role in creation. The final group (vv. 13-14) consists of the citation of Psalm 110:1, the biblical text that first prompted the preacher's reflections on the exaltation of the Son (1:3c), and a concluding exegetical comment on the inferior rank and status of the angels.

The seven quotations are cited as a succession of words spoken by God to the Son and to the heavenly hosts, words that the people of God are permitted to overhear. They establish that God's own witness is the decisive factor in the enthronement and exaltation of the Son. By implication, the auditors are invited to acknowledge the transcendent worth of the Son by affirming their full confidence in him (cf. 1:1-4; 3:1, 14).

The basis for the christological appropriation of these quotations is the Old Greek version of the text. This can be verified in a striking manner by reference to Psalm 102:25-27, which is introduced in 1:10-12 to specify the relationship of the exalted Son to the creation. The quotation develops the previous affirmation that the Son is the mediator and sustainer of the created order (1:2c, 3b).

In its original context Psalm 102:25-27 clearly refers to the immutable character of God. The psalmist contrasts the ability of Yahweh to stand above the change and decay of the created order with his own experience of affliction and exposure to death. In the Septuagint, however, a mistranslation of the unpointed Hebrew text made it possible to read the text christologically. The Hebrew radicals 'nh in verse 24 (English translations, v. 23), "he afflicted," were translated "he answered" (LXX *apekrithe*, Vg *respondit*), with the result that verses 23-28 become the response of Yahweh. Consequently, Psalm 102:25-27 (LXX) must refer to the creative activity of divine Wisdom or of the Messiah, rather than of God.[17] It is this understanding that stands behind the selection of this text for the chain of quotations developed in 1:5-13.

---

17. B. W. Bacon, 1902. "Heb. 1, 10-12 and the Septuagint Rendering of Ps. 102, 23," *Zeitschrift für die neutestamentliche Wissenschaft* 3 (1902): 280-85.

It may be assumed that the biblical passages cited in 1:5-13 were already familiar to the audience from the primitive liturgical tradition. All but one of the quotations were taken from the Greek Psalter, which was the hymnbook for both synagogue and the early church. The one exception is a quotation from the *Hymn of Moses*, which entered the worship of the Hellenistic synagogues as an ode appended to the Psalter.[18] The form of the quotation of Deuteronomy 32:43 in Hebrews 1:6 corresponds exactly to the translation provided in Odes 2:43.

Although in verses 5 and 13 the supporting quotations are introduced with a rhetorical question, the preacher is not concerned to set forth a formal proof in any strict sense of the word. The absence of logical argument and the observable fact that much of the content of 1:5-14 is not closely related to the further development of the address provide evidence that the quotations serve another purpose. The cited texts simply summarize the biblical testimony to Jesus' Sonship and rank and establish his superiority to the heavenly mediators of the old revelation. The quotations thus reinforce the community's confession (1:2b-4) and prepare for the solemn warning to respect the word of salvation proclaimed by the Lord (2:1-4).

A different use of Scripture is found in Hebrews 2:5-9. At this point the exposition is conformed to the tradition of homiletical midrash, in which key phrases of an extended quotation are taken up and expanded for the hearers (cf. 2:5-9; 3:7b–4:11; 8:6-13; 10:5-10, 15-18; 12:26-29). This approach to Scripture was developed in the homiletical practice of the synagogue in order to bring the biblical text into the experience of an audience through preaching.[19]

Both writer and audience were thoroughly familiar with homiletical midrash by virtue of their participation in the life of Hellenistic synagogues. When the writer of Hebrews resorts to homiletical midrash, it is done in continuity with peers in Hellenistic Judaism. The act of reflecting on Scripture and of interpreting Scripture presupposes certain shared assumptions about how the voice of God is recovered. It presupposes that Scripture announces a promise of future developments. This is a thoroughly Jewish understanding of Scripture.

The paragraph 2:5-9 is so dominated by the citation and explanation of Psalm 8 that it may be overlooked that the preacher is introducing a sec-

---

18. H. Schneider, "Die biblischen Oden im christlichen Altertum," *Biblica* 30 (1949): 32.

19. R. Bloch, "Midrash," in *Approaches to Ancient Judaism: Theory and Practice,* ed. W. S. Green (Calloway, Mont.: Scholars Press, 1978), 29-50; A. G. Wright, *Midrash: The Literary Genre* (Staten Island, N.Y.: Alba House, 1968), 52-59, 64-67.

ond string of biblical quotations (2:6-8, 12-13) that serves to complement the quotations in 1:5-13. The development in 2:5-9, however, is tied together by the word play on the verb *hupotassein* ("to subject," "to subordinate") and its derivatives. The declaration that it was not to angels that God subjected (*hupetaxen*) the heavenly world to come (2:5) anticipates the use of the same verbal form in the climatic refrain of Ps. 8:7 ("you subjected [*hupetaxas*] all things under his feet" [cited in Heb. 2:8*a*]). This in turn provides the writer with the key to the interpretation of the entire quotation:

> Now in putting everything in subjection (*en toi gar hupotaxai*) to him, he left nothing out of his control (*anhupotakton*). But in fact we do not see everything subject to his control (*hupotetagmena*).

The repetition, with variation in form, is rhetorically effective. It introduces an element of suspense that is not relieved until the emphatic and deferred statement of verse 9, "but we see the one who for a brief while was made lower than the angels—Jesus!" Here is first-century exegesis in the service of preaching.

The quotation of Psalm 8:5-7 (MT 8:4-6) conforms to the Septuagint version, but the clause "You made him ruler over the work of your hands" (Ps. 8:7*a* [MT 8:6*a*]) has been omitted. The omission is almost certainly deliberate. The writer regards the declarations of Psalm 8:6-7 as independent statements descriptive of three stages in the experience of Jesus: (A) incarnation and humiliation ("You made him for a little while lower than the angels" [v. 7*a*]); (B) exaltation ("You crowned him with glory and splendor" [v. 7*b*]); and (C) final triumph ("You put everything in subjection under his feet" [v. 8*a*]). By commenting on these statements in the order C (v. 8*b*-*c*), A (v. 9*a*), B (v. 9*b*), he made the entire exposition subservient to the perspective of the exaltation glory into which Jesus entered as a result of the death he suffered on behalf of others.

It is commonly held that the preacher found in the second line of the quotation is a reference to Jesus as the Son of Man or the Second Adam. In fact, this detail of the text encouraged this preacher to treat the quotation in an explicitly christological sense.

In the Gospels, however, the title by which Jesus designated himself is uniformly the articular expression *ho huios tou anthropou* ("The Son of Man"). The fact that *huios anthropou* is anarthrous in Psalm 8 supports the presumption that the preacher did not find a christological title in the designation. Psalm 8:5 was cited to emphasize that Jesus in a representative sense fulfilled the vocation intended for the human family. The preacher understood that the parallel expressions *anthropos* ("man") and *huios anthropou* ("son of man") were synonymous and were to be interpreted in terms of that fact. When the writer of Hebrews develops a midrashic commentary on this quotation, no interest is shown in the initial lines, but attention is confined exclusively to Psalm 8:6-7. The quotation of Psalm 8 may readily be applied to Jesus without finding in the vocabulary an implied reference to the Son of Man christology of the canonical Gospels.

The preacher's explanation of the text indicates precisely the point of his interest. It lies in the projection of an imperial destiny for the human family in the refrain "You have put everything in subjection under his feet" (v. 8*a*). This theme is taken up only to underscore the absoluteness of the language by resorting to a double use of the negative: God, in determining to put everything in subjection, left nothing that was not under his control (v. 8*b*).

The extravagance of the statement in verse 8*b* is mocked, of course, by human experience, so the preacher immediately adds, "we do not yet see everything subject to his control." The temporal expression *oupo* ("not yet") is crucial, for it indicates that the writer found in the quotation a prophecy that eventually will be fulfilled. He regarded Psalm 8:7*b* as a legal decree, the realization of which is yet deferred. The recognition of the present unfulfilled state of affairs prepares the preacher to see that the promised subjection has reference not to humanity in general (v. 8), but to Jesus (v. 9), whom God has appointed "heir of everything" (1:2).

This understanding is made explicit in verse 9, where it is evident that the writer interpreted the two lines of Psalm 8:6 without reference to the synonymous parallelism of the Hebrew text. From the perspective of the psalmist, to be made a "little lower" than a heavenly being is to be "crowned with glory and splendor." But for the preacher responsible for Hebrews, the two members of the parallelism expressed two successive phases in the life of the Lord. The first line is said to concern Jesus' temporary abasement, while the second speaks of his subsequent exaltation and glorification. This distinctly christological reading of the text also accounts for the omission of the first member of the following parallelism (Ps. 8:7*a*). The three lines cited by the writer combine to form a confession of faith that celebrates successive moments in the drama of redemption—incarnation, the exaltation, and the final victory of Jesus, the first pertaining to the past, the second to the present, and the third to the future. The departure from the original Semitic parallelism produced a distinctly confessional understanding of the quotation.

First-Century Light on Contemporary Preaching

In what way does this exegetical approach to Psalm 8 by the "sermon" of Hebrews serve the task of preaching? What light is shed on preaching and exegesis by this first-century model? What is taught that is of enduring proclamation significance?

1. In Jesus we see exhibited humanity's authentic vocation. In an extraordinary way he fulfills God's design for all creation and displays what had always been intended for the whole human family, according to Psalm 8. He is the one in whom primal glory and sovereignty have been restored. His experience of humiliation and exaltation is the guarantee that the absolute subjection of everything envisioned in Psalm 8:7 will yet be achieved.

2. An objection to Jesus' superiority to the angels on the grounds that he was made "lower than the angels" cannot be sustained. His abasement was only temporary; it lasted "for a brief while" and has already been exchanged for exaltation glory. In this regard, it is important to observe that when the line from Psalm 8:6*a* is repeated in verse 9, the word order is altered to bring forward the expression "for a brief while" into the emphatic position:

> v. 7 "You made him for a brief while lower than the angels."
> v. 9 "For a brief while [he] was made lower than the angels."

By this deliberate alteration, stress falls on the momentary character of the humiliation that was necessary to the accomplishment of redemption.

3. When the writer of Hebrews introduces the proper name "Jesus" for the first time in the homily (v. 9), it is assigned a deferred position in apposition to the clause *ton de . . . blepomen Iesoun*. The unusual word order is calculated to arouse attention; it conveys an element of surprise as well as emphasis (i.e., we see the one who for a little while was made lower than the angels—Jesus—dealing triumphantly with death on our behalf!). On seven subsequent occasions this preacher introduces the proper name "Jesus," and in each instance it is given a position of great emphasis by its syntactical lateness (3:1; 6:20; 7:22; 10:19; 12:2, 24; 13:20). There is nothing corresponding to this in any other New Testament document. This practice is characteristic of the writer of Hebrews, who exhibits sensitivity to the power of striking formulations in the service of preaching.

4. There is a profound note of anticipation in the Old Testament teaching about the human family. The words of the psalmist look forward into the future, and that future is inextricably bound up with the person and

work of Jesus. His condescension to be made for a brief while "lower than the angels" set in motion a sequence of events in which abasement and humiliation were the necessary prelude to exaltation. His coronation and investiture with glory and splendor provide assurance that the power of sin and death has been nullified and that the family of the redeemed will yet be led to the full realization of the intended glory. In Jesus, Christians are to find the pledge of their own entrance into the imperial destiny marked out for them by God in the Psalter.

These are only examples from Hebrews of one preacher's appropriation of Scripture in the service of preaching. They by no means exhaust the variety of approaches to Scripture illustrated in Hebrews. A more extended study is required to investigate the typological exegesis so important to the presentation of Melchizedek in Hebrews 7:1-10, or to the comparison between Christ and the Aaronic priesthood in 7:11–10:18. The use of a catalogue of attested witnesses in 11:4-38 entails a still different approach to Scripture. But sufficient has been said to demonstrate the importance of Hebrews to any serious discussion of preaching and exegesis in the first century.

Hebrews demonstrates that the biblical text remains a valid and significant witness to God's redemptive word and deed. Christians must grasp this witness in the light of God's decisive act of speaking through the Son (1:1-2*a*). The words of the Old Testament are quoted not for their significance in the past, but rather for their meanings in the present. All of Scripture remains a revelation of God's unalterable plan of salvation for the human family. Its relevance to the members of a house church in crisis is driven home forcefully by the writer's appropriation of the biblical text. Hebrews is a striking example of exegesis in the service of impassioned preaching, gospel proclamation designed to bring certainty in the context of an uncertain and hostile social climate.

Hebrews is one of the special gifts of God to his church. It is a gift to be appreciated especially when God's people find themselves prone to discouragement or distraction from any cause. James Earl Massey understands this and has brought to the text of Hebrews a sensitive appreciation for its value as a rich resource for the contemporary pulpit. His own powerful preaching is informed by the correlation between exegesis and preaching that is the hallmark of the preacher who crafted the sermon we call Hebrews.

PART · THREE

*Style
and
Rhythm*

CHAPTER SEVEN

PREACHING TO THE *VIDEO ERGO SUM* GENERATION

Al Fasol

P reaching is one of the integrative disciplines. H. C. Brown, Jr., summarizes what he calls the "true scope of preaching" as "correct use of Biblical content, hermeneutical principles, theological perspectives, [congregational] orientation, rhetorical rules, and oratorical principles." This chapter will focus on congregational orientation.[1]

Congregational orientation is undergoing the most rapid and radical changes at this time. The reasons for these changes are not fully understood. We do know that some perpetual tensions, such as generation gaps, egocentricities, and a sense of rebellion against the "old ways," are accentuated right now.

A study of congregational orientation and preaching raises a series of questions. Does the nature of the message dictate the form and content of the message, or does the congregation's cultural background dictate the form and content of the message? The answer always has been and will continue to be both. The nature of our message is kerygmatic. We wouldn't change the nature of the message if we could, and we couldn't if we would.

Using the analogy of the ambassador, one might think of Christian proclaimers as being sent to communicate a message from another as clearly and directly as possible. A good ambassador realizes that a set of language and other cultural barriers complicates the assignment. The

---

1. H. C. Brown uses "psychological" rather than "congregational." He regretted having used this term, however, and in a planned revision of *A Quest for Reformation in Preaching* (Waco, Tex.: Word, 1968), he intended to revise the wording to "congregational orientation." Unfortunately, he did not live to see this accomplished.

ambassador, therefore, seeks to overcome these barriers *without altering the nature of the message*. The ambassador may need to repeat the message, elaborate the message, or make adjustments in midmessage or later. Nonetheless, ideally the ambassador does this without changing or losing sight of the enduring nature of the message itself.

No Lambs in Alaska

While on a Bible study/preaching visit to Alaska in 1982, we stopped at a small village that I was told has no name. We stood by a small building that was an unused Russian Orthodox church. Nearby was a cemetery. The graves had miniature huts over them. Brightly colored blankets were stretched over the length of each grave. Two men walked to me from a nearby house. Soon perhaps twenty persons were present, most of the local men and children. The first sentence spoken by one of them was "We're a syncretistic lot, aren't we?" I responded, "Have Eskimos always covered their graves in this way? I noticed that some Alaskan Indians follow this practice. I presume they learned this from you Eskimos."

That was precisely the correct response on my part. The men smiled, talked among themselves with approving glances at me, and drew closer. The children, I noticed, took the cue and, with frowns rather than smiles, dropped some snowballs they had just made. Obviously, they had pelted "outsiders" before and were disappointed that we would not be more targets. My new Eskimo friend gratefully acknowledged that Alaskan Indians did borrow the custom from Eskimos. He proudly shared that, as far as he was concerned, Eskimos were the only true Alaskans.

To lighten the mood a little, I said, "Today, I will make all Eskimos happy." They looked quizzical, so I added, "I am from Texas. These two men with me are from Oklahoma. Today, we will drive to Anchorage. I, a Texan, will put an Okie under each arm, and we will fly out of Alaska on a Western Airlines airplane, and that is how I will make all Eskimos happy." I said that for humor. They did not laugh. They hugged me, patted me on the back, shook my hand, and most important, invited me into the old church building.

There were no seats and hardly any light. Fortunately, we were there early in the winter-shortened day. I asked how long it had been since they had heard a message from the Bible. The answer was "What you outsiders call July 1980." I asked what the previous preacher had told them. Wry smiles appeared. "He told us Jesus is the Lamb of God. We said we have never seen a lamb and if God did not put lambs in Alaska, maybe Jesus does not apply to us." All of a sudden I decided I would not talk about sheep, shepherds, vineyards, palm trees (Ps. 92:13), or streams in the desert. The point is that in an extremely brief exchange we had communicated a large amount of information about one another.

Conventional Communication Factors

Throughout this conversation with the Eskimos, I was doing what communication theorists call encoding. That is, I was preparing my message by choosing specific words, analogies, and paradigms. I had many from which to choose, but in my encoding I made specific and deliberate selections. What were my criteria for making these selections? In part they were influenced by the way I anticipated my hearers would decode what I planned to say. How could I, an outsider, anticipate their decoding? In this case I had read about native Alaskan cultures and had talked to people who had witnessed to native Alaskans.

The goal, of course, was for them to decode accurately what I had encoded intentionally. In the encoding process, I did not change the nature of the message I planned (which was John 3:7, 16-17). The content of the message was both directed by my biblical text and influenced by the cultural situation I was about to address. Again, the message was regulated or controlled by the biblical text, but the words, analogies, and other elements were chosen under the mostly invisible forces I felt exerted upon me by the cultural context of the Eskimo village. What I needed to say was formed by the biblical text. How I needed to say it (including delivery and content) was influenced significantly by the cultural context.

As always is the case in communications, other factors were at work. When we arrived, I think we were considered more likely to be a source for derisive fun (the children had their snowballs ready) than the source of a life-changing message. The attitude toward the outsiders changed when I referred to my hearers as Eskimos and suggested by my question that I knew they were not Alaskan Indians. Three important communication factors were working concurrently here.

First, my credibility rose dramatically in their eyes. Most outsiders would not have known the difference between an Eskimo and an Indian. This lack of knowledge typically is interpreted by the Eskimos as a lack of concern and, therefore, a lack of respect. Source credibility in communications is measured in three ways: expertise, integrity, and dynamism. (Dynamism means that a receptor should perceive that the messenger is so convinced that the message is vital to the receptor that the messenger communicates a sense of intensity, urgency, boldness, and persistence in the process of communicating.)

For my new Eskimo friends, my credibility probably rose in that chronological order: expertise first; then, since I knew how to distinguish an Eskimo and how to make an Eskimo happy, they were open to my being a person of integrity. Gaining respect for one's integrity is a process; it is part of what we call nurturing. It is a continuous action and not an aorist experience. When they heard me speak from John 3, these qualities were affirmed when I spoke with a sense of dynamism with which they were comfortable. They appeared to be more comfortable with low dynamism than with high. Therefore, I spoke slowly, intensely, and with indirect eye contact. In their culture, looking a person in the eye is impolite.

Each credibility factor in turn opened the door to the next one, and each factor served to affirm the others. If they had not accepted my expertise, they would have scorned my integrity and the communication opportunity would have been lost. Had my integrity not affirmed my expertise, they would have made snowballs with the children and later would have remarked that the outsider had almost conned them. Had I spoken with high dynamism, they would have been extremely uncomfortable and at best likely would have given me only polite attention.

Another factor that functioned simultaneously was "frame of reference," sometimes broadly called the "relational factor." With the Eskimos, my frame of reference was totally out of kilter. I was a white, too well-dressed (even in jeans) passenger in a recent vintage Ram Charger. Frame of reference involves the points the communicator has in common with the receptors. To different receptors some points of reference are more important than others. To some receptors a northern or southern regional accent is an automatic disqualification. For most receptors, credibility judgments are either helped or hindered until some points of reference have been established.

For Christians, our first point of reference with each other often is the salvation experience we share. Finding such points upon which a frame of reference can be built, however, is more challenging when talking to a non-Christian. Unless the receptor discovers a frame of reference with the speaker, the speaker is almost certain to fail. The receptor must feel a sense of relatedness to the communicator.

A third factor is the dual message concept. In any form of verbal communication, especially in oral communication, two messages are being conveyed at the same time. They are the intellectual message and the emotional message. The intellectual message refers to the words used in the communication process. The emotional message essentially is the way the receptor perceives that the communicator "feels" about the words being said. Pitch inflections, changes in volume and rate, body language, and even articulation are the primary indicators as far as the receptor is concerned.

There also are the denotative and connotative (especially, connotative) meanings of words. By my not looking at my hearers eye to eye, by my using a posture with head slightly bowed, by speaking slowly, and by my speaking with limited intensity, the Eskimos interpreted my emotional message as one of respect, politeness, sincerity, and self-assurance.

These three communication factors gained me the opportunity to speak a message from the Bible. First, I knew something of the cultural priorities and biases of my hearers, and I encoded my introductory sentences carefully so as to, second, establish myself as a credible person in their eyes. Third, I tried to communicate in such a way that the receptors would have no doubt that I sincerely meant what I said.

During the devotional time in the church, all of these communication factors remained active and crucial. However, my question about the date of the last "sermon" and what that preacher had said brought other communication principles into operation. When I asked about the previous speaker, I was interested not so much in these people's mnemonic capacities as I was interested in determining why the previous message to them did or did not have impact. The communication principle at work here is this: Impact is not equal to predictability and/or distance. This formula presumes that impact is positive until the impact is diminished by predictability (saying things the hearer knew in advance the communicator would say) and/or by distance (saying things that are out of the hearer's frame of reference).

The response I had received, "We said we have never seen a lamb," helped me both ways. In this case the predictability problem was subtle. They were still prepared for me to lose credibility by, predictably, saying something that was not only outside their frame of reference, but entirely outside their frame of experience (distance). They alerted me that various biblical analogies and metaphors would not communicate (e.g., Lamb), but various others would (salt, light). The challenge for the communicator, in part, was to avoid these pitfalls and maintain credibility so that a strong, positive message impact could occur.

The passage John 3:1-7, 16-17 seemed eminently workable to me. The birth experience is universal, and speaking of a second birth always inspires curiosity. Relating this second birth to Someone powerful enough to bring about such a thing, and with that power motivated by agape, is universally appealing. Even though love and a sense of belonging rate number three on Abraham Maslow's list of human needs, it is still a compelling need. He says that we all have five basic needs: physical (hunger, thirst, etc.); security; love; personal esteem; and self-actualization.[2]

The physical needs of the Eskimos seemed to be provided for adequately. I sensed no problem with their feeling of safety. Recall that they thought they would be pelting me with snowballs. I had already added to their self-esteem by acknowledging them as Eskimos. Self-actualization was not a problem. In fact, they felt their way of life to be far superior to ours. Love and a sense of belonging were things they already felt as a community. But to speak of God's love introduced a staggering new dimension for them.

Building on all of these principles, as I spoke I kept other factors in mind. In persuasive speech, I knew that they could respond with one of four attitudes: (1) the utilitarian, which is based on rewards and punishment; (2) the ego-defensive, which hides reality either by denial or rationalizing; (3) the value-expressive, which responds positively when such a response meets a self-image need; or (4) the knowledge-function, which responds to information, especially when such knowledge has not been confronted previously (e.g., the second birth).

From my perspective, the communication process at hand involved: (1) introducing the idea; (2) observing the behavioral attitudes at work—sensing from their feedback either acceptance, rejection, or puzzlement (which rather quickly will turn into rejection); (3) restatement or review as needed; and (4) invitation to act upon this new information. Their actual response was akin to those ancient receptors at Mars Hill. Mainly, the response was "I must think about this some more" (Acts 17:32). The knowledge-function approach usually has this result. Follow-up is critical. In this case it was done by our alumni and others.

To View Is to Be

The above are basic communication experiences that come close to being universal. We now turn to more recently identified communications factors studied to date only in the context of the forty-eight contiguous United States. These are new because we now are living through a communications revolution.

A person who celebrated a fifty-second birthday in 1505 would have lived when more books were produced (eight million) than had been produced in the previous one thousand years. The communications revo-

---

2. Abraham Maslow, *Motivation and Personality* (New York: Harper and Bros., 1954), 80-98.

lution, inspired by the invention of movable type, helped enable the Protestant Reformation, the rise of Western science, and the idealization of Renaissance art.[3] About fifty-five years now have also passed since the first commercial television program was broadcast. We are in the same position in relation to this new communications revolution as was our fifty-two year old born in 1453.

We are only now beginning to scratch the surface in discussing the consequences of this revolution. The consequences are as radical as the cultural changes that resulted from the invention of the alphabet. In an average American home, the television set is on for six hours and forty-four minutes each day.[4] First graders average twenty-four hours per week in viewing. Television watching now is second only to sleep and work as the most common activity. In excess of sixty million Americans are functionally illiterate[5] and another forty million choose to be illiterate.[6] Obviously this nation wants to view television, and will do so regardless of the price to its level of literacy.

What is the result for communications? Our culture is changed utterly. The way in which people now typically receive messages has changed utterly. That means that the way in which people receive sermons is changing dramatically.

These changes affect our very sense of consciousness. One change is that illiteracy will be much less a social pariah because habitual viewing makes illiteracy much less relevant. People now want books dramatized on the screen rather than written on pages. What money may have been budgeted for books is now budgeted for videotapes. Another change has occurred in our sense of community. People who do not own or who choose to remove TV sets from their homes are treated by many as deviants, cultural oddities, people who are, to use a currently devastating word, different. To be televisionless today is to be what illiterate was in the age of print.

A report on the BBC concluded: "British broadcasting in its existing public service mode should and did assert and reflect Britain as a community, society, and culture, and that it was the principle forum by which the nation as a whole was able to talk to itself. Television has a

---

3. E. L. Einstein, *The Printing Press as an Agent of Change* (New York: Cambridge University Press, 1979), 44.

4. Nielsen Survey, 1980, quoted in the *New York Times,* July 22, 1982, C15. The viewing rate is even higher in Japan—over eight hours.

5. *New York Times,* August 19, 1982.

6. *Books in Our Future* (Washington, D.C.: United States Government Printing Office, 1984), 12.

mirrorlike effect on our consciousness, especially because we find a sense of belonging in viewing what many other people are viewing. "To view is to be."[7]

Constant television viewing also changes the way we perceive reality. Marshall McLuhan was onto something when he asserted that a communication medium transmits a psychological message to us, and it is this medjum's message that alters our perception of reality. He judges that the content of what is received is much less important in transforming our consciousness than the form of the message.[8] "Sesame Street," for example, teaches a little about the alphabet and the formation of words and much that demonstrates how regular viewing can create an acceptance of the authority of television over every other authority and experience of life.

When viewers see a biblical drama or some historical drama, they are ready to ascribe accuracy and authority to the program even when that program disclaims such accuracy and authority. Whereas we formerly sought to correct the fallacy of "I read it in a book, so it must be true," we now strive to correct the fallacy of "I saw it on television, so it must be true." Such a correction is extraordinarily difficult to accomplish. The very nature of television as a medium works against its presenting factual or intellectual knowledge. The dialogue, the music, the graphics, the announcer, especially the editing all make for the presentation of emotional rather than intellectual information.

If the information that television transmits is predominantly emotional, the mechanism by which this information is transferred lies in a complex system of audiovisual codes. And of all the technical forms of television, the cut, I believe, is the most fundamental, the one that most determines the hidden message of the medium.[9] The power of television heightens the need for viewers to understand what selective editing does to our way of perceiving and thinking.

Words are paramount in a print culture. Words, however, become little more than a redundant tool that occasionally assists us in understanding the pictures on television. In comfortable surroundings, usually in our homes, we tend to exercise less critical thinking. We don't disbelieve our own furnishings, our family pictures on the wall. Therefore, it is difficult to disbelieve the visual stimuli we receive from our television set, which now is accepted as just another piece of furniture.

---

7. Jeremy Murray-Brown, "Video Ergo Sum," in Alan Olson et al., *Video Icons and Values* (Albany: State University of New York Press, 1991), 21.

8. Marshall McLuhan, *The Medium Is the Message* (New York: Random House, 1967).

9. Olson et al., *Video Icons and Values,* 23.

To state it positively, we are more willing to believe the reality of the image we receive in part because it is received in comfortable surroundings. The visual image itself would be dull. Therefore, the visual image must change constantly. With each change or cut, a message is sent to the viewer that assists the semipassive receptor in absorbing the emotional meaning of the new image. Our minds are thus compartmentalized and controlled in the comfort of our homes.

Let's look at one other change in our way of thinking before we assess what impact these changes have on Christian preaching. This next change is fragmented thinking, or the effect that prolonged viewing has on our ability to concentrate.

Research in this area began with the advent of cinematic movies. It is reported that William James asked one of his favorite students, Hugo Munsterberg, to examine what impact viewing of selected pictures from a film editor had on his ability to maintain attention in other forums (e.g., a lecture). Munsterberg was especially concerned with the passivity of the viewer. He viewed the "close-up" shot as "an externalization of the process of paying attention," and lamented that such viewing would cause people to be "ovine." That is, they would need constant supervision to assist in knowing when to pay attention. His observations may be prematurely alarmist, but I cite them as the first (c. 1920) time that a psychologist examined the relationship between viewing and the thinking process.

Most contemporary research on the relationship between prolonged television viewing and the attention span focuses on children (preteens). Young children seem compelled to view when the editing process includes rapid movement, rapid pacing (that is, numerous editing points or changes of picture), and loud music. Older children are less compelled to view the rapidly paced video, but not markedly so. This phenomenon bears a close relationship to what we know about our human perceptual system. Our eyes seem "hot-wired" to monitor change.[10] That is why our eyes stray back to the "tellie" even when we are in an enjoyable conversation.

The point is that television viewing fragments the attention span, making it possible to view in conjunction with other activities. This fragmented attention span has become the norm for a majority of people. The result:

Because we are used to receiving fragmented information in discontinuous form, we come to prefer that form; and information, such as a formal

---

10. Julian Hochberg, "Motion Pictures and Mental Structures." Paper presented at the 1978 meeting of the Eastern Psychological Association, Washington, D.C.

lecture, that requires sustained attention over a long period of time, becomes more difficult . . . for it is an adjustment that runs against the grain of discontinuity.[11]

Surviving the Morticians

By comparison with television editing, the "talking head" (lecturer, preacher) is boring in its sameness, since no visual monitoring is required. The peripatetic preacher is more popular (higher dynamism) because of the need for visual monitoring. This phenomenon has brought preaching into a transitional stage as now is evidenced in the differing worship styles, times of scheduling worship services, and attempts to make the local church "user friendly."

I have listened to a few tapes from pastors on the cutting edge of this movement. Remarkable, at least to me, is how recognizable the sermons are. I had expected only some trenchant remarks about issues that are of concern only to yuppies. What I find are biblically related remarks seeking relevant communication. I had originally feared that these user-friendly churches would have a chewing gum, rock-and-roll mentality. What I find instead are genuine attempts to subtly confront or introduce congregations to what light the Bible sheds on their specific concerns.

Preachers are attempting, albeit often obliquely, to help people come alive to the Bible. These preachers move from where people are to how the Bible helps them deal with where they are. We must sense where people are spiritually, make contact with them, and introduce them to the precepts of Scripture in ways that make them feel they have discovered the Bible on their own. Accordingly, inductive preaching rather than deductive preaching is much more appealing to our younger congregations.

What does the future hold for styles of preaching? Congregations always contain three types of receptors. The auditory receptors primarily want information. Usually, they sit toward the back to have space between themselves and the source. This allows them to ponder the data (the intellectual message) and minimize the emotional message. The visual receptors generally sit in the middle and to the side. They like the panoramic view and want (need?) illustrations and descriptive adjectives; otherwise they will say, "I just don't see what you mean." Kinesthetic receptors (backslapping, bear hugging, arm squeezing types) like

---

11. Renee Hobbs, "Television and the Shaping of Cognitive Skills," in Olson et al., *Video Icons and Values*, 37-38.

to sit close to the source. They want strong, direct application of the text so they can "feel" the message.

We are definitely in a visual/kinesthetic mode today. Many of us auditory types grew up in a strongly auditory age. We now must mellow our approach and work toward a visual/kinesthetic approach to gospel communication. As much as we can, we must move from behind the pulpit and give the congregation a change of picture! Removal of the pulpit works in auditoriums where the congregation is seated higher than the pulpit, but is awkward when the congregation is seated lower than the pulpit. Such changes are more extrinsic than intrinsic and, therefore, are not threatening to the integrity of preaching itself.

We have all heard and read eulogies of preaching. They are common these days. Nonetheless, preaching will survive extrinsic changes. Preaching may not have survived in the past had not extrinsic changes been made in previous times of significant cultural shift. We surely are in an era of radical change today. So far as I can see, preaching is adjusting and will survive its current morticians.

IMAGINATION: THE GENIUS OF CREATIVE SERMON CONSTRUCTION

Donald E. Demaray

Unconventionally, yet one hopes wisely and timely, we begin our approach to the genius of creative sermon construction by recalling children's stories and making ourselves freshly aware of critical assumptions that lie behind them.

The King's Questions

The Grimm Brothers left us a heritage of grand, classic stories: "Little Red Riding Hood," "Sleeping Beauty," "Rumpelstiltskin," and many more. These stories travel the world, are widely translated, and enjoy vigorous circulation.

Struggle, magical help, winning—especially winning—bring these tales to life and make them universal and enduring. They "ring the bell." The Brothers Grimm, in first writing out the fairy tales, touched the deep human feelings in all generations. They knew enough about all of us to plug into where we come from.[1]

Jacob and Wilhelm Grimm, wise and knowledgeable, traveled Germany to hear stories straight from country folk. A grandmother, the widow of a tailor, Katherina Viehmann stored dozens of such accounts in her head. Jacob and Wilhelm listened to her unfold the tales and then recorded them. They gave ear to other storytellers, too. The Brothers

---

1. Clifton Fadiman, *The World Treasury of Children's Literature*, with additional illustrations by Leslie Morrill, 2 vols. (Boston: Little, Brown and Company, 1984), 2:380ff. Fadiman's selection of material and explanations provide a magnificent source of great stories for little people and the child in all of us.

Grimm published their initial collection in 1812. The stories may well have come through hundreds of years by oral tradition. Their origins, lost in time, no one can trace. We do not know who first uttered them or how many now have repeated and enjoyed them.

One tale, "The Shepherd Boy," shows the rich use of imagination that characterized the Grimm stories. The delightful fable goes like this:

> Once upon a time, a shepherd boy became very well known because he could answer every question with wisdom. The king heard about his gift, but could not believe anyone so young could show such maturity. The king called for the lad and made an astonishing offer. "Answer three questions for me, and I will give you two rewards. First, I will make you my own son. Second, you will live with me in the royal palace."
>
> The young fellow, of course, wanted to know the questions at once. Question one was, "How many drops of water does the ocean contain?" The youth replied that if the king would dam all the rivers in the world so that not a single drop could run into the sea until he had counted them, he would tell him the number of drops in the ocean.
>
> The king then asked the next question: "How many stars does the sky include?" The young shepherd responded this way: "Give me a very big sheet of white paper and a writing instrument." The boy dotted the white paper with more tiny points than anyone could count. One could hardly distinguish the dots, and to look closely made one feel blinded. With that, the young man declared, "The sky holds as many stars as the dots on this paper. Count them." But no one could number them.
>
> The king asked a third question: "How many seconds of time does eternity hold?" The lad answered: "Diamond Mountain sits in Lower Pomerania. It stands two and a half miles high, its width measures two and a half miles, and its depth also is two and a half miles. Once each hundred years, a small bird sharpens its beak on the mountain. When the mountain wears away, the first second of eternity will have come to an end."
>
> The king admitted that the boy had answered the three questions like a wise and older man, and therefore could live with him in the royal palace as his very own child.

From this little fable we learn that profound truth is conveyed with skill by the provocative arena of imagination.

Gift, Sense, and Feel

The Gift of Seeing

Kentucky farmers surely can tell stories. Go to Hardees for morning coffee in Nicholasville, six miles from Asbury Theological Seminary in

Wilmore. Sit in a booth within earshot of one of many yarn spinners. Watch the plot unfold on the screen of your mind. Let your sensory apparatus respond to the stimuli of color, touch, smell, sound, and sight. Open yourself to the elements that characterize classic narrative with its life and charm. Follow the flowering of the story line.

Fantasy weavers use earth, kinfolk, and oral tradition to seed their imaginations. As great narrative artists do, they bring their stories to perfection. Rudyard Kipling serves as a good example.

Kipling's English home, Batemans, with its 300 acres, became exciting geography on which his children could romp and play. The little ones created their own adventures. While Kipling watched the acted-out imaginations of his offspring, fiction plots formed in his own imagination. Not surprisingly, he produced a series of fictitious tales about two children, modeled after his own Elsie and John. He used these narratives as a powerful way of teaching little people about the big moments in English history.

The territory around Bateman became the setting for many of these tales. By 1904, Kipling could publish *Puck of Pook's Hill*. Another collection, *Rewards and Fairies*, first saw the light of day in 1910.

Pook's Hill was a hill the kids loved to climb. The "old mill" Kipling purchased appears in some accounts, and nearby St. Bartholomew's Church shows its face in the story called "Hal O' the Draft."[2]

Notice what Jesus saw and talked about: soil, seeds, plants, harvest. He observed mothers, fathers, and their little ones. He watched children at their games and dances. He heard music, traced birds in flight, sensed the romance of sky and water. He observed struggle, hurt, love, resolution, and created stage settings as frameworks for unfolding his scenarios. The stories of Jesus go right to our deepest feelings, to the most vivid and basic realities of our lives as human beings. Who can miss the human drama of the prodigal son, for example?

Jesus' pictures stick like briars to clothes; they needle us, persist, and yield a succession of insights for a lifetime. The natural rhythms and flow of the parables and miracles embed themselves in our memory banks like a melody that won't go away, like Monet's water lilies that stay with us long after a visit to the museum, like a poem learned in elementary school that remains familiar for a lifetime.

Grimm, Kipling, and especially the stories of Jesus have given us narratives we label "classic" because they reflect life with uncommon per-

---

2. Mark I. West, "Batemans: Rudyard Kipling's English Haven," *British Heritage* (April/May 1994): 50-55. A delightful and well-researched piece on Kipling's English home and how that setting gave rise to some of Kipling's stories.

ception. The sense of reality grips us with enduring power because both form and substance move quickly to the theater at the center of our being. In a word, influential communicators do picture thinking. They see often what others overlook, and then paint their visions with unforgettable vividness.

The Sense of Wonder

Mr. Einstein gave his small son Alfred a compass. The five-year-old boy watched in astonished wonder as the needle pointed in the same direction no matter how he turned the device. Later, the young lad wondered why the moon did not fall to earth. Then came a question about light. Such boyhood queries would lead to one of the century's breakthrough discoveries: a new story about gravity and light.

Child developmentalists tell us that the sense of wonder plays a significant role in releasing young minds to growth. Wonder motivates questions, drives on to exploration, nourishes curiosity. Mozart never really left the wonder years of childhood, which accounts for the fascinating playfulness of his music. The philosopher Kant extended the spirit of his childhood when he exclaimed that two wonders never ceased to amaze him: the starry heavens above and the moral "ought" within.

Nature puts in us a necessary sense of the mystery of life. Human beings only really live when they hover on the edge of explanation. The frontier that calls for the exercise of faith points to the Sovereign God who creates and rules, and finally fulfills our capacity to wonder.

The Reverend Charles Lutwidge Dodgson loved children and told them stories. The first son in a family of eleven children, he grew up with games, tricks, and adventure. He became a pastor, but never preached much because of a stammer. He funneled his talents professionally into the teaching of mathematics at Oxford. The marriage of left and right brains brought to his life and thought a holistic wit that revealed a view of the world rich in imagination.

Nowhere do we see this rich imagination better than in Dodgson's *Alice's Adventures in Wonderland,* published under the pen name Lewis Carroll. George MacDonald, the man C. S. Lewis admired for his own storytelling, encouraged Dodgson to publish this work. Eric Malone calls Carroll "The Master of Wonderland."[3]

The wonderland master liked telling stories to children at a moment's

---

3. Eric Malone, "The Master of Wonderland," *British Heritage* (June/July 1994): 31-35. Well researched and interestingly written, the piece zeros in on Lewis Carroll.

notice, particularly to the three small daughters of Dr. Liddell, Dean of Christ Church, Oxford. They, along with an adult friend of Dodgson, used to take boat rides on the Thames. After picnicking, the girls would ask for a story. Only a little stimulus, like a rabbit running down a hole, could spin off a yarn.

One of the three girls, Alice, wanted Dodgson to write out the rabbit story. He did and presented it to her in his own handwriting at Christmas with the title "Alice's Adventures Underground." When Dodgson published a whole book about the rabbit, he changed the title to *Alice's Adventures in Wonderland.* The rest is history. The fact that a mathematician could write such a children's piece reminds one of J. R. R. Tolkien, a technical scholar, who could write *Lord of the Rings,* or C. S. Lewis, a medievalist who taught at both Cambridge and Oxford, who could pen the Narnia tales. Reason and hard facts cannot explain life. Tweedle-Dum and Tweedle-Dee, the Mad Hatter, the White Rabbit, Elsie, Lacie, and Tillie and more all give vent to Dodgson's intuitive knowledge that life adds up to more than mathematics. A celebration of Dodgson's rich fantasies finds expression in the Lewis Carroll window of All Saints Church, Caresbury, Cheshire, England.

What made Dodgson a genius of imagination? We have some hints. He loved what today we call the serendipitous. One doubts that he knew where his stories were headed. Surprise characterizes bright and fertile minds. Then, too, he was a photographer.

He has been called the most outstanding photographer of children in the nineteenth century. He took pictures of famous people and little children. More, he was an inventor, an inventor of games for children, of picture stories (he was the first to do story picture serials), of mathematical puzzles, and more. He did magic tricks, invented a circular billiards table, conceived a system for memorizing numbers. And the arts? Such a love! Opera, theater, literature. Still more, he published serious works on mathematics and logic, and wrestled with difficult problems that might find solution beyond conventional logical procedures (metalogic). Wisdom emerges from the sense of wonder.

The Feel for Rhythms

For those of us who live in an English-speaking culture, our elemental rhythm is the basic iambic of our language. We absorb it in childhood with the reading of the nursery rhymes. Soon we encounter Shakespeare. When we hear the King James Version of the Bible read and sample a contemporary translation done with sensitivity to flow, like the Revised Standard Version, we begin to catch the pulse beats of our language.

This native timing relates to our language as tonality relates to the Chinese language. Children who have the benefit of hearing rhythmic English read to them as they develop benefit from a conditioning to the natural cadences of language and often grow up to communicate well.

When Dylan Thomas talks excitedly about his youthful discovery of the mighty, cascading rhythms of English literature, he suggests that the tempos carry a powerful substance characteristic of the best in British insight. The marriage of the two rhythms—form and substance—identifies classic literature. William Wordsworth saw the two blended in nature, in head and heart, and he models both rhythms in his poem "I Wandered Lonely as a Cloud":

> I wandered lonely as a cloud
> That floats on high o'er vales and hills,
> When all at once I saw a crowd,
> A host, of golden daffodils;
> Beside the lake, beneath the trees,
> Fluttering and dancing in the breeze.
>
> Continuous as the stars that shine
> And twinkle on the milky way,
> They stretched in never-ending line
> Along the margin of a bay:
> Ten thousand saw I at a glance,
> Tossing their heads in sprightly dance.
>
> The waves beside them danced; but they
> Out-did the sparkling waves in glee;
> A poet could not but be gay,
> In such a jocund company:
> I gazed—and gazed—but little thought
> What wealth the show to me had brought:
>
> For oft, when on my couch I lie
> In vacant or in pensive mood,
> They flash upon that inward eye
> Which is the bliss of solitude;
> And then my heart with pleasure fills,
> And dances with the daffodils.

Nature helps us understand the underlying rhythms of life. Physician William Carlos Williams, who became a writer, saw pulses in the human body related to the pulse beats in poetry. One wonders whether Alexander Borodin, a professor of surgery, did not have some of the same perception when he turned composer. Borodin's second string quartet, for example, shows a profound understanding of life's rhythms.

Edmund Spenser believed that iambic pentameter dropped out of heaven, that nature created the heart throb of the English language. While this assumption begs critical dialogue, one wonders whether the therapist's advice in the following story shares the truth in this Spenserian idea: A psychologist told his patient to go to the country and lie on the ground in a quiet place with her ear to the ground. "Listen to the sounds," he advised. "The tiny creatures of the soil move to the beat of nature like the wind in the trees and the birds in flight. Stay quiet, one ear attuned to the ground, the other skyward. Stay still long enough to absorb the cadences of creation." He explained that our human mind and body rhythms can get out of sync. Chaotic living creates conflict.

As I write these lines, one of the biggest-selling compact discs in both Western Europe and America is "Gregorian Chant" done by the Benedictine monks of Santo Domingo De Silos. The genius of Gregorian chants goes beyond a mere device to accommodate sound in echoing medieval cathedrals. Its real genius lies in capturing one of heaven's rhythms.

This rhythmicity, so fundamental to our Western heartbeat, comes in an astonishing variety of formats. Mozart charms us with his six hundred and more compositions, and we broadcast him more than any other composer over classical radio stations in America. He traces the soul's flowing movements like exquisite Belgian lace, a Rubens masterpiece, Michelangelo's fresco ceiling in the Sistine Chapel, dancers performing *Swan Lake*, or Pavarotti singing an operatic aria.

The same sense of art and rhythm energized content and delivery in the preaching of James S. Stewart, that "Beethoven" of preachers. W. E. Sangster, with body language, tone, and semantics, could make eloquent a slice of biblical truth. E. V. Hill, with his undulations like a bird in flight, sings his soul into human hearts. James Earl Massey is a master of art and rhythm in delivering the content of the Christian gospel.

Applying the Imaginative

We move now from three representative commonalities of imaginative communication to three applications for Christian preachers: order, pictures, and music.

Order: Heaven's Law

A timeless proverb tells us that order is heaven's first law. Variety alone cannot create communication. System marks the successful articulation of revelation and life. But order by itself initiates and sustains boredom. An inviting mix of form, substance, and color works to get the message across.

Without order, chaos reigns. Scattered utterance leaves a kind of oblong blur on the psyche, rather than a clear and vivid declaration. Modern artists may try to communicate by helter-skelter expression, but that usually brings puzzled responses. It is not that we should frown unadvisedly on experimentation (Beethoven did not enjoy unabated affirmation in his day), but after the newness wears off, if enduring quality rings its bell, there has been some order that has characterized the communiqué. The true artist does not permit imagination to run away with itself lest creativity destroy creation.

The preacher needs to harness the imagination in order to create infectious art. Art is the exposé of the subliminal mind in meaningful form. The doctrine of privitism, that art exists for the artist and does not have to communicate to anyone else, is a teaching we cannot entertain. Jesus created the gospel for the world. Contagion sets in when listeners perceive in forms understandable to them.

Demosthenes knew about the order that comes across with power. He declared that "persuasion is as dependent upon the order of the arguments as upon the arguments themselves." Any number of delicious notions will not get through unless they come under the umbrella called arrangement. Sequencing material makes the difference between a tree and a brush pile. Horace, that fertile mind of ancient times, hit the nail on the head: "The beauty of order consists in saying just now what just now ought to be said, and postponing for the present all the rest."

The preacher may look at order from several vantage points. One is the opening of a flower in spring—tracing the emergence of bud, then color, and finally the full flower is a scenario printed in vivid sequence. Or consider the picture of parallel ideas: Each major concept appears in complementary form. James Stewart mastered this technique, and often used parallel language to shape his major concerns. His magnificent sermon "The Lord God Omnipotent Reigneth" models parallelism. What, he asks, is the biggest fact in life? Not home, not work, not health and happiness, but a profound truth that relates to and supersedes these. God reigns. And what does that mean? It means

The liberation of Life.
The doom of sin.
The comfort of sorrow.

Still another picture of order is a set of concentric circles, successive circles enlarging and expanding the single truth of a sermon. Part of the joy of creating homilies is the endless stream of possibilities for arranging ideas. Creative potential gathers force and enlarges the store of options the more years we invest in the exciting business of the preparation and delivery of sermons.

The sermon must march; it must move toward a specific goal and at its conclusion leave the clear impression of having arrived. Wesley's famous outline follows a progression that leads to a natural Christian climax:

> Gain all you can;
> Save all you can;
> Give all you can.

One can hardly miss the intended truth in its growing fullness.

Some preachers prefer not to announce points per se, but to unfold the single truth of the sermon, however subtly, until the material has come to a successful conclusion. This procedure can be visualized as unrolling an oriental carpet. Little by little its design appears until the entire piece lies open before us, making visible the whole pattern. However difficult this homiletical method may be for many preachers, it does work for some. The successful use of this methodology means clear perception and steady unfolding of the specific truth at hand.

By way of integrating the three characteristics of imaginative communication, then, we must see with penetrating eyes and arrange our material so that the audience will share in that vision. Creative design, imbued with freshness of thought, can open a whole new world of wonder, of "aha" moments, what psychologists call gestalts when truth emerges, dawns, and explodes on the inner mind. Finally, a steady beat, giving its marching orders, moves the sermon progressively to the rhythms of both form and substance.

Pictures: Heaven's Creation

"People do picture thinking" said veteran homiletician Albert Palmer. This recognition of the way the mind works, especially in listening settings, shows us an important law of communication. W. E. Sangster understood this principle and often used pictures. Someone once asked him if he didn't use too many illustrations. He said he did, then added: "I also know what communicates. Sermons seldom have too many pictures."

Spurgeon also knew the power of picture, and this, as much as his native gifts of public utterance, accounts for the oft-heard declaration that he stands as the greatest preacher since Paul. Interested students of

Spurgeon have sifted through his sermons and ferreted out illustrations to put into books.

In our own time, Charles Swindoll, a man Billy Graham listens to for personal growth, knows how to break apart a passage of Scripture and bring it to life with contemporary images, some of them very funny, nearly all of them telling.

Here, then, is the principle: Communicative preachers engage the right brain to make possible the processing of material in the left brain. To reverse that order will not work, because abstractions fall on deaf ears without the inviting and enlivening power of pictures. To preach the book of Romans, for example, in all its raw theological substance will appeal to almost no one. Best estimates indicate that only 7 to 10 percent of any population is primarily left brained, and even those who have left-brain occupations usually cannot comprehend theological declarations without picture material.

The challenge of picture preaching goes far beyond developing a file of illustrations. The more critical issue relates to the difference between sequential and simultaneous communication. The printed word calls for careful sequencing, especially in Western languages where word order is so important for understanding. Printed paragraphs govern the unfolding of ideas. Contrast a printed page with "The Young Girl at the Open Half Door," a painting that hangs over my desk as I write these lines. I can describe the painting in terms of light, shade, color, background, movement, and rhythm. But I cannot replicate the viewing experience by mere words, no matter how carefully sequenced. The impact of the Rembrandt we could term an experience of simultaneity or immediacy rather than sequence or word order.

Since preachers must mix sequential and simultaneous communication, space becomes very important. The public speaker cannot transpose mere words into an actual painting. The listener must have space to finish out the images suggested. To fill in too many details robs the listener of creative opportunity and, therefore, a sense of participating in the pulpit enterprise.

Painting pictures, then, requires giving freedom to listeners to finish out the images. This explains Robert Louis Stevenson's comment that if he knew what to omit he would be a genius. While we can never perfectly exercise selectivity and economy, we do know the force of suggestion and understatement. We also know that when we deliver sermons, we can pause and slow down speech at appropriate places to help our people track with us and have time to fill in the spaces.

Herein lies the suggestion of an important theological truth: The Holy

Spirit shapes messages to individual human needs. People come to church with different agendas; God knows that and tailors applications to suit personal requirements. To rob the Spirit of this particularized communication opportunity, either by filling in too many details or by exaggerating and twisting truth, leads to serious consequences. Television ads, notorious for their half-truths, make us laugh; we know that they are designed to con us. Manipulative preachers, because of their authoritative position, may even lead Christians astray.

Luke helps us to integrate our three marks of imaginative communication. An ancient tradition is that Luke was a painter. One can believe that Luke's Gospel and Acts read like an art gallery, one picture after another. We know Luke was a doctor as well, and maybe because of this he gives a fuller account of Mary's virginal conception of Jesus than does any other Gospel writer. The sacred mystery, the sense of wonder at God's creative work, comes through loud and clear. Note, too, the rhythms and music of his writing—the Magnificat, e.g., the flow and cadence of Luke 15 with its three "losts"—and more, much more. Luke saw with spiritual eyes; he stood in awe at the wonder of God and life; he felt the rhythms of the music of the good news in Christ. Luke stands as a model of imaginative preaching.

Music: Heaven's Cadence

"The music of the Gospel leads us home," wrote F. W. Faber. Gospel preaching, by its very nature, sings its way into human hearts. The Psalter, the hymnbook of the Israelites, stands as the stalwart model. The song of Moses, the Pauline hymnlike expressions, Luke's music—no wonder the Christian faith expresses itself in music as does no other religion.

Home, indeed! Warmth, security, fresh insight, the stretch of growth, new awarenesses—all and more describe the heart's definition of *home*. This explains why listening to Handel's *Messiah*, Bach's B Minor Mass, or Beethoven's Ninth Symphony brings a deep sense of home. This is precisely what happens when we hear the Christian gospel in the music of heaven. This explains why singing and preaching always go together in the Christian faith.

Listen to the Beaux Arts Trio's recording of Beethoven's Triple Concerto. Daniel Guilet, violin; Menahem Pressler, piano; and Bernard Greenhouse, cello, have worked together so long and assiduously that they play as a single soul. With them we have no quick rehearsal of artists coming from hither and yon to do a one-night stand, but musicians who play together with a consistency that opens the very door of heaven.

I listened to that Triple Concerto recently while driving to town. The fountains of my inner being broke loose as heaven spoke. I knew that Beethoven's own suffering—the suicide of his adopted nephew, his own deafness, his old-age diseases—all now had found resolution. Ah, resolution! There you have it. The conflict, the disharmonies in his music, always find resolution. Perhaps no composer treated suffering so creatively as did Ludwig von Beethoven. He knew the music of the gospel had power to carry him home.

God has given us three vehicles of communication: words (semantics), tone (tonics), and body language (kinetics). When the three work together in a kind of Beaux Arts Trio oneness, the music of the gospel may well find engaging expression. Add to the teaching power of experience and effort the all-important work of God's Spirit, and preaching penetrates lost souls and enlightens hurting people.

J. S. Bach believed, with Martin Luther, that "music's only purpose should be for the glory of God and the recreation of the human spirit." Often Bach put "J. J." at the top of an unused manuscript sheet—*Jesu Juva* ("Help me, Jesus"). Sometimes he initialed "I. N. J." (*In Nomine Jesus*, "In the name of Jesus"). Always at the close of a score Bach inscribed "S. D. G."—*Soli Deo Gloria* ("To God alone the glory"). No wonder history sees Bach as the foremost Christian composer and that musicians call him their patron saint.[4]

With the Spirit comes freedom, joy, and the gift of humor. Schubert's "Trout" Quintet ripples along with incomparable delight. Haydn's "Surprise" Symphony makes us smile to hear the unexpected. Haydn loved life and his vocation, and he could say with utter sincerity, "God gave me a cheerful heart, so He will surely forgive me if I serve Him cheerfully." Preaching in such a spirit, with wit, wisdom, and humor, carries testimony to the liberating force of the gospel.

Mozart's childlike playfulness opens windows on insights, truth, and the wholeness of liberated life. We get some of the same feelings and reactions listening to children play and talk. In the compositions of the classic musicians, often we confront what Liszt called "Programme Music," music that tells a story. Playful or sober, calm or stormy, the narrative finds expression in color, tone, and rhythm. "Programme Preaching" does the same, but always with faith, hope, and love, the gospel that leads people home.

---

4. Patrick Kavanaugh, *The Spiritual Lives of Great Composers* (Nashville: Sparrow Press, 1992), 12, 13. Kavanaugh, Executive Director of the Christian Performing Artists Fellowship and a well-known conductor, reveals the seldom heard truth about the deep spirituality of great composers. Well worth reading.

When the vision of God comes to the preacher, he or she stands in wonder and awe in the divine presence. When wonder and sight move to the rhythms of heaven's cadence, we hear music. It is the music of truly good news! Our call is to share heaven's music.

Suggested Reading

Alinder, James, and John Szarkowski. *Ansel Adam's Classic Images*. New York: Little Brown and Co., 1994. The genius of Adams lies in where he stands when he takes his pictures.

Augustine. *The Confessions*. Translated with introductory materials by E. M. Blaiklock. Nashville: Thomas Nelson, 1983. Augustine's remarkable commentary on human memory in Book X provides a launching pad for understanding the database from which imagination makes constructions. Elsewhere, Augustine talks about revelation, significant for a Christian understanding of imagination.

Bailey, Colin B., Joseph J. Rishel, and Mark Rosenthal, with assistance of Veerle Thielemans. *Masterpieces of Impressionism and Post-Impressionism: The Annenberg Collection*. Philadelphia: The Philadelphia Museum of Art, 1989. The color photography reveals even brush strokes and gives the viewer the sense of seeing texture almost as if one were standing in front of the pictures at the museum.

Boorstin, Daniel J. *The Creators*. New York: Random House, 1992. The great range of Boorstin's work, coupled with theological underpinnings, makes this a seminal volume.

Cameron, Nigel M. de S., et al. *Dictionary of Scottish Church History and Theology*. Downers Grove, Ill.: InterVarsity Press, 1993. The remarkable contribution of the Scots to theology and preaching calls for a work of this dimension. Note the consistent and imaginative influence of Scottish exegesis (see the article on biblical exegesis) and the freedom of thought in doing theology (see, e.g., the article on James Denney).

Carpenter, Humphrey. *The Inklings: C. S. Lewis, J. R. R. Tolkien, Charles Williams, and Their Friends*. Boston: Houghton Mifflin, 1979. Carpenter, known for his biography of Tolkien and other penetrating works, exposes through his writing his own gift for imagination, while helping us understand the creativity of the C. S. Lewis literary circle.

Carroll, Lewis. *The Annotated Alice: Alice's Adventures in Wonderland and Through the Looking Glass, by Lewis Carroll*. Notes editor Martin Gardner. Illustrated by John Tenniel. New York: Bramhall House, 1960. A handbook for seeing into the mind of a great imaginer.

Chilvers, Ian, and Harold Osborne, eds., with consultant editor Dennis Farr. *The Oxford Dictionary of Art*. New York: Oxford University Press, 1988. Remarkable for the range of articles, although disappointing that no specific treatments of art, painting, image, sculpture, or architecture appear.

Duduit, Michael, ed. *Handbook of Contemporary Preaching*. Nashville: Broadman Press, 1992. Chapters, in order of appearance, relative to the subject of the imagination, are by Calvin Miller, Lloyd John Ogilvie, Stephen Brown, James Earl Massey, Peter Rhea Jones, Roy DeBrand, and Ralph Lewis.

Gardner, Howard. *Creating Minds: An Anatomy of Creativity Seen Through the Lives of Freud, Einstein, Picasso, Stravinsky, Eliot Graham, and Gandhi*. New York: Basic Books, 1993. The Harvard developmentalist shares his perspective on the dynamics of innovative minds.

Jones, Ilion T. *Principles and Practice of Preaching*. Nashville: Abingdon Press, 1956. A practical textbook on the preparation and delivery of sermons.

Keck, Leander E. *The Church Confident*. Nashville: Abingdon Press, 1993.

_____. *The Lyman Beecher Lectures*, Yale Divinity School, 1992. Dr. Keck helps us get under the skin of contemporary communications challenges.

Kennedy, Michael, ed. *The Oxford Dictionary of Music*. New York: Oxford University Press, 1993. Like the Oxford Dictionary of Art, the scope of the work impresses the researcher. Articles relevant to the imagination include those on images, impressionism, and programme music.

McArthur, Tom, ed. *The Oxford Companion to the English Language*. New York: Oxford University Press, 1992. A hefty volume covering about every topic one can think of relating to our language. See articles on imagery, images, and imagination.

Merton, Thomas. *A Thomas Merton Reader*. Edited by Thomas P. McDonnell. London: Lamp Press, 1989. Merton's extraordinary, in-depth analysis of life and God, along with wonderfully fresh and descriptive language, make him one of the century's great minds. The Reader provides an introduction to the vast body of writings that have emerged from his pen.

Parris, Leslie, and Ian Fleming-Williams. *Constable*. New York: Cross River Press, 1993. John Constable, father of English impressionism, created on canvas sky, clouds, water, trees, and steeples, with sufficient impact to make his paintings some of the most desired in history. This volume contains a vast collection of data and fine reproductions.

Peterson, Eugene H. *The Message: The New Testament in Contemporary English.* Colorado Springs: Navpress, 1993. Peterson generally reads Old and New Testaments in his Hebrew and Greek Bibles. Here he brings his fertile mind to rendering the Scriptures in language that ordinary readers can visualize.

"Sounding a Note of Hope," *Lexington Herald-Leader*, June 20, 1994, A3. This is a remarkable account of Zubin Mehta, Jose Carreras, and other musicians bringing hope through music to Sarajevans.

Thielen, Martin. "Beyond Infosermons." *Leadership* (Winter 1994). Raw data and cold outlines will not, of themselves, communicate.

Wynne-Davies, Marion, ed. *Prentice Hall Guide to English Literature: The New Authority on English Literature.* New York: Prentice Hall, 1990. After a dozen essays to give the feel of literary contexts, a rich reference section, alphabetical and often with graphics, brings data within reach.

LAUGHING WITH THE GOSPEL

David G. Buttrick

T he preacher laughed out loud. So did the congregation. He had just spoken of power brokers, the big shots in high places who actually think they run the world. Well, no wonder the congregation laughed. They knew better because, according to the apostle Paul, as believing Christians they were somehow in on the ways of God.

Again and again, black preaching contrasts the foolish, delusional pretensions of the world—often a well-off white world—with the special insight granted to God's people, specifically to God's oppressed people.[1] So African American congregations will laugh out loud in the middle of sermons. Although the experience is seldom met these days in mainline white congregations, it has been a distinctive feature of Christian preaching since the time of the earliest church.

To honor a remarkable colleague, James Earl Massey, I want to explore what Ralph Ellison once labeled "the confounding, persistent, and embarrassing mystery of black laughter" in preaching.[2]

---

1. Dick Gregory, a profoundly religious man, observes, "When it comes to our humor, the white man is our greatest clown." Quoted in Nat Hentoff, "Goodbye Mistah Bones," *The New York Times Magazine,* April 27, 1975, 40.

2. Ralph Ellison, "The Extravagance of Laughter," in *Going to the Territory* (New York: Random House, 1986), 190. For a recent comprehensive study of African American humor, see Mel Watkins, *On the Real Side: Laughing, Living, and Signifying—The Underground Tradition of African-American Humor That Transformed American Culture from Slavery to Richard Pryor* (New York: Simon and Schuster, 1994).

Homiletic Laughter

What are we talking about? Can we describe the phenomenon? Here is a brief sample provided by Dr. Wyatt Tee Walker, pastor of the large Canaan Baptist Church of Christ in New York City.

> Queen Esther is facing a terrible decision: Will she reveal her Jewish identity and risk the loss of her position and possibly her life? Esther goes into her walk-in closet and looks at the gowns designed by Balenciaga and Yves St. Laurent; then she turns quickly to the window and sees her silver-grey Mark VI sitting in the driveway of the palace and wonders, how on earth can I give up all this?[3]

Walker's congregation would laugh at the references to gowns by Yves St. Laurent and the silver-grey car in the drive. They would be laughing at worldly values compared to the purposes of God.

Here is a somewhat more sophisticated example provided by a brilliant preacher, Dr. Mack King Carter of the Mount Olive Baptist Church in Ft. Lauderdale, Florida:

> The greatest threat to America and its brand of Christianity was never Communism, but the fact that Jesus might have been a Black man. If this could be proved photographically, Christianity would last only seventy-two hours: twenty-four hours to embrace the shock, twenty-four hours to pack its icons and religious paraphernalia, and twenty-four hours to deal with massive clerical unemployment. The dispersive power of ebony pigmentation is awesome! Just think of it, the Nigger from Nazareth is Lord![4]

According to Dr. Carter, his congregation laughed as he preached this powerful section from his sermon. Actually, they were laughing at the racism of American religious institutions compared to a God who has been choosing the socially rejected for centuries. Examples can be brief or can comprise major sections of a sermon. Always they are freely imagined, but designed with careful rhetorical skill. And, always, there is laughter, from the pulpit as well as from the pews.

---

3. Wyatt Tee Walker, *The Soul of Black Worship* (New York: Martin Luther King Fellowship Press, 1984), 22.
4. Mack King Carter, excerpt from the sermon "Why America Rejects the Biblical Christ" (Text: 1 Cor. 1:18, 22-24). Delivered October 5, 1987, in the Martin Luther King, Jr., Chapel at Morehouse College, Atlanta, Georgia.

Insight and Oppression

Now what exactly is going on? What is the source of laughter? Initially the laughter is established by a contrast between power and powerlessness. Langston Hughes put it bluntly: "Humor is laughing at what you haven't got when you ought to have it."[5] Obviously the people who suppose they control the human world are people in power. Some drink coffee midmorning on "Main Street" America; others toss back martinis at lunch in World Trade Towers; but all regard themselves as powerful. They have the cash or the clout to order and sometimes even dominate the lives of others. Moreover, they have social status; their names show up in the papers—on news pages, financial pages, or society pages. They are the movers, the shakers, the go-getters, the pacesetters, the shapers of public opinion.

By contrast, the average African American congregation has not exactly been "mainstream." From the time of the Civil War until the 1960s, most black congregations were busy surviving.[6] They were an "in group" that was socially excluded from cash, power, and status by American racism. What's more, the African American congregation was usually quite aware of both its isolation and its exclusion, not to mention its own special in-group Christian character—the songs, the responses, the community ethos that comprised a distinctive black church in America.[7] So, at the outset we can note two kinds of groupings within the mind of an average black congregation—namely, themselves and those in power. Now, please note, the same sort of awareness is certainly to be found in the New Testament church. Doesn't the apostle Paul distinguish his Corinthian congregation from the powers of the world? He is candid with the people of Corinth. From a worldly point of view, they were not much: "Not many smart, not many powerful, not many well-born," he remarks (1 Cor. 1:26),[8] and you can imagine members of the congregation looking around and nodding their heads in honest agreement. The con-

---

5. Henry D. Spalding, *Encyclopedia of Black Folklore and Humor* (Middle Village, N.Y.: Jonathan David, 1972), 428.

6. See E. Franklin Frazier, *The Negro Church in America* (New York: Schocken Books, 1974), and C. Eric Lincoln, *The Black Church Since Frazier* (New York: Schocken Books, 1974), 35-51. See also Gayraud S. Wilmore, *Black Religion and Black Radicalism: An Examination of the Black Experience in Religion* (Garden City, N.Y.: Doubleday, 1973), 187-227.

7. Melva Wilson Costen, *African-American Christian Worship* (Nashville: Abingdon Press, 1993), 91-117; William B. McClain, *Come Sunday: The Liturgy of Zion* (Nashville: Abingdon Press, 1990), 45-58.

8. All Scripture quotations in this chapter are the author's translations.

---

gregation in Corinth was not exactly an advertisement for "lifestyles of the rich and famous."

By contrast, Paul seems to poke fun at those in power. Discussion of the word *power* in Pauline thought is complex, for Paul speaks of "principalities and powers" in a peculiar way.[9] The "powers that be" are transsocial in character; they seem to be somewhere "above" in the layered heavens.[10] Yet they are definitely connected to earthly powers—political, economic, and religious. They appear to be structured in a manner similar to patterns described by sociologists of knowledge.[11] The human world projects customs, attitudes, cultural assumptions to a common level of affirmation. These take on an aura of divinity; they become sacred social affirmations of faith and practice. In turn they tend to dictate to the human world that this is the way we ought to act, believe, value, and so on. The "powers that be," as transsocial powers, are mere projections—they are human products—but as they act on us, influence our behavior, control our social ways and means, they can become demonic. They are "no-powers" that nonetheless can be devastatingly influential in human affairs.[12]

The power-elite of the world are definitely related to the powers that be. But, according to Paul, the world powers are ignorant of God's purposes; they crucified the "Lord of glory" because they didn't know what was really going on—that is, going on in God's hidden purposes. Notice, however, that in 1 Corinthians 2:6-13 God's servant people do know; they have the wisdom of God:

> We do speak wisdom among the mature, not the wisdom of this world nor of the powers that be who soon will be has-beens. We speak God's mysterious wisdom, the hidden wisdom that God proposed for our glorification

9. For a recent study of the "principalities and powers," see Walter Wink's trilogy, *Naming the Powers* (1984), *Unmasking the Powers* (1986), and, most recently, *Engaging the Powers: Discernment and Resistance in a World of Domination* (1992), all published by Fortress Press.

10. Clinton D. Morrison, *The Powers That Be* (London: SCM Press, 1960), 102-29.

11. For example, see Peter L. Berger and Thomas Luckmann, *The Social Construction of Reality: A Treatise in the Sociology of Knowledge* (Garden City, N.Y.: Doubleday, 1967). They are drawing upon the social phenomenology of Alfred Schutz.

12. Peter Berger describes the sequence: "Society is a human product. Society is an objective reality. Human beings are a social product" (Berger and Luckmann, *The Social Construction of Reality*, 67). He means that "society" is a system of customs, attitudes, ideas, rituals, and the like, projected by human beings. But society can become a separate "objective" reality that, in turn, shapes human beings. The Bible seems to understand "the powers that be" in much the same way.

before the world began. Not one of the powers of the world understood; if they had, they would not have crucified the Lord of glory. . . . But God has disclosed [it all] to us through the Spirit. . . . We have not received a worldly spirit, but the Spirit from God so we can grasp the graces God has so freely given us, and which we talk about, not in words of human wisdom, but as we are taught by the Spirit—words of the Spirit from the Spirit.

The Corinthians may have had no power, no cash, no smarts, no status, but they knew what God was doing because they were aware of saving grace moving through their own impotent, impoverished community.[13] So Paul tells them of the powers that be who soon will be "has-beens," and you can almost hear the congregational laughter in Corinth. People who are socially helpless understand how God's hidden grace can function; they are seldom deceived by overt displays of power.

Ordinary people cannot grasp things of the Spirit of God; to them, it's all nonsense. Because such things can only be explored by the Spirit, they simply do not know. But those of the Spirit can judge such things, while they themselves are beyond judgment (1 Cor. 2:14-15).

According to Paul, the Corinthian congregation actually had "the mind of Christ!" So in African American congregations, the preacher, like the apostle Paul, will contrast foolish, blind, worldly "wisdom" with the truly savvy faith of God's people who, acquainted with grace, can see through the pretensions of power and can know what's truly going on in the hiddenness of God's purpose. God's people can laugh, and their laughter is based on the joke of power and the insightful giggle of the powerless.

The Promise of the Cross

There is another source for laughter—namely, the witness of the cross. Earlier, in 1 Corinthians 1, Paul draws a sharp contrast between (1) "Jews who need a sign and Greeks who want wisdom" and (2) the cross of Jesus Christ, a cross that is impotency to Jews and stupidity to Greeks. Nevertheless, says Paul, to us who are being saved, the message of the cross is truly a message of liberation. The paradox of the cross—Christ

---

13. Paul argues that God uses the "foolish" to shame the wise, the "weak" to shame the strong, the low-born to veto "those that are." His descriptions, of course, match the Christians in Corinth who, he has said, are short of smarts, power, and status. But God has chosen the Corinthians, Paul claims, so that no one will boast. Instead, he says, "Whoever may boast, boast in the Lord."

horribly crucified like a renegade slave—is that a foolish, impotent Christ is nothing less than the unconquerable power of God's love. Thus, eschatologically, Paul affirms the fact that God's odd, seemingly impotent power is the only true power, and the seeming foolishness of Christ's sacrifice is God's true wisdom. Paul looks to the ultimate victory of love. He knows what all Christians know, that God's silly, senseless, seemingly overwhelmed love is actually unconquerable.

So African American congregations laugh because they know how God's story will come out. They know by gazing at the cross that a broken, crucified, but self-giving people are bound to triumph in God's purpose. We can describe the laughter in black sermons, then, as eschatological laughter. Black congregations, socially denied, abused, and discriminated against, identify with a Savior who was also put down and nailed up by people who were in charge of the world. But if Christ has been raised by the power of God, then oppressed believers will also be raised up—it's a sure thing! If the world doesn't know how God's story will end, then more's the pity to the world. If the world will not know, then, well, all we can do is laugh at their wised-up foolishness!

A sense of eschatological reversal fills the New Testament writings. The poor, denied property now, will fill God's new-order world. The meek, kept in place now, shall "inherit the earth." The blues singers, repressed now, will cakewalk with joy. The great reversal of the cross informs us all: Jesus, who was condemned under law and strung up by a first-century lynch mob, has been raised by God to rule the new order. Thus, by analogy, if in our cruciform lives we are unjustly hassled by law and murderously abused, we can be sure that God intends to reverse our destiny. Now, even now, we can celebrate and do so with a kind of impudent glee.

But we must be cautious; eschatology can be perverse. Listen to James Cone:

> If eschatology means that one believes that God is totally uninvolved in the suffering of men because he is preparing them for another world, then Black Theology is an earthly theology! It is not concerned with the "last things" but with the "white thing."[14]

---

14. James Cone, *Black Theology and Black Power* (New York: Seabury Press, 1969), 123. Cone's position has been modified. For example, he has more recently written: "I contend that black people's experience of liberation as hope for a new heaven and a new earth represents a new mode of perception, different from the experience of white people" (James Cone, *God of the Oppressed* [New York: Seabury Press, 1975], 159). For discussion, see James H. Evans, Jr., *We Have Been Believers: An African-American Systematic Theology* (Minneapolis: Fortress Press, 1992), chapter 7.

Did not Karl Marx castigate the church for handing out pie in the sky while at the same time piously supporting economic oppression of the poor? But in the best of the black preaching tradition, a vision of God's new order seems instead to have encouraged social action. Gayraud Wilmore admits that while black preaching can tumble toward the Marxist accusation, properly a vision of "last things" should be both politically potent and a judgment on our present social order.[15]

When the island of Jamaica was granted independence from British rule, an official date, August 6, 1962, was announced some weeks ahead of time. As a result, the population began celebrating, partying in advance because they knew they were de facto free. Is it possible that what Henry Mitchell and others have described as "celebration" in the black sermon is somewhat similar?[16] Insofar as an African American congregation can see a vision of God's new social order, what the Bible calls "the kingdom of God"—a sure-thing vision guaranteed by the life and death and resurrection of Jesus Christ—naturally the congregation can "celebrate" in advance. Moreover, such celebration can be socially dynamic as Christians begin to live freely according to patterns of life in God's new order. "New World A-Coming," sang the great African American editor and reformer Roi Ottley, and his phrase captures the power and the joy of black social vision.[17]

What are the sources of laughter in black preaching? Laughter comes from being oppressed while at the same time, in grace, knowing God's purposes for the human enterprise. Black homiletic laughter is generated by a sure faith in the cross of Jesus Christ. Of course, beneath these obvious realities is a deeper reality—the working of the Holy Spirit in the African American community of faith.

Laughter in the Gospel of John

We find similar structures in the Gospel of John. There are several "mystery dialogues" between Jesus and persons who represent worldly thought and religion.[18] Read the dialogue between Jesus and Nicodemus

---

15. Gayraud S. Wilmore, *Last Things First* (Philadelphia: Westminster Press, 1982), 77.

16. See Henry H. Mitchell, *The Recovery of Preaching* (San Francisco: Harper & Row, 1977), 189-95; *Black Preaching* (New York: Lippincott, 1977), chapter 4.

17. See Roi Ottley, *New World A-Coming* (New York: Arno Press, 1968).

18. The form of these dialogues may be prompted by the repartée of rabbinic instruction or, more likely, by gnostic writings in which a "revealer" will disclose arcane truth to ordinary mortals. See Pheme Perkins, *The Gnostic Dialogue: The Early Church and the Crisis of Gnosticism* (New York: Paulist Press, 1980).

(3:1-15). "Unless a person is born from above, he cannot see the kingdom of God," says Jesus. "How can a man be born when he's old?" answers an obtuse Nicodemus. "Can he enter into his mother's womb a second time and be born?" The first-century Johannine congregation would be giggling with delight. They know. They know but, rather obviously, old Nicodemus does not know.

The same sort of phenomenon occurs with the woman at the well (4:7-30). She simply doesn't understand, does she? Jesus offers her living water, and all she says is, "You've nothing to draw with, and the well is deep." She is even scornfully sassy: "Mister, where are you getting your 'living water'?" When Jesus replies, saying that anyone who drinks the water he gives will "never thirst again," she misses the point completely, saying in effect, "Okay, give me your water so I won't have to come down to this old well all the time!"

Again, you can almost hear the first-century Christians chuckling at her ignorance. The same sort of pattern occurs with Peter, who is seldom accorded too much respect in the Gospel of John (13:3-16). Peter cannot feature Christ bending down to scrub his feet: "You'll never wash my feet, not now, not ever!" he protests. Then, when Jesus warns him that unless he allows himself to be washed he will have no share in salvation, dumb Peter wants the full treatment: "Lord, don't just wash my feet, but my hands and face as well." So Jesus has to remind him that forgiven people do not require repeated scrubbing. The dialogue is howlingly funny if, underscore the if, if you are where the Johannine community was—namely, on the lee side of the cross enjoying free, forgiven, eternal life in the Spirit.

So what is the source of laughter? It has to do with location. Christian congregations live on the far side of the cross. They know that Jesus has died, rejected by the world. They also know that the same God who has raised Jesus Christ is truly in charge of the world. As a result, they know what the world cannot know. Christians know that the end of the human story is salvation and that the Savior is the same Jesus whom the world has rejected. Nicodemus, the woman at the well, even Peter at the supper table—they are all still living in a precross world and have not yet entered the joyful community of the Spirit. So they are dumb, but the Johannine congregation, remembering the cross while living a new life in the Spirit, can understand.

Kind Bemusement

Now, please note the quality of black Christian laughter. Although it laughs at the pretensions of the worldly (often white) world, it is not a gloating, vindictive laughter. Yes, the power brokers of the world are dense, misguided, and vain; they are laughable. But at the same time black congregations can remember that the world is a world God wants to save, indeed a world that, according to John 3:16, God loves. So the laughter is honest. The world is wretched, sinful, prejudiced, and stacked against God's people; but it is our world and our common sinful humanity that is being foolish. There is a kindness lurking in the homiletic joking and the congregational laughter. Again, the question: How come?

Many persons have noticed that African American preaching often works out of a large narrative sense. What prevents black laughter from becoming cruel pleasure or common vindictiveness (like the rather nasty twentieth chapter of Revelation!) is the scope of the story that the black church tells. Although the story of the exodus is especially significant to the black community—the paradigmatic narrative of an enslaved people—even the exodus account is held within a wider story, a story that begins in creation and ends in a vision of God's "Holy City." In other words, the African American community lives in a biblical "myth" that is the whole human story and not a parochial narrative of blackness alone.

Thus the power brokers of the world are framed within the same story of creation and eschaton, of sin and salvation, as are members of the black world. We are all created children of God, and we are all poor sinners in need of saving grace. The difference? The difference is that the black congregation is in the know; they have a wisdom of God, given by the Spirit. But the common definition of humanity within the biblical story means that congregational laughter can never be nasty. No, we are all sinners and all need to be saved by the cross. If poor, deluded power people don't know what's going on in God's world, they are foolish and laughable; but ultimately, in God's large mercy, even they may be saved! So let us describe carefully the laughter engendered by black preaching. Surely it is a kind, generous laughter.

Liberating Laughter

Note a final feature of laughter in an African American congregation: The laughter is liberating because the congregational giggle is based on what might be termed "gospel knowledge." We live in a world dominated by what Paul has termed "powers that be." Such powers can take people in, even Christian people such as the bone-headed Galatians (3:1-5; 4:8-10) or the cowed Colossians (2:8-23), who end up overscheduled by "new moons and sabbaths." The powers that be in our modern world have an advantage—namely, public media and advertising. Most of us want to be someone, get somewhere, and have something. Thus the powers that be can con us into the captivity of sin. But the laughter of an African American congregation is bemusement over the pretense of power on the part of the powers that be; they have no ultimate power.

As Paul says—was he giggling as he wrote the words?—the powers that be soon will be has-beens, for the powers that be are illusionary. Romans 8:31-39 says emphatically that they cannot separate us from God's love. According to the witness of 1 Corinthians 15:24-28, they will be redeemed by Christ and, ultimately, brought under God's control. So, like the familiar fairy tale of the "Emperor's New Clothes," black laughter strips the powers of their pretended power. After all, in the sight of Christ, they are naked. Thus laughter in the black sermon can set members free from the illusionary sway of the powers that be.

We have explored a special phenomenon, the profound humor of black preaching and the liberating laughter that it invokes. Actually, such laughter is a singular feature of Christian preaching and Christian congregations and has been present with the church for sixteen centuries. Have we not spotted it in the New Testament writings? Of course, the laughter can be lost should congregations fall under the influence of the powers that be. And lost laughter is a Christian tragedy. Lost laughter will soon give way to the terrible sighs of captivity.

These days the sighs may be white.

PART · FOUR

Harmonizing

THE CATHOLICITY OF BLACK PREACHING

Frederick W. Norris

T hat sounds like great black preaching." The comment came from a white D.Min. student from North Carolina in response to my reading a selection from an oration by Gregory Nazianzen, one of the pillars of Eastern Orthodoxy.[1] When Gregory preached those words he lived in fourth-century C.E. Constantinople and spoke Greek. He was no African American, yet he was preaching to a minority in a small chapel. His opponents had the basilicas.

How could his oration, read in English, sound like great black preaching? The passage came from Oration 29 in which Gregory was trying to remind his audience that Jesus Christ is both divine and human. He is not to be likened to a created being who is less than God the Father just because Scripture speaks of his weakness.

Feel the Cadence Build

To get the full effect of this passage, you need to do two things. First, read it aloud and listen for the cadence. It is not poetry in the sense that every line rhymes or that every sentence is rhythmically balanced. But you can feel it build on itself, then relax and rebuild the tension again. When you have felt the force of that, then think about the fact that at least 125 passages of Scripture have been carefully woven together to

---

1. Gregory Nazianzen, Oration 29.19-20, in *Faith Gives Fullness to Reasoning: The Five Theological Orations of Gregory Nazianzen,* intro. and commentary by Frederick W. Norris, trans. Lionel Wickham and Frederick Williams (Leiden: E. J. Brill, 1991), 257-60. I have adapted the selection to highlight its poetic character.

present a picture of Jesus the Christ.[2] Gregory gave his best to depict the God-man in terms of the Bible.

> He was begotten of a woman.
> > Yet he was already begotten.
> > > And yet she was a virgin.
> > That it was from a woman makes it human,
> > > that she was a virgin makes it divine.
> On earth he has no father,
> > but in heaven no mother.
> All this is part of his Godhead.
> He was carried in the womb,
> > but acknowledged by a prophet as yet unborn himself,
> > > who leaped for joy at the presence of the Word
> > > > for whose sake he had been created.

> He was wrapped in swaddling bands,
> > but at the Resurrection he unloosed
> > > the swaddling bands of the grave.

> He was laid in a manger,
> > but was extolled by angels,
> > > disclosed by a star
> > > > and adored by Magi.

> Why do you take offense at what you see,
> > instead of attending to its spiritual significance?

> He was exiled into Egypt,
> > but he banished the Egyptian idols.

> He had no form or beauty for the Jews,
> > but for David he was fairer than the children of men
> and on the mount he shines forth,
> > > becoming more luminous than the Sun,
> > > > to reveal the future mystery.

> As man he was baptized,
> > but he absolved sins as God;
> > he needed no purifying rites himself
> > his purpose was to hallow water.

---

2. These scriptural references are identified in Norris, *Faith Gives Fullness to Reasoning.*

As man he was put to the test,
    but as God he came through victorious
    yet bids us be of good cheer,
        because he has conquered the world.
He hungered,
    yet he fed thousands.
  He is indeed living, heavenly bread.

He thirsted,
    yet he exclaimed:
        Whosoever thirsts, let him come to me and drink.
Indeed he promised that believers would become fountains.

He was tired,
    yet he is the rest of the weary and the burdened.

He was overcome by heavy sleep,
    yet he goes lightly over the sea,
        rebukes winds,
            and relieves the drowning Peter.

He pays tax,
    yet he uses a fish to do it;
    indeed he is emperor over those who demand tax.

He is called a Samaritan, demonically possessed,
    but he rescues the man who came down from Jerusalem
      and fell among thieves.

Yes, he is recognized by demons,
    drives out demons,
        drowns deep a legion of spirits
        and sees the prince of demons
            falling like lightning.

He is stoned,
    yet not hit.

He prays,
    yet he hears prayer.

He weeps,
    yet he puts an end to weeping.

He asks where Lazarus is—he was man.
    Yet he raises Lazarus—he was God.

He is sold, and cheap was the price—
    thirty pieces of silver;
    yet he buys back the world
        at the mighty cost of his own blood.

A sheep, he is led to the slaughter—
    yet he shepherds Israel
    and now the whole world as well.

A lamb, he is dumb—
    yet he is word proclaimed by
        the voice of one crying in the wilderness.

He is weakened, wounded,
    yet he cures every disease and every weakness.

He is brought up to the tree and nailed to it,
    yet by the tree of life he restores us.

Yes, he saves even a thief crucified with him;
    he wraps all the visible world in darkness.

He is given vinegar to drink, gall to eat—and who is he?
    Why, one who turned water into wine,
        who took away the taste of bitterness,
        who is all sweetness and desire.

He surrenders his life,
    yet he has power to take it again.

Yes, the veil is rent,
    for things of heaven are being revealed,
        rocks split,
        and dead men have an earlier awakening.

He dies,
    but he vivifies and by death destroys death.

He is buried,
    yet he rises again.

He goes down to Hades,
    yet he leads souls up,
        ascends to heaven,
        and will come to judge the quick and dead,
        and to probe discussions like these.

> If the first set of expressions starts you going astray,
> the second set takes your error away.

You certainly could call Nazianzen's preaching great. Most of what we have from him are orations, along with some letters and a good bit of poetry. He is so influential among the Orthodox that they give only him and the apostle John the title "The Theologian."

Gregory Nazianzen and Black Preaching

For centuries the Eastern Orthodox Church has understood that there is a direct connection between great preaching and great theology. The three hierarchs of Eastern Orthodoxy—Basil of Caesarea, John Chrysostom, and Gregory Nazianzen—were all grand preachers. They are looked to regularly as guides in theology. Yet, to make that greatness of patristic preaching clearer, we can look at five particular aspects that Nazianzen's preaching and black preaching share.

First, the cadence of the excerpt reprinted above from the Theologian was what caught the D.Min. student's ear. As a good rhetorician, Gregory heard the drum beat of human life. Phrases and clauses were balanced not only when their poetry was beautiful, but also when their tempo made you sway.

In recent years, rap has arisen as a common music form in black communities. Sometimes the poetry is bad, but the beat is always there. I first heard it in a German airport two decades ago when a couple of African American soldiers were talking with each other in a ticket line. I was mesmerized. Their conversation wasn't violent, oversexed, or racist; it was the talk of two young men enjoying each other's company and expressing it in rhythm and rhyme.

Whatever empowers that rhythm in black communities should be caught, taught, perhaps even flaunted. Ancient rhetoricians who taught the Church Fathers knew that the will could not be moved until the emotions had been kindled. Part of the parallel between Gregory Nazianzen's homily and black preaching is cadence, an aspect of human speech that draws people in and moves them—in song, in poetry, in rap, in great preaching.

Second, Scripture dominates this passage. Take the Scripture away, and not much else is left. These sections from Gregory are more densely biblical than most of his sermons, but the bulk of early Christian homilies consist of weaving Scripture together, warp and woof, to make not only a tapestry of beauty, but also a blanket of warmth. Black preaching is also

dominated by Scripture. Years of biblical preaching and home Bible reading or memorization within African American churches have led to chains
of reference that strengthen the bond between preacher and congregation.

Not long ago I heard about another accomplished African American
who laughed heartily when asked about being taught to read by his
grandmother. This wonderful black woman made him read from her
worn King James Bible. When he got it wrong, she thumped his head
and had him read it again. Not until after he graduated with honors from
college did he find out that his grandmother could not read! She fingered
that Bible as she prayed with it in her lap. She had memorized so much
Scripture by hearing it that she could watch over him as he tried to read
and correct him when he made a mistake. That kind of saturation with
Holy Writ is all too rare in churches, but it was so very common in the
early church where many who worshiped still could not read. Listening
to Scripture read aloud and being enmeshed in sermons may at times
bring the message into the heart more readily than merely reading.

The allegorical interpretation of Scripture is also shared by early Christian homilies and black sermons. Much modern Western seminary education dismantles any allegorical orientation as a destruction of the text.
The teaching of Scripture is most often done in categories that make it
difficult to get from the historical-critical study of the text to devotional
reading and to a sermon.

The Interpreter's Bible tried to remedy that by providing two types of
treatments, one historical-critical, the other homiletical. But that division
probably showed more clearly the depth of the fissures between the two
kinds of approaches than how easily one could move from scientific
commentary to spiritual homily. *The New Interpreter's Bible* puts these
tasks in the hands of one person, not two. The change shows the editors'
sense of wanting the tasks to be unified.[3]

Yet the allegorical interpretation of Scripture marks much of the work
from the early Church Fathers. They at times overdid it. Origen warned
that when Jesus told the people to sit on the grass as he was preparing to
feed the five thousand (Matt. 14:19), he made no off-hand remark. Isaiah
40:6 says that all flesh is grass, so Jesus was not wasting his time giving a
mundane command. He was preaching about how we need to put off the
flesh.[4]

---

3. James Earl Massey is a member of the editorial board for *The New Interpreter's Bible,* a commentary in twelve volumes, published by Abingdon Press.
Volume 1 appeared in September 1994, with two volumes scheduled to be published each year thereafter.
4. Origen *Commentary on Matthew* 11:3.

The richness of Scripture, however, is often recovered only through some kind of allegorical interpretation. The musical group Take Six creates some of the best harmonies ever heard from human voices. Six black men singing a cappella—or most recently with instrumental accompaniment—send chills up your spine. The song that struck me most on one of their early tapes has these lines:

> Oh Mary don't you weep, don't you mourn.
> 'Cause Pharaoh's army's been drowned.

Lazarus's sister Mary should not cry because God drowned Pharaoh's troops. Much scientific biblical study argues against juxtaposing the biblical text and such current application, but the Negro spiritual on which Take Six's rendition is based depends on it. Don't be shattered by death; God saved Israel, and he will save you. For many African American churches, all through their existence the allegorical claiming and naming of biblical texts about suffering helped keep them alive.

A third aspect, hinted at above, is the narrative and liturgical quality of Gregory Nazianzen's preaching. The bulk of his orations are centered around the great festivals of the church year. Many black churches do not practice that wonderful tradition, but I do not know any of them who cannot rehearse the great stories of God's people, particularly the escape from Egypt and the central events of Passion week. For some of the so-called African American low churches, the cycles of the church year may not be in evidence, but narrative theology—so new in seminaries—is old stuff. How could you preach without telling the stories of the Bible? How could you possibly live without knowing that those great narratives are tales of your life, of our life together? Liturgy is enacted story; it is dramatized narrative. African American churches breathe story and drama.

Fourth, Nazianzen insisted that the best theologians were the ones who could give us new images by which to understand the faith. African American preachers are noted for their poetic ability, their gifts for turning a phrase. Often the images are taken from Scripture itself, but they are shaped in beautiful ways for an audience that demands such beauty.

A friend of mine in college preached for a small black church about ten miles from our dorm. He listened and learned. His poetic sensibilities improved much more while worshiping with that church than they did when he took English courses. The hymns, the prayers, the responses let him know that language lives. It took him a while to know the difference in these responses. The first few months he heard a number of requests: "Help him, Lord." "Lead him, Jesus." But later, as he became more at one with his congregation, he heard, "Preach it, brother!" Each shout was a pointed cry, clear in its simplicity. Strunk and White, C. S. Lewis, or T. S. Eliot could not write cleaner lines. James Weldon Johnson is no oddity of genius without progeny in the black community.

A fifth aspect, communal interdependence of preacher and congregation, reaches across racial lines and addresses a problem that sets one culture against another. Charges of plagiarism by Martin Luther King, Jr., are themselves deeply set within an educational community that does not know or does not accept parts of its own history. Of course, stealing someone else's written work is unworthy and must be avoided. But the charge of plagiarism itself subtly honors individual effort over communal work. It is set in a context in which group projects, like encyclopedias or multi-author books, often are not given appropriate recognition by academic committees on promotion and tenure. No credit is given for words that are not clearly yours and yours alone. True cooperation is discouraged.

Ancient writers put the names of their teachers on their writings to honor those forebears. There has been a persistent, I believe mistaken, suggestion that Evagrius of Pontus, a monk of considerable spiritual insight who studied with Gregory Nazianzen, may have written some of Gregory's most important orations. I do not think that is true, but it points up again how much our own age is titillated by individualism and looks for star talent. Our age would say that if Gregory wrote it, it doesn't belong to Evagrius. If Evagrius wrote it and put Gregory's name on it, he is a liar.

Yet when you read biographies you often find that great people defer to the influence of their families, their teachers, and their colleagues. Modern literary theory suggests that the search for the author of a text may be essentially pointless. Readers bring to the text their own community values. The author does not totally disappear, but individuality, particularly when emphasized among Christians, often becomes sinister.

What do great black preachers do when so much of their preaching has been absorbed from the worshiping community? How much of any preacher's sermons should be marked by originality that points to the preacher and not to the message? When you speak from the Bible, should you end every sentence with a footnote about chapter and verse?

From Communities of Suffering

The five points examined in the previous section may help us to see similarities between the styles of Nazianzen and black preaching, but the reasons why the D.Min. student heard black preaching when I read Nazianzen aloud are wider than any attempt to justify the use of the word *great*. There are what appear to be great differences as well.

Gregory was one of the best educated men of his era. His family had money, and he took advantage of it. He spent eleven years in Caesarea, Alexandria, and Athens with some of the finest professors available. Many black preachers have been poor and thus could not afford to be well educated according to North American cultural standards. Nonetheless, the tradition of African American preaching is so strong that those raised within the congregations learn how to preach well by paying attention and modeling what works well for other preachers. The tradition is electric, moving, memorable. Indeed, great black preachers are often that way before they receive their highest formal educations. Some tend to be weakened by modern education's ideals and only return to their ability to preach when they have repented and followed the leadership of their people.

For me, the fifth aspect of similarity is the most important. In some deep and unexpected ways, the well for great preaching is the congregation itself. That white friend of mine in college who preached for a black church was a fair preacher, but among that congregation, under their wing, he grew wings and flew. They took a preacher boy and made him a preacher man.

When you read the sermons of Martin Luther King, Jr., the best-known black preacher among white audiences, you hear the old words of Scripture made vitally new again because they create a whole different world. When you hear and see his sermon at the Lincoln Memorial replayed on television, or the one preached in Memphis just before his murder, the words still leap out at you no matter what your race. And a good case can be made that those two sermons were not necessarily his best. He learned that style of preaching from great churches as a boy, and as an assistant in Birmingham.

Despite obvious differences, great black preaching so resembles great patristic preaching that it is to be seen as catholic in character, universal at its best. Recognized in these five features, it appears within a broad spectrum of churches. Christian communities have quite often found these characteristics to be parts of their preaching in different times and among different cultures. These aspects are part of what I would call the *consensus fidelium* of proclamation, the consensus I read throughout the history of the Christian community as it listens to the Word of God and witnesses to its faith.

African American churches are to be emulated in keeping the proclamation of the good news live. Their preaching has risen from the bowels of suffering; theirs is no health and wealth gospel—may that not infect them. Their preaching has grown from within their communities. It has looked at the Bible and known that it is the Word of God for us today. So it sings the songs of allegory, not in some uncritical, stupid sense, but in that deep critical conviction that God's Word will teach us something important. As more black preachers have gone to seminary, there has been a richness that has taken seriously some of historical criticism, but the best preaching of their best educated is not a sterile exercise in rationalistic lecturing.

When James Earl Massey gave lectures on homiletics at the seminary where I teach, he was critical, careful, and aware. These lectures drew more and more students as word got around that Massey could not keep from preaching. He explained his main points in all the ways considered significant by modern Western educators. Yet he persuaded his hearers most deeply when he preached in those styles that the Church Fathers knew from their rhetorical educations and their communities of faith, and he knew of both from his education and his church. Massey was always lucid in these lectures, but when he broke into preaching the earth moved!

Just Listen to That Nubian!

Among Massey's sermons is one entitled "The Face of Jesus." It was not presented in the midst of a hostile polemic against those who taught that the church and its Scripture presented Jesus as secondary to God, in nature less than the Father. (The words I chose from Gregory deal with such opponents.) Massey had no need to anchor every matched phrase to some Bible text so that it would not wash away. His homily referred to the history of Christian art in a manner that only an educated person and an audience interested in such things make possible. In that sermon, we can hear the same concern for the Christ, that cadence and poetry that marked the preaching of Gregory Nazianzen—the minority stance, the acceptance of suffering, the saturation with scriptural story, the ability to be shaped by and to shape the text for a contemporary church.

Once again I have arranged the sermon as the poetry it is and ask you to read it aloud. Listen to its movement, the building of tension, its relaxation and renewal. Then think about the many passages from the Old Testament and the Gospels that are woven into this picture.

After reminding us that the face of Jesus was a Semitic face, one we too often refuse to recognize, Massey continues:

The face of Jesus was also the face of a sufferer.
It is interesting that the portraitures of Jesus
  do not usually show this.
In their attempts to portray the human Jesus,
  artists have evidently been led
  by other considerations,
    casting his countenance to reflect
      serenity,
        warmth,
          poise,
            and tenderness.

Very few artists depict the feature of pensive suffering
  which must have been there facially
    because of his miseries as
      a poor and underprivileged Jew—
      not to mention his lot as a subjugated member
        of a minority group in a land
          tyrannized by Roman rule.

Consider also that Jesus was constantly opposed in his
  work by religious bigots who held power.

Jesus was a sufferer.
  Poor,
    harassed,
      sometimes helpless in the face of despots.

Jesus of Nazareth knew the torments that etch lines
  into the human face—
    lines of concern,
      lines of resistance,
      lines of longing,
        lines of sorrow and suffering.

It is possible to trace this consideration about Jesus in
  the views of certain Church Fathers.
Influenced by the facts of his life,
  together with reflection on Isaiah 53:2-3,
    Justin Martyr, for instance, thought of Jesus
    as a man of frail body,
      weak,
        small in stature,
        and of a deprived countenance.[5]

---

5. Massey cites the discussion of this controversy in Charles Guignebert, *Jesus*, trans. S. H. Hooke (New Hyde Park, N.Y.: University Books, 1956), esp. 164-69.

The same reasoning appears in the thought of Clement of Alexandria,
Origen, and a few others.

. But some other Church Fathers were impressed with the notion
of a physically attractive Christ,
and they searched the Old Testament for passages
to support that concern.
They found Psalm 45:2:
Thou art fairer than the children of men (KJV),
which they interpreted to show his gainly grace.

So the ensuing centuries have brought us both sides of
the question in the portraitures we view.

The first-century believers who had seen Jesus in the
flesh left us no portraits of his physical manhood,
and the New Testament writings give us no
word description of his facial cast.

But the record of his poverty,
his struggles,
his disinheritedness,
strongly suggest a countenance of serious cast,
with lines of decisiveness
by which to handle the falsities
and contradictions
that would have otherwise beset him.

The face of Jesus was the face of a sufferer.

Jesus was a man of set face.

I have spoken about lines of decisiveness in his face.

There is an enlightening verse in Luke 9:51 about this:
When the days drew near for him to be received up,
he set his face to go to Jerusalem.

That expression set his face is a Semitic way of saying
that Jesus firmed up his intention,
strengthened his will,
and bolstered his determination.

He had to do so!
There was so much calculated activity against Jesus
as he did his work.

Except for calculated steadfastness Jesus
could not have endured.

Jesus had to be a man of firm purpose and strong intention.
It had to be so with him from the very first:
from the time he deliberated in the wilderness
weighing the issues of how he would serve,
up to the time he struggled so resolutely in
accepting the way of the cross.

Jesus saw the masses of people abroad in the land.
He saw a people needing a true leader,
a people whose frenzied concern for freedom
from Roman rule made them
open prey to false messiahs.
He saw them as sheep having no shepherd.
The people he saw as he began his work were leaderless,
vulnerable,
and potentially dangerous
because of their state of mind and affairs.

He had to plan wisely for what he would say.
He had to make precise calculations
about their attitudes
and plan with acuteness
about what to dare and do.

Some issues he would only touch,
and some others he would outrightly handle;
he would discuss values in the light of Scripture and
he would press for scriptural solutions to problems.

Jesus knew that a national uprising was possible, and
that someone could take the command post
by popular acclaim.

He set himself against false routes to power,
and that decision did not ever change.[6]

Had we a time machine and Massey the ability to speak Greek fluently, we just might send him back to fourth-century Constantinople to preach

---

6. Maurice Berquist, ed., *The Christian Brotherhood Hour Pulpit: Notable Sermons of W. Dale Oldham, R. Eugene Sterner, James Earl Massey* (Anderson, Ind.: Warner Press, 1972), 107-9.

---

these words. He would need to recast some things and not confuse his audience with future Christian art or quotes from the fathers as long-dead friends. His etched black face might remind those in Gregory's small chapel, called The Resurrection, that Jesus' face was not like theirs. But I would expect to hear someone, so struck by the unexpected, say: "Just listen to that Nubian. That sounds like great Greek preaching!"

CHAPTER ELEVEN

GOD'S TROMBONES: VOICES IN AFRICAN AMERICAN FOLK PREACHING

Cheryl J. Sanders

The origins of the traditional folk sermons of African Americans can be traced as far back as the 1700s. Significant numbers of blacks, including slaves, were converted to Christianity in response to the revivalistic preaching of George Whitefield and others in the American colonies. Black Christian leaders such as George Liele and Richard Allen began establishing their own churches and denominations in the eighteenth century, and these Baptist and Methodist pulpits emerged as permanent platforms for the propagation of the gospel of Jesus Christ in harmony with the language, culture, and aspirations of black people.

Because of the efforts undertaken by the slave South during the antebellum period to prevent slaves from conducting their own meetings and gatherings, there arose what historians have called the "invisible institution." It was a network of black Christians forced underground by racist laws and police practices designed to guard against slave uprisings. These people worshiped secretly in slave quarters after midnight and at any time or place where they could hope to escape detection and punishment. Their preachers were brave souls, often victims themselves of illiteracy, forced labor, and the other indignities of slave life. They brought hope and encouragement to the suffering slaves by telling the biblical stories of salvation and deliverance in the light of their own struggle against the evils of white brutality and terrorism.

In the aftermath of slavery, the folk-preaching tradition flourished as the former slaves were legally freed to choose and develop their own places and practices of worship. In the twentieth century, the tradition survives in many of the urban, suburban, and rural churches of the United States and remains vital for national audiences reached by evangelists and conference preachers. Today, folk preaching is especially valued by people who have childhood and ancestral memories of the Southern peasant culture of an earlier era.

The title of this chapter, "God's Trombones: Voices in African American Folk Preaching," is adapted from James Weldon Johnson's *God's Trombones*, a collection of poetry first published in 1927 as an eloquent tribute to the aesthetic force and lyricism of the black preaching tradition. Following Johnson's lead, a variety of twentieth-century writers, scholars, and activists have attempted to transcribe, interpret, and/or emulate the folk sermons of African American preachers. Motivated by a host of factors stated and unstated, these individuals have sought to present folk preaching, originally conceived and performed as oral tradition, in forms and forums accessible to audiences beyond the immediate context of black worship.

A survey of some representative efforts to focus broader attention on the tradition reveals at least seven different types of transcripts of African American folk sermons—poetic, literary, musical, structural, hermeneutical, ethical, and political—each of which will be discussed here in turn. This introduction to the nature of African American folk preaching as genre will be followed by a brief analysis of ways in which male and female homiletical voices are finding current expression in black churches and culture, drawing upon James Earl Massey's own incisive insights into the black preaching tradition. Finally, a concluding perspective will be offered on the future of the tradition in view of the rapidly changing educational, ethical, and cultural sensibilities of African American congregations.

Transcripts of the African American Folk Preaching Tradition

Foremost among the interpreters of the African American folk preaching tradition is the African American poet James Weldon Johnson (1871–1938). His book *God's Trombones* provides a poetic transcript of the tradition. Johnson used poetry to capture the imagery, drama, and rhythm of black preaching as he experienced it. In the book's preface, he describes the preaching performance that inspired him to write and name the collection:

> He [the black preacher] was wonderful in the way he employed his conscious and unconscious art. He strode the pulpit up and down in what was actually a very rhythmic dance, and he brought into play the full gamut of his wonderful voice, a voice—what shall I say?—not of an organ or a trumpet, but rather of a trombone, the instrument possessing above all others the

power to express the wide and varied range of emotions encompassed by the human voice—and with greater amplitude. He intoned, he moaned, he pleaded—he blared, he crashed, he thundered. I sat fascinated; and more, I was, perhaps against my will, deeply moved; the emotional effect upon me was irresistible. Before he had finished I took a slip of paper and somewhat surreptitiously jotted down some ideas for the first poem, "The Creation."[1]

"The Creation" remains a favorite selection from the collection, one that is still memorized and recited by African Americans. A brief excerpt illustrates the artistry, eloquence, and cultural authenticity of black folk preaching as poetic transcript:

> Up from the bed of the river
> God scooped the clay;
> And by the bank of the river
> He kneeled him down;
> And there the great God Almighty
> Who lit the sun and fixed it in the sky,
> Who flung the stars to the most far corner of the night,
> Who rounded the earth in the middle of his hand;
> This Great God,
> Like a mammy bending over her baby,
> Kneeled down in the dust
> Toiling over a lump of clay
> Till he shaped it in his own image.

Johnson's choice of the trombone as a metaphor for the black folk preacher was made with full appreciation of that instrument's specific harmonic qualities, uniquely comparable to the human voice and the violin, and of its value to the orchestra.[2] Thus by using the term "God's trombones," Johnson conjures vivid images of the black folk preacher making use of the full tonal and dynamic range of the human voice as an instrument of divine call and human response. These poetic transcripts mark the black preacher's mastery of "all the modes of eloquence" and the convergence of Negro dialect, biblical English, and traditional African speech in the folk sermon: "They were all saturated with the sublime phraseology of the Hebrew prophets and steeped in the idioms of King James English, so when they preached and warmed to their work they spoke another language."[3]

---

1. James Weldon Johnson, *God's Trombones: Seven Negro Sermons in Verse* (New York: Viking Penguin, 1927; 1990), 6-7.
2. Ibid., 7.

Johnson is fully aware of the limitations of the poetic transcript. He warns the reader of his inability to recreate the atmosphere of black folk preaching, with its fervent amens and hallelujahs, the sung responses, the preacher's physical magnetism, gestures, and syncopation of speech. He suggests that these poems "would better be intoned than read." Notwithstanding the wisdom of this directive, *God's Trombones* has been appreciated as both a silent and a spoken poetic transcript of African American folk preaching; it is a black literary classic, remaining in print for over six decades, to the continuing delight and inspiration of several generations of readers and hearers of the preached word.

Not only have African American folk sermons been transcribed in poetic form, but literary transcripts of these sermons also appear in novels, plays, essays, and other prose writings by African American authors. Zora Neale Hurston (1901–1960), a contemporary of James Weldon Johnson and the daughter of a Baptist preacher, incorporated literary transcripts of folk preaching into her anthropological and artistic works. The text of a sermon she heard preached by C. C. Lovelace in Eau Gallie, Florida, in 1929 appears in a posthumously published collection of her prose essays, *The Sanctified Church*. It also is in her 1934 novel *Jonah's Gourd Vine*, in which it is attributed to a fictional character, the Reverend John Buddy Pearson.

Hurston's literary transcript is divided into two parts—the spoken introduction is written in prose form, and the chanted body of the sermon is recorded in poetic form. The sermon begins with an introduction of theme and text:

> Our theme this morning is the wounds of Jesus. When the Father shall ask "What are these wounds in thine hand?" He shall answer, "Those are they with which I was wounded in the house of my friends" (Zach, xiii. 6). . . . Jesus was not unthoughtful. He was not overbearing. He was never a bully. He was never sick. He was never a criminal before the law, and yet He was wounded. Now a man usually gets wounded in the midst of his enemies; but this man was wounded, says the text, in the house of His friends. It is not your enemies that harm you all the time. Watch that close friend, and every sin we commit is a wound to Jesus.[4]

The transcript shifts into poetic form and is recorded in Negro dialect, as illustrated in this brief excerpt:

---

3. Ibid., 9.
4. Zora Neale Hurston, *The Sanctified Church* (Berkeley, Calif.: Turtle Island, 1981), 95.

I heard the whistle of de damnation train
Dat pulled out from Garden of Eden loaded wid cargo goin to hell
Ran at break-neck speed all de way thru de law
All de way thru de prophetic age
All de way thru de reign of kings and judges—
Plowed her way thru de Jordan—
And on her way to Calvary when she blew for de switch
Jesus stood out on her track like a rough-backed mountain
And she threw her cow-catcher in His side and His blood
ditched de train,
He died for our sins.
Wounded in the house of His friends.
Thats where I got off de damnation train
And dats where you must get off, ha!
For in dat mor-ornin', ha!
To dat judgment convention, ha![5]

Katie Geneva Cannon, a contemporary ethicist and preacher, lifts up Hurston's literary transcript of the "The Wounds of Jesus" as a pivotal text in African American letters. Cannon observes that this sermon was disclaimed by the *New York Times* as "too good, too brilliantly splashed with poetic imagery to be the product of any Negro preacher."[6] She cites a letter Hurston wrote to James Weldon Johnson expressing her own evaluation of the authentic artistry and brilliance of the black folk preacher:

> [The preacher] must also be an artist. He must be both a poet and an actor of a very high order, and then he must have the voice and figure. [The *New York Times* critic] does not realize or is unwilling to admit that the light that shone from God's Trombones was handed to you, as was the sermon to me in Jonah's Gourd Vine.[7]

Clearly, the black folk sermon that Hurston committed to writing was subjected to critical scrutiny that was both unfair and uninformed. She and Johnson openly acknowledged that their literary and poetic transcripts had been directly borrowed from living oral tradition.

5. Ibid., 102.
6. Katie Geneva Cannon, " 'The Wounds of Jesus': Justification of Goodness in the Face of Manifold Evil," in Emilie Townes, ed., *A Troubling in My Soul* (Maryknoll, N.Y.: Orbis, 1993), 223.
7. Ibid.

Poets and essayists have given attention to the musical qualities of African American folk preaching, a feature that is difficult to transcribe using only words. The musical transcripts of Jon Michael Spencer make use of musical notation in order to do justice to the rhythm and tonality of the tradition. Spencer, an ethnomusicologist who is also an ordained minister in the African Methodist Episcopal Church, compiled, transcribed, and published a collection of chanted sermons in a 1987 book entitled *Sacred Symphony*. Spencer's book documents one hundred musical transcripts of folk sermons, which he refers to as "modern spirituals," collected from sixteen well-known contemporary preachers representing Baptist, Methodist, Holiness, and Pentecostal denominations from various regions of the United States and the Caribbean. The transcripts are not complete sermons; rather, they record in musical form that portion of the sermon that is referred to as whooping, intoning, chanting, moaning, and tuning, a particular style of melody that is defined "as a series of cohesive pitches which have continuity, tonality, quasi-metrical phraseology, and formulary cadence."[8]

The musical transcription of the folk sermon is provided by jazz composer and artist Wynton Marsalis, whose recent release *In This House, on This Morning* uses the idiom of jazz and blues to frame a musical statement of the dynamics of folk worship and preaching. In short, the composition is structured like a typical worship service in the African American folk tradition. In the selection entitled "Sermon," Marsalis's jazz septet features "shouting horns that project an intensity unusual even for jazz," according to the liner notes.[9] Indeed, this jazz transcript gives musical voice to James Weldon Johnson's concept of *God's Trombones*, as the trombone, trumpet, saxophones, piano, bass, and drums play out the entire drama of folk preaching, prayer, and worship.

Folklorist Gerald Davis has produced one of the most comprehensive studies to date of the black preaching tradition. He devotes most of his attention in the book to a detailed analysis of the preaching of Bishop E. E. Cleveland, pastor of Ephesians Church of God in Christ in Berkeley, California. Based on a structural transcript of Cleveland's sermon "You're Not Ready," Davis outlines a general scheme for the evaluation of African American folk preaching:

---

8. Jon Michael Spencer, *Sacred Symphony: The Chanted Sermon of the Black Preacher* (Westport, Conn.: Greenwood Press, 1987), 1.

9. Stanley Crouch, "In the Sweet Embrace of Life," liner notes to compact disc recording by Wynton Marsalis Septet, *In This House, on This Morning*. Sony Music Entertainment, Inc., 1994.

In the key sermon in this study . . . formula, theme, and bridge are readily identifiable. Cleveland's theme is preparation for entry into the Kingdom of God. There are four major formulaic units in the Cleveland sermon. Each unit has its own function in terms of amplifying an aspect of the theme. Additionally, each formulaic unit manifests the required sacred/ secular polarity, or tension.[10]

The first formulaic unit expresses the sermon's basic theme in terms of a general commentary on a biblical text. The second unit expresses the theme in the sacred context. The third unit shows how the theme finds application in everyday existence (i.e., in secular contexts). In the fourth and final formulaic unit, the sermon theme statement is summarized and reiterated in sacred terms.[11] Davis's purpose is to create a procedure for evaluating folk sermons on the basis of how successfully they conform to African American aesthetic criteria, and also to allow for the comparison of sermons with other African American narrative systems or genres.[12] In addition, he has produced a one-hour documentary film on black preaching entitled *The Performed Word.*

One of the first efforts to fashion a hermeneutical transcript of black folk preaching was undertaken in 1970 by black theologian Henry Mitchell in the book *Black Preaching.* Referencing the school of thought promoted by Gerhard Eberling and others as the "new hermeneutics," Mitchell describes two hermeneutical principles that he regards as essential to black preaching:

> The first is that one must declare the gospel in the language and culture of the people—the vernacular. For some this involves resistance to a temptation to be learned and "proper." . . . The second hermeneutic principle is that the gospel must speak to the contemporary man and his needs. . . . As I have used it, "hermeneutic" is a code word for putting the gospel on a tell-it-like-it-is, nitty-gritty basis.[13]

Notwithstanding Mitchell's use of the gender-exclusive language characteristic of the times, these are valid hermeneutical principles with great significance for the proclamation of the gospel within (and outside) the black churches. However, the actual transcript he provides in the last

---

10. Gerald L. Davis, *I Got the Word in Me and I Can Sing It, You Know: A Study of the Performed African-American Sermon* (Philadelphia: University of Pennsylvania Press, 1985), 56.
11. Ibid., 49ff.
12. Ibid., 46.
13. Henry H. Mitchell, *Black Preaching* (Philadelphia: J. B. Lippincott, 1970), 29-30.

chapter of the book attempts to juxtapose a white sermon alongside a black sermon. The former is the text of a sermon actually preached by Ernest Campbell at Riverside Church in New York in 1969. The latter is Mitchell's own translation of the white sermon into the black vernacular, point by point. Unfortunately, the hermeneutical transcript does not work here because the black "sermon" has no integrity or authenticity of its own—it is merely Mitchell's hip and humorous rendering of what the white preacher said. A more useful approach might be to compare sermons preached on the same text or topic by preachers from different traditions, and to ask whether the sermons satisfy the hermeneutical criteria of vernacular translation and addressing human needs.

The one African American sermon that is best known in American society is the "I Have a Dream" sermon preached by Martin Luther King, Jr., from the steps of the Lincoln Memorial in Washington, D.C., during the historic March on Washington in 1963. It takes the form of an ethical transcript. Although Davis sees this sermon as "the quintessential adaptation of the performed African-American sermon structure to national and international political purpose," it seems that its ethical concerns greatly outweigh the political, especially given the fact that the sermon is continually cited, replayed, and analyzed as a nonpartisan ode to the most cherished values in American civil existence—freedom, justice, and equality.[14]

Note how King uses the rhythmic refrain "I have a dream" to set up a string of rich incarnational images of the ethic of racial reconciliation:

I have a dream that one day on the red hills of Georgia, sons of former slaves and sons of former slave-owners will be able to sit down together at the table of brotherhood.

I have a dream that one day, even the state of Mississippi, a state sweltering with the heat of injustice, sweltering with the heat of oppression, will be transformed into an oasis of freedom and justice.

I have a dream my four little children will one day live in a nation where they will not be judged by the color of their skin but by the content of their character. I have a dream today![15]

As an activist, theologian, and preacher with deep roots in the black Baptist churches of the South, King found in black preaching the ideal vehicle for public proclamation of his ethical ideas with regard to the pursuit of human and civil rights.

---

14. Davis, *I Got the Word in Me and I Can Sing It, You Know*, 11.

15. Martin Luther King, Jr., "I Have a Dream," in *A Testament of Hope: The Essential Writings of Martin Luther King, Jr.*, James Melvin Washington, ed. (San Francisco: Harper & Row, 1986), 219.

The political transcript of the African American folk sermon is perhaps more aptly ascribed to the preaching of Reverend Jesse Jackson, a colleague of King's who retains high visibility as a civil rights activist. Davis describes the dilemma faced by Reverend Jackson at the 1984 Democratic National Convention when he had to decide whether to give a political speech or a spirited sermon as his keynote address to a sea of delegates before a nationally televised audience:

> Apparently deciding that he was a national candidate for the American presidency, Jackson assumed all of the trappings of that august image and began fumbling his way, ineptly, through his prepared speech. But part of the genius of the African-American performed sermon is that, in the hands of a talented preacher, it permits and allows for instant adjustment.

Realizing that his speech was not having the intended impact, continues Davis, Jackson adjusted his oratorical style.

> Jackson regained confidence as he reclaimed his preaching metier. His moral sense of outrage found a glorious articulation base in the African-American sermon structure that it could not find in the more restrictive American speechmaking style. Hardened delegates—all hues of his "Rainbow Coalition"—began weeping and cheering, seemingly involuntarily, as Jackson's preaching began to roll over the vast assembly. And at that moment, it became clear to all that Jackson was no longer a candidate for the presidency. He had become, at that moment of his transition, a superordinate moral voice for the redress of the gross insensitivities of the Reagan Administration and the inadequacies of the federal polity.[16]

Jackson's performance in this situation exemplifies the "inescapable opportunism, deep-seated moralism, and aggressive pessimism" that philosopher Cornel West associates with the prophetic tradition of African American Christians.[17] Understanding the sermon as political transcript, Jackson continues to merge the folk sensibilities and techniques of the black preacher with the savvy of the politician and policymaker in his frequent public appearances as a human rights activist.

Male and Female Homiletical Voices

James Earl Massey, himself a bearer of the highest forms and interpretations of the art of preaching, has shared some of his own insights from

---

16. Davis, *I Got the Word in Me and I Can Sing It, You Know,* 12.
17. Cornel West, *Prophetic Fragments* (Grand Rapids: Eerdmans, 1988), 41.

---

the black preaching tradition. He lists five characteristics of the black sermon.[18] First, the sermon is functional "in its intent to liberate the hearer's spirit, give him life and sustain his faith." Second, the sermon is festive, meaning that it is an "invitation to joy" and "an open expression of faith that has worked its way through." Third, the sermon is communal, a characteristic he describes in relation to function and festivity. Frequently "audible expressions of response will occur in most black settings where the preacher speaks with festive bearing, for a functional purpose, and with a sense of community with his hearers." Fourth, the sermon is radical, in the true sense of the word, taking the hearer to the "roots" of personal life and vital response.

Finally, black preaching is intended *to produce a climax of impression for the hearer:*

> Scripture, interpretation, zestful speech, a concern for community, mind-engaging lines, controlled imagination—all these are calculated to incite the hearer to participate as well as listen, leading him to a climax of impression for faith and life.

Massey's explanation of this fifth characteristic succinctly summarizes the basic elements and intentions involved in black preaching, understood in the light of the preacher's vital leadership role in the community of faith.

In his study of the charismatic aspects of black preaching, Massey acknowledges the connection between African American folk preaching and African traditional religion. The black preacher usually has

> given himself to his preaching task with such abandon that a heritage of freedom and involvement continues to characterize Black Church worship. This worship freedom is not purely Christian in origin—related as it is to an ancient African belief in being possessed by the deity.[19]

This connection is significant for at least two reasons. First, many African American scholars and preachers are rethinking the value and relevance of African religious traditions to the practice of Christianity, aided by an increased awareness of the negative impact white racist biblical hermeneutics and theology have had on black Christian identity. Second, the concept that the performed sermon is an experience of possession by

---

18. James Earl Massey, *The Responsible Pulpit* (Anderson, Ind.: Warner Press, 1974), 102-8.

19. James Earl Massey, *The Sermon in Perspective: A Study of Communication and Charisma* (Anderson, Ind.: Warner Press, 1976), 107.

the divine places an increased weight of responsibility upon both the preacher and the hearer of the word. Reports Massey:

> Black Church tradition carries the concern for possession by deity one step further in expecting the claim upon those who hear and accept his message. In Black Church life, then, the preacher becomes the agent of contact with divine will and holy word.[20]

Massey warns that we should not "unwisely associate God with only one worship style, nor . . . mistakenly associate Him with only one people," a word that needs repeated proclamation in a church and society beset by racial strife and cultural conflict.[21]

Most of the works cited thus far in this discussion focus exclusive attention on the folk preaching of African American males. While the vast majority of pastors and preachers in the black churches are indeed male, women have contributed to the tradition in the role of both performer and respondent.

Gerald Davis interviewed Bishop Cleveland's daughter, Pastor Ernestine Cleveland Reems, whom he identifies as pastor of the Center of Hope in East Oakland and preacher, and asks her to compare her preaching with her father's.[22] However, he does not transcribe or analyze any of her sermons. Johnson acknowledges the role of women in leading chanted prayers in the black churches (the first poem in *God's Trombones* is "Listen, Lord—A Prayer"). He writes: "One factor in the creation of atmosphere I have included—the preliminary prayer. The prayer leader was sometimes a woman. . . . These preliminary prayers were often products hardly less remarkable than the sermons."[23]

In the twentieth century, gospel music has emerged as a significant vehicle for women to perform sermons. Beginning with the pioneering singing style of Mahalia Jackson, African American women gospel singers have incorporated folk preaching styles into their music. Shirley Caesar, pastor, evangelist, and gospel artist, has made numerous recordings in which she offers a preached interlude (including "No Charge"; "Don't Drive Your Mama Away"; and "Hold My Mule"). Aretha Franklin, best known as the "Queen of Soul," has released several highly successful gospel recordings. Her chanted account of the resurrection of Lazarus in "Oh, Mary Don't You Weep" on the recording *Amazing Grace*

---

20. Ibid., 107.
21. Ibid., 108.
22. Davis, *I Got the Word in Me and I Can Sing It, You Know*, x-xi.
23. Johnson, *God's Trombones*, 11.

demonstrates the extent of Franklin's competence in "telling the story" in a manner reminiscent of her father, the Reverend C. L. Franklin, who is widely regarded as one of the great folk preachers of this century.

In my own comparative study of sermons by both male and female black preachers, drawn from published collections, I discovered elements of folk preaching even in the carefully edited transcripts of sermons produced by groups comprised primarily of theologically educated ministers. I concluded that men and women were more alike than different in the content and intention of their preaching.

> Women and men preach the same types of sermons, from the [same] biblical texts, but differ slightly in their choices of themes and tasks, and differ greatly in their talk about God and persons in inclusive terms. . . . Women tend to emphasize the personal and men the prophetic.[24]

Women who perform their sermons in the folk tradition are often criticized for trying to "preach like a man." This is not surprising in view of Massey's description of the climactic characteristics of the black preaching performance, the dynamics of which are experienced exclusively by some as sexual interplay between a male performer and his congregation, which typically is predominantly female. By clearly distinguishing between proper and improper presentation of the performed sermon, Massey elevates the concept of a "climax of impression" from the sensual level to a plane of preaching excellence attainable by thoughtful preachers of both sexes (presumably, if one can excuse his use of gender exclusive language in the 1974 text):

> It is true that art can be exploited and turned to the false end of exhibitionism. But the prostitution of an art must not blind us to its proper end and effects. A preacher must not ignore the soundness of the theory and insistence that his sermon should produce a climax of impression for his hearers. Preaching at its best involves this, and more; but if it lacks this ability, no matter whatever else it has, such a sermon will make no difference.[25]

A Perspective on the Twenty-first Century

At the end of his preface to *God's Trombones*, written during the decade when the last generation of African Americans born into slavery was

---

24. Cheryl J. Sanders, "The Woman as Preacher," *Journal of Religious Thought* 43, 1 (Spring-Summer 1986): 22.
25. Massey, *The Responsible Pulpit*, 110.

approaching old age, Johnson laments the prospective demise of the folk preacher and offers his poems as a means of preserving the tradition. He observes that the "old-time Negro preacher is rapidly passing. I have here tried sincerely to fix something of him."[26]

However, as the twentieth century draws to a close, folk sermons are yet being preached in the African American churches. Thanks to the contributions of many writers, scholars, and activists, only a few of whom have been cited in this discussion, the tradition is being preserved in fixed transcripts of various sorts. These poetic, literary, musical, structural, hermeneutical, ethical, and political transcripts of the African American folk sermon have been presented here as evidence that the tradition is alive and thriving in its complexity of expression and development.

What will be the value of folk preaching to the African American churches of the twenty-first century? This question appears especially pressing in view of the rapidly changing educational, ethical, and cultural sensibilities of its constituents.

One of the most negative assumptions often made about folk preaching is that it is motivated by ignorance and a lack of education. Some would condemn the tradition as unethical insofar as it lends itself to exploitation of black congregations by preachers seeking financial gain, opportunities for sexual exploitation, and/or satisfaction of ego needs. The cultural sensibilities of upwardly mobile middle-class African American churchgoers are greatly influenced by pressures to adopt the attitudes, tastes, and demeanor of the white majority, especially with regard to worship.

Today's black preachers and theological educators are challenged to follow Massey's lead in pursuing the high ground of artistic and homiletical excellence in the continued performance and study of folk preaching. African Americans must resist the temptation to adopt uncritically negative attitudes toward their own religion and culture that are characteristic of the dominant culture, and are often based on ignorance and prejudice. Instead, it is imperative to uphold meaningful standards for evaluating preaching competence and to encourage the people in the churches to become intelligent and culturally sensitive consumers of sermons.

Henry Mitchell has offered this interesting proposition to black and white preachers in view of the changing conditions of American society:

---

26. Johnson, *God's Trombones*, 11.

The depersonalized condition to which Black proclamation has been directed is more and more the condition of all colors and cultures in this mass society. White Christianity seems to be losing the battle to reach the crucial needs of the people who have to live in the kind of world we have fashioned for ourselves. A Blacker hermeneutical style among white preachers just might help to reverse the trend.[27]

Christian preachers of all races who are willing to progress toward racial reconciliation in America may discover new sources of inspiration both by experiencing black folk preaching and by engaging its hermeneutical, ethical, and political transcripts. Folk preachers who are willing to carry to its fullest fruition this task of preaching for communal empowerment will work toward equipping the churches to meet human needs in a manner consistent with the word being preached. They will dedicate some of the same creative energies and gifts used in preaching to the broader ministry of salvation and human wholeness.

---

27. Mitchell, *Black Preaching*, 31.

THE CHALLENGE OF PREACHING ON RACIAL ISSUES FOR EURO- AMERICAN PREACHERS[1]

Ronald J. Allen and Jicelyn I. Thomas

The eminent African American philosopher and historian W. E. B. DuBois wrote prophetically that "the problem of the twentieth century is the problem of the color line."[2] Between the time DuBois wrote (1903) and today, overt Jim Crow policies and legal segregation have faded. The African American middle class has grown. Opportunities in education, employment, and housing have increased for African Americans as well.

However, a growing number of interpreters agree with Peter Paris that "by all the social and economic indices our people [African Americans] are worse off today than we were thirty years ago."[3] Cornel West speaks of our time as an "African winter."[4] In some ways these are the best of times for the African American middle class, but the worst for many others.[5] Furthermore, as Katie Cannon says, while the United States has

---

1. For a powerful statement of James Earl Massey's perspective on these matters, see his *Concerning Christian Unity* (Anderson, Ind.: Warner Press, 1979).

2. W. E. B. Dubois, *The Souls of Black Folk* (Greenwich, Conn.: Fawcett, 1961), 23.

3. Peter Paris, "In the Face of Despair," *The Christian Century* 111 (1994): 439.

4. Cornel West, *Prophetic Fragments* (Grand Rapids: Eerdmans, 1988), 35-37.

5. See Cornel West, *Prophetic Thought in Postmodern Times* (Monroe, Maine: Common Courage Press, 1993), 59. However, the gains in these and other arenas have not been as widespread or as fast as envisioned by the leaders of the civil rights movement in the midcentury. In the latter years of the twentieth century, many gains are actually being reversed by changes in government policy and by a resurgence of racism. For a review of relative progress and decline in key issues, see Bernard R. Boxill, *Blacks and Social Justice*, rev. ed. (Lanham, Md.: Rowman and Littlefield Publishers, 1992).

become desegregated in many sectors, it is still not a truly integrated society.[6] Outside the workplace, Euro-Americans and African Americans have relatively little interchange. Suspicion and tension often characterize the relationship between the races. Such tensions become especially visible in major public events, such as the uprising that followed the Rodney King beating trial verdict in Los Angeles. This situation is far from the hope of the Christian gospel for unconditional love and unfailing justice in all human relationships.[7]

In this chapter, we will explore some of today's basic challenges when Euro-American pastors preach on racial issues. We focus on Euro-Americans for two reasons. First, this allows a maximum focus for a short chapter. Second, racism is primarily a Euro-American phenomenon. African Americans may respond to racism in ways that Euro-Americans designate reverse racism. But by definition (as we shall see below) racism in the United States is principally practiced by Caucasian people. A similar chapter for African American pastors might be entitled "The Challenge of Responding to Racism."

We briefly review the history of the relationship between Caucasians and African Americans and the character and manifestation of racism today. We turn then to the mandate on pastors to preach and teach on race and to practical guidelines for doing so.[8]

These are deeply personal concerns for us. Jicelyn Thomas is an African American who is ordained in The United Methodist Church. She taught preaching jointly with Ronald Allen at Christian Theological Seminary before enrolling in the Ph.D. program at Vanderbilt University. Ronald Allen is a Euro-American minister in the Christian Church (Disciples of Christ), a teacher of preaching, and a parent of five children, two of whom are African American.

---

6. Katie Cannon, unpublished lecture. Indianapolis, Ind.: Christian Theological Seminary, 1992.

7. We agree with Clark M. Williamson's summary of the gospel. The gospel is "the good news that God graciously and freely offers the divine love to each and all (oneself included) and that this God who loves all the creatures therefore commands that justice be done to them. This dipolar gospel (a) promises God's love to each of us as the only adequate ground of our life and (b) demands justice toward all others whom God loves." See Clark M. Williamson, "Preaching the Gospel: Some Theological Reflections," *Encounter* 49 (1988): 191.

8. We recognize that in the United States the relationships among Euro-Americans and other races are also often problematic. However, in this brief chapter we can address only African American and Euro-American concerns. For a basic guide to issues arising in connection with different groups, see Harry H. Kitano, *Race Relations*, 3rd ed. (Englewood Cliffs, N.J.: Prentice-Hall, 1985).

Race in Antiquity

In the Mediterranean world of antiquity, people were often classified. For instance, without purporting to be exhaustive, Colossians 3:11 speaks of "Greek and Jew, circumcised and uncircumcised, barbarian, Scythian, slave and free" (the better known Gal. 3:28 adds "male and female"). None of these classifications refers to skin pigmentation. In Greek society, a barbarian was anyone who was not inculturated in Greek ways. Scythians were thought to be especially violent. The basic divisions of the human family in ancient society were along the lines of gender, ethnicity, economic and political status, culture, and religion.

In the ancient world, people were not classified racially along the lines of color as they are today. To be sure, ancient societies noticed skin pigmentation. Frank Snowden's thorough examination of the place and valuation of black persons and societies in the world of antiquity finds that blacks were regarded much like other peoples. African peoples established large, thriving, economically and politically powerful nations. They traveled extensively and without bias. They participated freely and fully in all aspects of ancient life. Some writers in antiquity even praised the beauty of dark-skinned people. Black peoples produced their share of reprobates, but they were regarded with no more disdain than light-skinned reprobates.[9] Likely, color prejudice existed in the Mediterranean world, but much less so than today.[10]

Several biblical scholars are recognizing the foundational importance of Africa and African peoples.[11] Egypt and Cush—located on the continent of Africa—appear in the Table of the Nations in Genesis 10.[12] Like many other nations in the Bible, these are evaluated both positively and negatively according to the role they played at particular moments. Egypt, for example, was both the source of Israel's survival (Genesis 46) and the agency of Israel's enslavement (Exodus 1–4). Hagar was an Egyptian (Gen. 16:1). Moses' wife was a Cushite (Num. 21:1). Solomon

---

9. Frank Snowden, Jr., *Blacks in Antiquity* (Cambridge: The Belknap Press, 1970).

10. Cornel West, *Prophesy Deliverance!* (Philadelphia: Westminster, 1982), 64.

11. Some anthropologists trace the beginning of humankind to Africa. For example, the Gihon River (Gen. 2:13) is thought to be a reference to the Nile in Africa. See Robert Davidson, *Genesis 1–11*, Cambridge Bible Commentary (Cambridge: Cambridge University Press, 1973), 33.

12. Sheba may also have been located in Africa. See Randall C. Bailey, "Beyond Identification: The Use of Africans in Old Testament Poetry and Narratives," in *Stony the Road We Trod*, ed. Cain Hope Felder (Minneapolis: Fortress Press, 1991), 171-72.

married the daughter of Pharaoh (1 Kings 3:1). Zephaniah looked forward to the day when many would come from beyond the rivers of Ethiopia to bring an offering to God on the day of the Lord (3:10).[13] Simon, who carried the cross of Jesus was from Cyrene (Matt. 27:32; Mark 15:21; Luke 23:26). The eunuch converted on the road from Jerusalem to Gaza was an Ethiopian (Acts 8:26-40). Acts 13:1 mentions two African persons in leadership in the church at Antioch, Simeon and Lucius.[14]

Nonetheless, Cain Hope Felder notices that people of African descent are somewhat marginalized in the New Testament. Few Africans are mentioned, and their roles are seldom crucial to the story presented. However, Felder sees this less as an indication of systematic prejudice against people of color on the part of the writers of the New Testament and more as the result of the church's need to find ways to live in a society dominated by the Roman government. In any event, the major eschatological visions of the New Testament (e.g., Rev. 7:9) envision a coming age in which people of all colors are drawn together in the presence of God.[15]

Racism in Europe and North America

The history of the relationship between the races took a decisive turn in European society during the Enlightenment and the birth of the industrial age. Four factors combined to bring about contemporary racism.[16]

(1) The industrial revolution and the expansion of the world economy created a need for cheap labor. Western Europeans and North Americans quickly exploited Africa as the source of inexpensive slave labor. (2) The slaveholders disenfranchised the enslaved people. This was necessary to establish superior sociopolitical status and to enable slaveholders to maintain control over their enslaved communities. (3) Powerful psychosexual factors were also at work. Racism provided both immediate physical chains and enduring psychological chains. People of European culture "endow non-European (especially African) men and women with sexual prowess; view non-Europeans as either cruel, revengeful fathers, frivolous, carefree children, or passive, long-suffering mothers; and iden-

---

13. Charles B. Copher, "The Black Presence in the Old Testament," in Felder, *Stony the Road We Trod*, 153-64; Bailey, "Beyond Identification," in ibid., 170-73.
14. Cain Hope Felder, "Race, Racism and the Biblical Narratives," in Felder, *Stony the Road We Trod*, 141-45.
15. Ibid., 144-45.
16. West, *Prophesy Deliverance!* 47.

tify non-Europeans (especially black people) with dirt, odious smell, and feces."[17] Europeans thus assuaged their consciences and felt justified in consigning non-Europeans to subhuman status. (4) Cornel West contends that the structure of Western discourse had an inherent inclination to lead to racism. The scientific method, based on the principle of an alleged value-free observation of data, became the standard way of interpreting the world and its inhabitants. Unfortunately, unconscious biases of the interpreters were either overlooked or suppressed. It was in this milieu of the seventeenth century that race as a way of categorizing the human family according to skin color came into vogue.

In 1684 a French physician was the first to associate the term *race* with skin color. In 1735 the famous scientist Carolus Linnaeus canonized skin color as the distinctive element in racial classification.[18] About the same time, Europeans came to regard the Greco-Roman society of antiquity as the cultural norm for truth and beauty. Major thinkers used the scientific method to compare persons of African origin with the Greco-Roman ideal and found Africans wanting. Major shapers of European and North American thought (e.g., Voltaire, Hume, Kant, Jefferson) concluded that black inferiority is built into the fabric of dark-skinned being itself.[19]

The church helped to provide theoretical support for racism and slaveholding by misinterpreting the curse of Ham as dark skin. The church also noted that slavery is not expressly forbidden in the Bible. Many Euro-American Christian pulpits emphasized the codes in the New Testament that authorize slavery in Christian households (e.g., Eph. 5:5-8; Col. 3:22-25; 1 Pet. 2:18-25).[20]

The legacy of this history is achingly familiar. The United States continues to be a racist society. Social structures systematically are biased against giving African Americans and other racial and ethnic minorities access to power and resources (such as money, housing, food, health

---

17. West, *Prophetic Fragments,* 102. Some scholars think that European racism emerged in conjunction with the institution of slavery. Others are convinced that racism in Europeans preceded (and caused) slavery. See Carl Degler, "Slavery and the Genesis of American Race Prejudice," in *The Making of Black America,* ed. August Meier and Elliott Rudwick (New York: Atheneum, 1969), 1:91-108. Cf. Philip S. Foner, *History of Black Americans: From Africa to the Emergence of the Cotton Kingdom* (Westport, Conn.: Greenwood Press, 1975), chapter 4; George P. Rawick, *From Sundown to Sunup: The Making of the Black Community* (Westport, Conn.: Greenwood Press, 1975), chapters 7–8.

18. West, *Prophetic Fragments,* 100.

19. West, *Prophesy Deliverance!* 47-65.

20. See H. Shelton Smith, *In His Image, But . . .* (Durham, N.C.: Duke University Press, 1972).

care, and education). Social systems erode self-confidence, self-regard and self-esteem.[21] Institutional racism is manifest, for instance, in the limited role of African Americans in shaping economic life and in the disparity between incomes in Euro-American and African American households. According to one projection, the median incomes of households in these two communities is not expected to be the same until the year 2420.[22] This pace of development "gives a new meaning to the term gradualism."[23] Few educational systems take into account the learning needs or styles of African American children or young people.[24]

Further, all Euro-American individuals in the United States are implicated in racism to one degree or another. This is true even of those who are deeply committed to a liberated social world and who actively resist racism. As Rufus Burrow, Jr., summarizes: "Whites, by virtue of their white skin, benefit from the system of racism and economic exploitation even though they are against racism and do not practice it."[25] The painful fact is that to be Euro-American is to be an agent of racism and to be complicit in a racist social world.[26]

In this context, Cornel West finds that nihilism is an expanding threat in the African American community. "This threat is not simply a matter of relative economic deprivation and political powerlessness. . . . It is primarily a question of speaking to the profound sense of psychological depression, personal worthlessness, and social despair so widespread in

---

21. See West, *Prophetic Thought in Postmodern Times,* 11; Rufus Burrow, Jr., *James H. Cone and Black Liberation Theology* (Jefferson, N.C.: McFarland and Co., 1994), 38–41.

22. Theodore Cross, *The Black Power Imperative* (New York: Faulkener Books, 1987), 208.

23. Clark M. Williamson and Ronald J. Allen, *A Credible and Timely Word* (St. Louis: Chalice Press, 1991), 63.

24. See Boxill, *Blacks and Social Justice;* Louis L. Knowles and Kenneth Prewitt, eds., *Institutional Racism in America* (Englewood Cliffs, N.J.: Prentice-Hall, 1968).

25. Burrow, *James H. Cone and Black Liberation Theology,* 111. This statement needs to be tempered by Peter Paris's observation that "America is no longer dependent on a black laboring class, reserve or otherwise" (Paris, "In the Face of Despair," 438). Some Euro-Americans are, therefore, likely to regard African Americans as completely dispensable. This represents another obstacle that the Euro-American preacher must overcome on the way to helping the congregation repent of its collusion in racism.

26. James Cone points out that some Euro-Americans can so identify with the African American struggle for liberation that they become "ontologically black." See James H. Cone, *A Black Theology of Liberation* (Philadelphia: J. B. Lippencott, 1970), 27. Yet, even ontologically black Euro-Americans are complicit in racism by virtue of being Euro-American.

---

black America."[27] According to Cornel West, the African American community, therefore, has two basic tasks. For one, African Americans need to become self-determining, to gain "significant control" in the institutions that shape daily life. This is necessary for sociopolitical and economic liberation. The other is for African Americans to continue to develop strong self-images in the face of continuing racism. These are necessary for African Americans to survive in the face of racism and to have the strength necessary to struggle for liberation.[28]

The African American community, like most other groups, is not monolithic but is multivocal. African Americans continue to offer various strategies on how best to renew self-image or how to become self-determinative or how to relate to Euro-American culture and power.[29] Four relating patterns can be distinguished.

Some African Americans wish to *assimilate* into Euro-American culture by minimizing their African American culture and by adapting to the ways of Euro-Americana. E. Franklin Frazier was an assimilationist. The *exceptionalists* have a very positive view of African American culture and believe that it can preserve its distinctiveness while contributing to the larger Euro-American culture and allowing African Americans to benefit economically and politically in the larger culture. Martin Luther King, Jr., is a prime example.

Marginalists are individualists who highly value African American culture, but regard themselves as being on the edges of both African American and Euro-American communities. They see themselves in revolt against Euro-American racism and against aspects of African American life. They live on the margins. James Baldwin and Toni Morrison are marginalists.

The *humanist* tradition regards African American people and culture as human—with strengths and weaknesses. An unflinching examination of African American history and life will find neither unrelenting heroism nor unrelenting lament. Such introspection can provide the resources for personal survival and can generate the hope of a new social future in the United States that is shaped not by racial concerns but by human ones. Such a future calls for more participatory social, political, and economic practices in the United States. The exceptionalists want to open the present social order to African Americans. Humanists wish fundamentally to reshape the social order. This tradition is represented by Zora Neale Hurston, Ralph Ellison, and Malcom X.

---

27. Cornel West, *Race Matters* (Boston: Beacon Press, 1993), 11-12.
28. West, *Prophesy Deliverance!* 22.
29. Ibid., 69-91.

Although we have listed only four categories, the astute reader will recognize that many more fall between the labels. The relationship of African American communities and Euro-American communities is thus very complicated.

The Mandate of the Euro-American Preacher

The basic call of the Christian preacher is to interpret the world in terms of the gospel of Jesus Christ. The preacher announces the promise of God's unconditional love for each person and God's will for justice for each person.[30] Issues related to race take their place within this vocation. Racial matters come to expression in the pulpit not as special pleading but as an irrestible part of the preacher's concern for the gospel to be manifest in all human arenas. As Cornel West indicates, *"We need to begin with a frank acknowledgement of the basic humanness and Americanness of each of us."*[31] In particular, Euro-Americans need to acknowledge the humanity of African Americans. And many African Americans need to embrace their own humanness.

In regard to both the general relationship of the races and specific issues and situations, the preacher announces God's unconditional love for all people and clarifies God's will for justice for all people. In the United States, the pastor's portfolio on race has two basic parts. The first is to help the congregation understand the dynamics of racism and its inappropriateness in the light of the gospel. The second is to help the congregation envision patterns of relationship between individuals of the races and the larger social patterns that are shaped in all respects by mutual love and justice.

Thus the preacher's general mandate is clear. The preacher is to identify attitudes, values, behaviors, or systems that are inappropriate or unjust. The pastor also should point to God's vision for a humanity that is free of racism and that is marked by mutuality, encouragement, and support. But the preacher may find it difficult to describe that vision in specific terms. As the reader can gather from our survey of the history and status of racism earlier in this chapter, we live in a time of variety and transition. In the previous generation it seemed clear that racism should give way to integration; African Americans should have equal access to the rights and institutions of our land that were founded and run principally by Euro-Americans (schools, political influence, health

---

30. In this context, justice is the enactment of love in all relationships.
31. West, *Race Matters*, 4, italics added.

care, jobs, housing, social opportunities). Humanist African American communities insist that something more is needed: a new social world. However, the full, specific outlines of this more radical vision have yet to be clarified.[32] The Euro-American preacher will not always be able to say confidently that a particular idea, strategy, or event partakes of the new world. But, as Joseph Sittler once noted, preachers must sometimes "declare as a gift of God" that which they "do not fully possess."[33]

Even when the preacher cannot confidently commend a particular strategy, the preacher can keep before the congregation the promise of God's love for all and the challenge of God for justice for all. Peter Paris's injunction is applicable to pastors of all races. It is crucial "to keep alive the discourse about racism as a formidable organizing principle in our common life."[34] The shape of the new world will likely become clearer as we talk about it.

The preacher ought to help the congregation develop a realistic sense of the extent of its immediate hope. As long as our society is racist, Caucasian people will be racist. Rufus Burrow, Jr., offers a sober but realistic expression for what a Euro-American can become given our present racist world. She or he can at least be a recovering racist.[35] Even Euro-Americans who are converted from racism to a gospel world still participate in a racist society. Until the coming of a new world, and the end of the oppressive structures of the present one, Euro-Americans will always be recovering racists.

What, then, are some practical possibilities for the Christian sermon that can help ministers fulfill their calling in the pulpit?

Possibilities for Preaching on Race for Euro-American Pastors

As a matter of respect, the preacher should refer to the African American community by the nomenclature that is preferred by that community. In midcentury, the term *Negro* was widely used, but it gave way to the word *Black*. Today, the expression *African American* (or Afro-American) has joined Black as an acceptable designation. However, the pastor needs to keep alert for possible changes.

---

32. For two statements of this emerging vision, see James Cone, *For My People* (Maryknoll, N.Y.: Orbis Books, 1984), and Manning Marable, *How Capitalism Underdeveloped Black America* (Boston: South Beacon Press, 1983), 255-62.
33. Joseph Sittler, *The Care of the Earth* (Philadelphia: Fortress Press, 1964), 81.
34. Paris, "In the Face of Despair," 439.
35. Burrow, *James H. Cone and Black Liberation Theology*, 181.

Euro-American pastors need to preach frequently and substantially on issues of race. The gospel requires this. African American concerns now become especially visible at certain days or times of the year. The Euro-American pastor can easily take the birthday of Martin Luther King, Jr., Black history month (February), and the celebration of Kwanzaa as starting points for preaching. The Euro-American preacher may need to study the background of these persons and events in much the same way that one does background exegesis of a biblical text. Others, less well known in the Euro-American community but providing significant points of entry into the discussion of race for the preacher, include Jubilee, Junteeth, Malcolm X, Nkrumah, Marcus Garvey, and the anniversary of the assassination of Martin Luther King, Jr.[36]

Some denominations observe a race relations Sunday or season. Many local communities have other events that bring African American concerns into public view. For instance, in Indianapolis Black Expo, a huge exposition of African American life, takes place every summer. Local media coverage provides data about African American life on which the preacher and congregation may reflect. Race can easily become a central focus of discussion on the Sunday nearest July 4 or on the anniversary of the Emancipation Proclamation or landmark decisions and events from the civil rights movement. The appearance of African Americans in broadcast news reports (for example, the election of an African American to lead a national corporation) is a point at which the preacher can tap into a consciousness that is already developing in the congregation.

The preacher certainly will want to lead the congregation in thinking critically about dramatic situations such as those surrounding Rodney King and the Los Angeles uprisings of 1992. But the preacher needs to be careful not to allow such negative incidents to become the only occasions to focus on race relations in the Euro-American congregation. That would leave the impression that racial issues are primarily crisis affairs and are worthy of Euro-American attention only when racially related matters become threatening. Frequent preaching about race can create a climate of understanding within which to interpret crisis situations.

Furthermore, the preacher needs to bring African American successes to the attention of Euro-American congregations. This avoids the impres-

---

36. The Euro-American preacher would be well served to have a calendar that lists days important to African Americans and a desk copy of a history of African American life. For example, see Lerone Bennett, Jr., *Before the Mayflower: A History of the Negro in America*, rev. ed. (New York: Viking Penguin Books, 1993); idem., *Wade in the Water: Great Moments in Black History* (Chicago: Johnson Publishing Co., 1989).

sion that racial issues are always negative. It gives the Euro-American congregation the opportunity to celebrate African American successes and to increase the depth of human bonds between the two communities.

The minister can also draw upon African American people and communities as illustrations and images of subjects that are not directly related to race. For example, when preaching on justification by grace, the preacher might tell about an African American congregation that rediscovered this important doctrine and its implication for their lives.

Euro-American pastors can inventory how often they preach on race by periodically reviewing their sermons to see how often (and in what ways) they mention racial issues. Any quantification is somewhat arbitrary, but we think that a Euro-American pastor could include a significant discussion of an issue related to race at least once a month. This seems modest in the light of the urgency and complexity of the issue. A whole sermon might focus on race, or the preacher might use material from the African American world in the context of discussing another point (e.g., as a case study or illustration).

Insofar as possible, the Euro-American pastor needs to help the congregation understand what it means to live as people forced to the margins in a racist society. What are the feelings of African Americans? What do they experience in the everyday world? What are African American fears and hopes? Toward developing such empathy, the pastor can help the congregation hear African Americans in their own voices. This both minimizes the possibility of the Euro-American preacher's distorting African American experience and enlarges the horizon of the congregation by bringing it into an unfamiliar world.

Regular pulpit exchanges can bring a physical African American presence into the sanctuary (and can send the Euro-American pastor into an African American community). Congregational exchanges can send Euro-Americans to visit African American churches, and vice versa. Joint services provide opportunities for each community to listen to the other. While such exchanges are good, racism is a Euro-American problem and cannot be addressed adequately by guest African Americans. Euro-American preachers must take up the issue. For help in hearing the African American voice, the pastor can draw upon conversations with African American friends and on material from African American books, speeches, interviews, media appearances, movies, and sermons.

The preacher needs to help the congregation understand the systemic nature of racism and its depth and extent. Many Euro-Americans appear to think of racism as a collection of regrettable actions by a few individuals. Many also think that if all African Americans would simply exert the required initiative, they would be free of poverty and would make their way into the middle and upper classes where all would be well.

Initiative is never to be discouraged. The African American community certainly would be economically improved if all of its members could be in the middle and upper classes. But without a profound change in the larger culture, racism would still oppress the African American community and eat like a cancer at the soul of Euro-America. Indeed, the cover of a recent news magazine focused on "The Hidden Rage of Successful Blacks."[37] Under present conditions, many African Americans in the middle and upper classes are perpetually angry by the slights, unspoken policies of discrimination, and patronizing they often encounter when working and living in businesses and communities dominated by Euro-American presence and values. The conversion of the culture is needed in its fundamental valuation of color as well as in its economic, social, and political organization.

The preacher also needs to help the congregation recognize its participation in racism. Our impression is that relatively few Euro-Americans think of themselves as racist. Most would deny being prejudiced or being implicated in the repression of the African American community.

The Euro-American congregation needs to understand that the church itself manifests racism. The members of a local congregation, of course, would deny that the congregation is racist. "Anyone is welcome here." Middle- and upper-level judicatories work hard to include representative African Americans on boards and in staff positions. But the racism of the larger culture typically taints local and denominational Christian bodies. African Americans appear to be welcome in most Euro-American churches when African Americans are willing to accept the customs and practices of the Euro-American church. To be candid, Euro-Americans appear willing for African Americans to assimilate into the dominant church, but do not appear eager to share power or to reshape congregational and denominational life in order to celebrate African American traditions and values.

If real change is to occur in the church and culture, the congregation must confess this aspect of its sin and repent. As long as Euro-Americans deny complicity in racism, racism works as an unrecognized disease in the unconscious shaping of Euro-American values and practices. Unrecognized sin is the most sinister because it can work its destructive ways unnoticed and unchallenged. Only when the Euro-American community

---

37. *Newsweek*, November 15, 1993.

---

is aware of its inherent racism can the community become critical of its participation in racism and start down a healthy road to recovery.

In the Christian community, repentance is largely a positive act. Repentance begins with confession of sin. But the heart of repentance is turning to embrace God and God's ways. Thus the pastor needs to emphasize the positive vision of a transformed human community. As noted earlier, the preacher might not be able to describe this community in detail, but the preacher can point toward its essential characteristics. The preacher can appeal to the congregation's sense of adventure. "We have the opportunity to join God in creating fresh forms of community life. This can be an adventure of the highest order. Of course, there are uncertainties and risks. But the trail leads in a promising direction." As a matter of integrity, the congregation needs to confess its sin. But people are motivated to change and to move toward a different future less by guilt and more by the promise of a better world. The more attractive the vision, the more likely Euro-Americans are to embrace it.

Euro-Americans need to understand that, while many in the African American community will welcome Euro-American efforts to end racism, many African Americans initially will be reserved. The legacy of alienation is deep. Broken promises and dreams denied are many. Based on four centuries of bitter experience with Caucasians, many African Americans view Euro-American overtures with suspicion. Rufus Burrow, Jr., puts the matter succinctly: "Whites must earn the trust of African Americans."[38]

Of course, congregations need solid data about the concrete manifestations of racism in our culture. But more than information is needed. The preacher needs to put a face on racism. As long as the preacher speaks generically about racism, the congregation can leave the phenomenon at arm's length. The preacher needs to help the issue get under the skin of the congregation. Telling stories is one of the best ways to do so. At the simplest level, stories add interest to the sermon. Beyond this, the congregation often identifies with characters or plot; the listeners then relate the story to their own experience. When a story is internalized, it becomes a part of the reservoir of experience of the listener. It then can contribute to the lens through which the hearer views the world. It allows the members of the community to "try on" a world that is different from its own.

Telling stories from African American history and culture helps the preacher to introduce Euro-American people to African American experi-

---

38. Burrow, *James H. Cone and Black Liberation Theology*, 49.

ence. Stories also can have uncanny revelatory power; they can lead Euro-Americans to recognize their own complicity in racism. Euro-Americans who deny the proposition "I am a racist" might come much closer to the truth if they encounter it in the context of a story in which they have identified with persons or situations that reveal racism.

Christians are especially touched by the pastor's own story. Euro-American preachers might trace segments of their own journey into transformed racial consciousness. "Throughout much of the first part of my life, I thought . . . and felt . . . and acted . . . but, then, I discovered . . . and now I think . . . and feel . . . and act." Listeners especially want to know what brings about a change of heart, mind, and will.[39]

The preacher is called to help the congregation envision practical steps that it can take to embody a transformed racial consciousness and commitment. People who claim a theology of solidarity must ask themselves, "What am I willing to do, or not do, to set at liberty the captives, who through no fault of their own are crushed to the earth?"[40] Cornel West believes that many Euro-Americans are "hungry" for "genuine human interaction among black and white folk in struggle where bonds of trust are displayed."[41]

Unfortunately, relatively few Euro-Americans seem able to identify occasions or organizations in which such interaction takes place. The preacher can suggest such opportunities. These venues can be as simple as resolving to greet African Americans on the sidewalk and in the mall or attending an African American cultural event (such as Indianapolis' Black Expo) or inviting African Americans for dinner. They can be as public as joining in demonstrations to protest racist policies or becoming a member of the NAACP. They can be as complicated as critiquing capitalism and imagining an economic order in which all citizens of the land have a say in the control of the means of production and consumption.

Along the way, the preacher can warn the congregation about the consequences that result from racism. Peter Hodgson insightfully points out that racism is characterized by deceit and idolatry.[42] These invidious qualities result in interior rot in a community. Not only is God glorified, but also the human community's best interest is served when Euro-Americans destroy the idol and replace the lie with the truth.

---

39. Bonita Benda, "The Silence Is Broken: Preaching on Social Justice Issues" (Th.D. diss., The Iliff School of Theology, 1983), 257, 265-66; Hans van der Geest, *Presence in the Pulpit*, trans. Douglas W. Stott (Atlanta: John Knox Press, 1981), 143.
40. Burrow, *James H. Cone and Black Liberation Theology*, 43.
41. West, *Prophetic Thought in Postmodern Times*, 75.
42. Peter Hodgson, *Children of Freedom* (Philadelphia: Fortress Press, 1974), 23-30.

The Christian congregation cannot rely on the sermon alone to raise its consciousness about race. Concern for racism needs to be integrated into the systemic life of the congregation. The pastor and the leaders of the congregation should see that race is included in study material for classes and in other aspects of the congregation's life, such as community outreach, congregational dinners, and leadership meetings.

Conclusion

Pastors who respond affirmatively to the mandate to preach on issues of race need to be creative, inviting, and visionary in order to do all that they can to receive a positive hearing in the congregation. However, the Euro-American preacher who addresses the subject of race runs a risk. Robert McAfee Brown notices that such a preacher takes issue with "the assumptions, norms and values of the society that supports us, feeds us, and pays us."[43] The pastor who comes into conflict with the congregation may need to remember that the promises of God ultimately are guaranteed by the inexhaustibility of the divine life.

Furthermore, the preacher is not alone. The preacher is joined by many, both African Americans and Euro-Americans, who have greeted the new world from afar. As the preacher joins in singing an old African American song, "Hold my hand, while I run this race," the great cloud of witnesses extends its hands in solidarity and support. At the head is the living Christ, ever present, the pioneer and perfecter of the coming world. The Euro-American pastor who addresses issues of race in the pulpit is in good company.

---

43. Robert McAfee Brown, *Gustavo Gutiérrez* (Atlanta: John Knox Press, 1980), 71.

PART FIVE

Tuning
for
Tomorrow

CHAPTER THIRTEEN

MINORITY PREACHING IN A POSTMODERN AGE

Justo L. González

As the twentieth century draws to a close, many observers are announcing the end of the modern age. This age referred to as "modern" is one in which objectivity has been taken to be the highest goal of intellectual discourse. It is the age of "science," when the unprecedented success of technology has led to the belief that all problems and questions are approached best through the "scientific" method of objective observation and experimentation. Even in those fields where experimentation is impossible, it has been supposed that the best understanding is achieved when a method of scientific, objective observation and analysis is applied.

Flawed Ideals

This modern age has been the "golden age of reason," on which Mexican-American theologian Virgil Elizondo has commented that it "was well named: gold could buy reason."[1] Although Elizondo makes this statement in connection with the manner in which the thirst for gold seemed to justify the greatest atrocities of the Spanish conquest of the Western Hemisphere, his statement is true in more subtle ways. It could be argued, indeed, that modernity and its ideals were the expression of the goals and perspectives of the rising bourgeoisie, first in Europe and then across the Atlantic. What modernity deemed universal was in fact the projection and imposition on others of the perspectives and under-

---

1. Virgil Elizondo, *Galilean Journey: The Mexican-American Promise* (Maryknoll, N.Y.: Orbis, 1983), 9.

standings of the suppressing group—and, in a different way, of males within it.

The so-called objectivity of modernity involves the suppression of all subjectivities and subjects that do not agree with the standards set by those in control. The suppression of both/and thought and the reign of either/or modalities has meant that all who did not agree with the rising science and technology were absolutely wrong and could be ignored. The values of such minority people, and the objections they might raise as a result of their values, were judged to be of no significance, for they are "primitive," "unscientific," and "premodern." Thus mass production and mass exploitation of the earth's resources could proceed apace, with no other critique than that raised from within the centers of modernity itself.

For these reasons, it has been well said that colonialism is the armed version of modernism.[2] What the colonial enterprise did was to suppress all who did not agree with the interests and perspectives of the colonial powers, and to do this in the name of progress and science. What the colonized persons thought and valued could be ignored, for it was primitive and unscientific. By forcing on them the results of Western advances, presumably they too would be led to progress. By joining the mainstream of modernity, they would be better off. To bring them to see this, by persuasion or by force, by hook or by crook, was "the white man's burden."

Needless to say, there was enough truth in the promises of modernity to make them believable. Medical technology saved many a life. The ideals of democracy and freedom, although seldom allowed full rein in situations in which they would threaten the economic power and profit of international investors, have been generally well received and affirmed by people in various parts of the world and at various levels in society. At the same time, however, this acceptance was gained at the expense of much that is valuable in suppressed cultures and traditions.

In the North Atlantic, similar processes were taking place. The wisdom, values, and perspectives of those who did not control the means of culture formation were ignored and often suppressed. The values and perspectives of the rising bourgeoisie found willing support in academic circles, where the ideal of objectivity soon reigned supreme, and where this objectivity was in fact the expression of the values and perspectives of the controlling elements of society.

---

2. Ashis Nandy, *The Intimate Enemy: Loss and Recovery of Self Under Colonialism* (Delhi: O.U.P., 1983), xiv.

The Troubling Dichotomy

All of this shaped the sort of biblical scholarship in which most of us were schooled. Norman Gottwald has expressed it this way:

> Biblical scholars from the Renaissance to the bourgeois revolutions of the seventeenth through the nineteenth centuries were generally the intellectual adjuncts of monarchic, aristocratic, or clerical class interests. Increasingly in the nineteenth century, they became one functional group among many academicians and intellectuals who shared in the bourgeois revolutions against monarchic and aristocratic domination. A broadly bourgeois democratic political and cultural perspective shaped their outlook.... By and large the position of biblical scholars, as a professional and intellectual elite, was oppositional both toward the declining monarchies and aristocracies and toward the rising underclasses of the industrial proletariat and, later, the peasantry. In contrast to the formerly dominant classes, they were liberative and progressive, but toward the classes below them they were conservative and reactionary.[3]

Hence the dichotomy, which many seminary professors noted and bemoaned, between what was learned at school and what was preached in church—particularly in the case of ethnic minority and poor white churches. In school one learned to read Scripture according to the historical-critical method and its many later variations—form criticism, redaction criticism, and the like. In church one preached that God delivered Moses and the people of Israel by parting the waters of the Red Sea.

In school one learned of a closed universe, patterned after the great machines that modern technology had produced, a universe where all is cause and effect and where divine intervention is unthinkable. In church and in ethnic minority communities one experienced and preached an open universe that is constantly in God's hand, a universe where hope is still possible precisely because the present is open to God's intervention. Our teachers believed, and told us, that this contrast was the result of our communities' still living in premodern conditions, that they were primitive, ignorant, "fundamentalistic."

Our professors told us that, and we believed it. Some of us even taught it. And yet, the dissonance continued, for no matter what "objective" modern knowledge told us, we knew a different reality and a different experience—a reality and an experience that could not be poured into the wineskins of modernity. Our community was basically formed of people

---

3. Norman Gottwald, *The Tribes of Yahweh: A Sociology of the Religion of Liberated Israel, 1250–1050 B.C.E.* (Maryknoll, N.Y.: Orbis, 1979), 10.

whom modernity excluded, whom modernity oppressed and suppressed, and who, therefore, insisted on finding their hope in views that the dominant intellectual groups dubbed "premodern."

Then along came the postmodern critique of modernity. Much of what postmodernity proposes as an alternative is what marginalized people have believed and practiced all along. As one who has lived for decades in the tension between (1) studying and teaching a modern reading of the Bible and (2) believing and preaching a "premodern" one, I resonate with a postmodernity described as a "shift away from modernity's universalizing and totalizing drive . . . [an] assertion of the value of inclusive 'both/and' thinking [which] deliberately contests the exclusive 'either/or' binary oppositions of modernity . . . [a position where] paradox, ambiguity, irony, indeterminacy, and contingency are seen to replace modern closure, unity, order, the absolute, and the rational . . . [one] valuing the local and the particular, the provisional and the tentative."[4]

It is immediately obvious that the current debate regarding postmodernity, now lodged at the traditional centers of learning—at the very universities and seminaries that still dub preaching in ethnic minority churches as primitive and premodern—is related to the dichotomy described above. Much of what those very scholars called primitive is very close to what they now call postmodern! Therefore, much of what they now have to say will help us to understand and even to a measure justify the seeming dichotomy between our preaching and our "scientific" learning.

For instance, as I read Lyotard's discussion of the relationship between narrative language and scientific discourse, I begin to understand how it is possible for many Hispanics and other minorities to make the biblical narratives part of their own lives and hopes, without thereby rejecting scientific discourse. In brief, what Lyotard claims is that narrative and scientific discourse do not function at the same level. While the latter must reject the former as unscientific, the former can accept the latter as one more narrative. Explains Lyotard:

> I have said that narrative knowledge does not give priority to the question of its own legitimation and that it certifies itself in the pragmatics of its own transmission without having recourse to argumentation and proof. This is why its incomprehension of the problems of scientific discourse is accompanied by a certain tolerance: it approaches such discourse primarily as a variant in the family of narrative cultures. The opposite is not true. The

4. J. Natoly and L. Hutcheon, eds., *A Postmodern Reader* (Albany: State University of New York Press, 1993), ix.

scientist questions the validity of narrative statements and concludes that they are never subject to argumentation or proof. He classifies them as belonging to a different mentality: savage, primitive, underdeveloped, backward, alienated, composed of opinions, customs, authority, prejudice, ignorance, ideology. Narratives are fables, myths, legends, fit only for women and children. At best, attempts are made to throw some rays of light into this obscurantism, to civilize, educate, develop.[5]

Our reading as narrative—as authoritative narrative that relates and guides our own narratives—is radically different from the objectivizing reading of modernity—or, as Lyotard would say, from scientific discourse. It, therefore, has that "certain tolerance" that allows us to accept both that reading of the Bible and the historical-critical readings we were taught by the academic tradition.

Being Metamodern

By the same token, we are not fundamentalists. Fundamentalism is a reading of the biblical narrative as scientific discourse, and hence lacks that "certain tolerance." For the same reason, the "scientific" reader—that is, the liberal, white, "objective" theologian or biblical scholar—cannot see the difference between the position of most Hispanics and other minorities and classical fundamentalism and must declare that we are "savage, primitive, underdeveloped, fundamentalistic." But most Hispanics and other minorities in the church are not fundamentalists. Fundamentalism is a modern phenomenon. Most minorities are simply outside the scope of modernity—rather, at its edges—and are, therefore, what I would call *metamodern.*

That is not to say that postmodernity will necessarily make it easier for these metamodern minorities. Lyotard gives us a hint of this when he speaks of postmodernity as something taking place "in the most highly developed societies."[6] The hint is that, while he has much to say about the failures of modernity, he still seems to accept modernity's understanding of "highly developed." Highly developed are the white societies of the North Atlantic and those in other parts of the world that emulate them. Thus, while proclaiming the demise of modernity, Lyotard and many others still accept the oppressive premises of modernity. Therefore, not only African Americans, but all minorities as well, would do well to follow the example of Cornel West: "I do not displace myself

---

5. Natoly and Hutcheon, *A Postmodern Reader,* 83.
6. Ibid., 71.

from the post-modernism debate, I simply try to keep my distance from its parochialism and view it as a symptom of our present cultural crisis."[7]

This could be stated in terms of the way in which modernity and postmodernity deal with metanarratives. Modernity questioned all metanarratives as subjective, partial, and primitive. One should approach reality with no metanarratives seeking to explain it. Rather, one should simply observe reality as it is in itself, objectively, apart from all preconceived notions or metanarratives. The problem is that modernity itself had its own metanarrative, albeit hidden to itself.

The presuppositions of modernity had no greater basis in reality than the other metanarratives that it so dogmatically denied. Hence the need to exclude the metanarratives of ethnic minorities, of all oppressed groups, and of the biblical tradition. In this regard, the major contribution of postmodernity has been to make it quite clear that there is no such thing as an objectively verifiable metanarrative. It has liberated us from the modern metanarrative, which served to justify the existing order as the inevitable result of mechanistic forces, and which had no place for metanarratives of faith.

On the other hand, the notion that all metanarratives are equally sustainable, or that one has no right and no basis to claim a particular metanarrative, is the metanarrative of postmodernity. The fact that all knowledge is perspectival does not mean that all perspectives are equally valid, and certainly not that knowledge is reduced to perspective.

It is at this point that I find it necessary to part company with postmodernity, for as a Christian, and as a Latino Christian, I claim a metanarrative from which I must interpret all of reality. I claim that metanarrative in such a way that it is not simply interchangeable with all others. Our communities, which have been excluded from and by modernity, and which have survived thanks to their sustaining metanarratives, must not now capitulate to the postmodern notion that all metanarratives are the same and that, therefore, a text (in our case, the biblical text) has no particular authority.

Stephen Slemon is speaking of a similar issue when he proposes a "post-colonial" reading of texts, meaning by that something similar to what I mean by a metamodern reading. Argues Slemon:

> Whereas a post-modernist criticism would want to argue . . . the constructedness of all textuality and thus call down "the claim to unequivocal domination of one mode of signifying over another" . . . an interested post-

---

7. See ibid., 394.

colonial critical practice would want to allow for the positive production of oppositional truth-claims in these texts. It would retain for post-colonial writing, that is, a mimetic or referential purchase to textuality, and it would recognize in this referential drive the operations of a crucial strategy for survival in marginalized social groups.[8]

Preaching as Countercultural

The implications of the postmodern critique of modernity for preaching should be obvious. Walter Brueggemann describes the new situation by proposing that "the shift from an objective claim of hegemony to a contextual, local perspective accurately describes our pastoral situation." He then affirms that "in this post-Cartesian situation, knowing consists not in settled certitudes but in the actual work of imagination . . . to picture, portray, and practice the world in ways other than it appears to be at first glance when seen through a dominant, habitual, unexamined lens."[9]

What this means is that the act of preaching—and the hermeneutics that precedes and shapes it—is in itself a countercultural act, one in which, making use of the freedom granted to us by postmodernity, we propose a reading of the world, of life, and of reality that is quite different from both the modern reading and the postmodern view that all readings are equally valid. In other words, we propose a metamodern reading not only of Scripture, but also of the world, of life, of culture.

In this regard, all preaching is cross-cultural, for it proposes a different reading, a different way of being, a different world, and, therefore, a different culture. All preaching confronts the church (including the preacher) with the contrast between the world as read by unbelieving eyes—no matter whether modern or postmodern—and the world as it is read through the eyes of faith. Indeed, the very fact that we tend to reserve the title "cross-cultural preaching" for what takes place in the presence of persons of different cultures is an indication of the degree to which, in so much of its preaching, the church has capitulated to the influences of the culture around it.

The metamodern preaching of ethnic minorities has always been cross-cultural. It has been cross-cultural, first of all, in the sense that it has never been able to ignore the dominant culture that is the context of the life of parishioners. An African American preacher in a black church is

---

8. Ibid., 431.
9. Walter Brueggemann, *Texts Under Negotiation: The Bible and Postmodern Imagination* (Minneapolis: Fortress Press, 1993), 10, 12-13.

---

still preaching in a cross-cultural situation, for the congregation, and the preacher too, live in a situation in which they cannot avoid dealing with a culture other than their own.

But the metamodern preaching of ethnic minorities has been cross-cultural in a deeper sense. It has cut across the grain of the dominant culture and dared to proclaim a reality that that culture tended to suppress. What could be more cross-cultural than to preach hope in the midst of slavery, or in an exile of generations, or on a reservation, or in an internment camp?

Obviously, in each of these situations different perspectives are brought to bear on the text of Scripture as well as on the world. Yet there is also a convergence, for the text of Scripture provides a common metanarrative. Although this metanarrative is nuanced by its intersection with the narratives of each ethnic group, and thus each contributes something significant to the reading of the text, in principle we affirm that this is the same metanarrative, and thus we are able to acknowledge each other as part of the same history and the same hope.

Most important, however, is the question "What does this sort of preaching have to contribute to the preaching of the church at large, and especially to those of the dominant culture?" The answer depends to a large measure on the degree to which that church and those preachers are willing to let go of their moorings in the dominant metanarrative and set sail in quest of a different reading of the world and of Scripture.

As I travel throughout the country, I find that much of the church and its preaching is still tied to modern paradigms of supposed objectivity, chained to a shallow scientism that often translates into psychologism. Scripture is not allowed to speak a word of genuine challenge to the individual, and much less to society. Rather, it is tamed into a book of religious observances, moral platitudes, and psychological banalities. The cause is not lack of imagination. Rather, it is caused by an imagination so bound by the canons of modernity—and of its accompanying laissez-faire capitalism—that all it can imagine under different canons is disaster.

It is at this point that ethnic minority preaching and hermeneutics can make a valuable contribution. Having always existed at the margins of modernity—and of its accompanying laissez-faire capitalism—it has at least the possibility of offering a different reading. It offers a hopeful reading in a world that seems to be closed to all but the most fatalistic laws of cause and effect. It offers a truly liberating reading in a world enslaved by its own lack of imagination. That, and nothing else, is the preaching of the Christian gospel!

CHAPTER FOURTEEN

PREACHING GOD'S FUTURE: THE ESCHATOLOGICAL CONTEXT OF CHRISTIAN PROCLAMATION

Thomas G. Long

Several years ago, when Leslie Stahl was a White House correspondent for CBS News, she prepared a story for the evening news on some controversial problem developing in the administration of President Ronald Reagan. She wrote the script for her report, but for the visual background she used video footage borrowed from the White House Office of Communications. Thus, when the piece was aired, viewers heard Stahl's commentary, but they saw the administration's pictures—vigorous and colorful shots of President Reagan riding a horse, tossing a football around on a beach, chopping wood, and standing reverently in front of an American flag.

The next day, Michael Deaver, Director of the Office of Communications, phoned Stahl to praise and thank her for the story. Stahl was surprised by the commendation, since, to her mind, the report had been critical in tone. She asked Deaver why he was applauding her for an unfavorable story about the president. Deaver replied that, yes, he knew that her words were negative, but she had used his pictures. "In the battle between the eye and the ear," he said, "the eye wins every time."

"The eye wins every time." Few communication experts would challenge Deaver's point. It is common wisdom that, in the race to transmit information clearly, memorably, and persuasively, visuals outpace aurals without even breaking a sweat. A politician can produce indifferent yawns all day long with endless blab about inflation and consumer purchasing power, but show a little pie graph on television about how much of a weekly paycheck it takes to buy groceries and the voters snap to attention. Whether the issue is learning how to swing a golf club or deciding guilt or innocence in a jury trial, people trust, value, and believe what they see over what they hear. Communicationally, we are all from Missouri—"Show me." In communicational terms, Michael Deaver is clearly right: "In the battle between the eye and the ear, the eye wins every time."

But what about in homiletical terms? Deaver's claim forms an intriguing and rather daunting challenge for preachers, since words are finally all we have. Despite many attempts to "improve" preaching by transforming it into a visual art, the fact remains that preaching is, irreducibly, an oral event. No backdrop of stained glass, no vivid vestments, no overlay of liturgical dance or dramatic gesturing, no number of visual aids or color slides projected onto a scrim can obscure the brute fact that sermons are essentially made out of words spoken into the air and into the ear.[1]

If that is so—if preaching is irrevocably oral—then what hope is there for the preacher in an image-saturated, MTV world, a world where influence peddlers like Michael Deaver know all too well that "in the battle between the ear and the eye, the eye wins every time"?

Beyond the Naked Eye

One obvious response to this challenge is that preachers must learn how to touch the eye through the ear, must learn to use words to form images. That is, we need to discover the way, as the *Reader's Digest* puts it, "toward more picturesque speech." Preaching is not visual in the tech-

---

1. I am aware of the objection that restricting the definition of preaching to the spoken word alone runs into difficulty when one considers the proclamation of the gospel to those who physically cannot hear sound. Is there, then, no preaching among the deaf? The problem, it seems to me, is not with an oral/aural definition of preaching, but with a too literal, and thus a too oral, interpretation of the theological metaphor "Word of God." The category "Word of God" embraces all acts of God's self-disclosure, and careful theologians have never collapsed "Word" into "words" nor limited the breadth of events implied in "Word of God" only to acts involving speech.

Preaching, however, is that expression of the "Word of God" essentially bound to the spoken word. Of course, preaching is not the only form of the "Word of God," but it is that form that seeks and hopes for God's action through faithful human speaking and hearing. To push matters somewhat, if the Eucharist has bread and wine as its sacramental elements, preaching has sound and human speech. Can we imagine celebrating the Eucharist in a culture that knew no bread or wine? Yes, of course, but we would have to recognize that no easy and obvious substitutions could be made for these primary and multivalent symbols. The same is true for the problem of preaching in an environment lacking oral communication.

nical sense, but spoken language has the capacity to form powerful images in the mind's eye. In some contexts, it may be true that "a picture is worth a thousand words," but preachers can also be confident that a few aptly chosen words can generate a thousand pictures in the imagination. Much recent homiletical work has, in fact, been aimed directly at the goal of recovering the imagination and visual potential of the spoken word.[2]

At another and deeper level, however, Michael Deaver's flippant comment on the superiority of the eye over the ear is a superficial expression of what is, at root, the gravest threat in the contemporary world to the proclamation of the gospel. Deaver's assertion that what we see is more trustworthy than what we hear is popular wisdom's legacy from a long philosophical and epistemological tradition, cresting in Cartesian empiricism, that values tangible, immediate, and observable personal experience over all other forms of knowing. The "eye" takes in the world at hand, what is available in the present and sensuous world. The gospel, however, as Moltmann and others have reminded us, is a word of promise; and promise, whatever else one may say, transcends tangible, immediate, and observable personal experience.

Indeed, among New Testament documents, the epistle to the Hebrews can be understood precisely as a sermon addressed to the conflict between the ear and the eye—that is, as a sermon preached in defense of sermons, in defense of the claim that the gospel promises heard in the ear are to be trusted over what is seen by the naked eye. What is seen by the eye is a world in which evil triumphs over good, cruelty over kindness, and injustice over righteousness. To the eye, Jesus is but a tragic historical figure, a person whose lofty goals and noble message were finally crushed under the heavy wheel of suffering, a sad and defeated person whose last hours were filled with pain and "loud cries and tears." To the ear, though, this suffering was priestly, this pain was divine compassion, and this defeat was the source of eternal salvation.

If the eye is all we have, then the faith cannot be maintained. The hands of charity will inevitably droop, and the knees of mission will buckle under the stress. "Therefore," preaches the author of Hebrews, "we must pay greater attention to what we have heard" (Heb. 2:1). The truth about the world is not available to the eye; only a spoken word can

---

2. Among those homileticians who have helpfully emphasized the role of image and imagination in preaching are Patricia Wilson-Kastner, *Imagery for Preaching* (Minneapolis: Fortress, 1989); Thomas Troeger, *Creating Fresh Images for Preaching* (Philadelphia: Judson, 1982); and Paul Scott Wilson, *Imagination of the Heart* (Nashville: Abingdon Press, 1988).

express it, and, in order to make this point, Hebrews abounds with oral symbolism. "Long ago God spoke to our ancestors in many and various ways by the prophets, but in these last days he has spoken to us by a Son" (Heb. 1:1). Or "Let us hold fast to the confession of our hope without wavering, for he who has promised is faithful" (Heb. 10:23) and "Remember your leaders, those who spoke the Word of God to you" (Heb. 13:7). And again, "See that you do not refuse the one who is speaking" (Heb. 12:25).

It is no surprise that one of the favorite Old Testament quotations of the author of Hebrews is Psalm 95:7: "O that today you would listen to his voice." Only if the community of faith can trust the spoken promise of the gospel's eventual triumph more than the visual evidence of defeat right before their own eyes can they lift their drooping hands and strengthen their weak knees and join the great cloud of witnesses in running with perseverance the race set before them. In the battle between the ear and the eye, the radical claim of Christian preaching is that, though the world seen through the "eye" may seem to hold all the cards, the eschatological promises that only the "ear" can hear are to be trusted, and God will eventually triumph in the end.

Dale Aukerman makes a similar eschatological point in his recent treatment of the relationship between apocalyptic hope and Christian ethics:

> Biblical hope is directed toward promise, that is toward One who has promised and is able to fulfill his promise. All other hope is at bottom wishful thinking. In Christian faith what is decisive is not projections about the future that humans come up with but rather God's promises about the good future he brings in. The many pictures of that future given in scripture are to be seen, not as visions born of human longing, but as expressions of the utterly trustworthy promise of God. Paul S. Minear writes: "Every genuine promise comes from God. He alone is absolutely dependable in doing what he says he will do. . . . This is why his promise is the only sure basis of hope."[3]

The Eschatological Nature of Preaching

The essential homiletical argument I want to make in this chapter is contained in the famous definition of faith in Hebrews 11:1: "Now faith is the assurance of things hoped for, the conviction of things not seen." Preaching is precisely about those truths that cannot be seen, but can only be heard. Preaching speaks to the ear the promise of that which is

---

3. Dale Aukerman, *Reckoning with Apocalypse: Terminal Politics and Christian Hope* (New York: Crossroad, 1993), 210-11.

not yet available to the eye but, nonetheless, will surely come to pass— the assurance of things hoped for.

It is no accident, then, that preaching, phenomenologically, is oral in character, that it is not an entirely visual event since the oral medium itself embodies some of the key characteristics of promisemaking. If you and I gaze at a Rembrandt in the Metropolitan Museum of Art or contemplate a lovely yellow willow blowing in the wind beside a brook, there is, to be sure, great profundity in these visual experiences. To be sure, even if we summoned the most sophisticated and picturesque language we possess, neither of us would be able to exhaust the depth of meaning present in either the great painting or the beautiful tree. But the fact remains that the meaning is present there—that is, there in the present—to be grasped. We may lack the skill or the time to get at the fullness of either visual event, but everything is available, potentially at least, to be seen. In other words, the painting and the tree do not make future promises; they disclose everything in the present.

If, on the other hand, you say something to me, the words you speak are gone as soon as you speak them. The waves of speech instantly dissipate; nothing remains of the actual sound of your words to be probed and dissected. This is why Ricoeur, among others, makes much of the hermeneutical shift from speech to writing.[4] Speech is fleeting and ephemeral; writing is fixed and permanent. A document can be held in the hand; speech, however, both literally and figuratively, cannot be fully grasped. Like a promise, speech is not captive to the present tense. Spoken words enter the present and do their work, but they are not depleted by the present; there is more there than the present tense can hold.

The main point to be made here, however, is not one about the phenomenology of oral communication, but a more basic one about the theological character of preaching. True gospel proclamation is always thoroughgoingly eschatological. That is, Christian preaching is not only a word about God's future, but it is also a word from God's future that interrupts and disrupts the expectations of the present tense with the crisis of God's advent. The gospel, notes Karl Heim, forces us to

> reckon with the end of the whole temporal form of the world as earnestly and soberly as we reckon with our own death. We must approach every crisis of politics, every social revolution, with the question, What light is thrown on this event by the End?[5]

---

4. See, for example, Paul Ricoeur, *Interpretation Theory: Discourse and the Surplus of Meaning* (Fort Worth: Texas Christian University Press, 1976).
5. Karl Heim, *The New Divine Order* (London: Student Christian Movement, 1930), 87.

Whenever preachers lose sight of the eschatological nature of preaching, they inevitably become shills for the status quo, spokespersons for the prevailing powers and principalities of the present age. They may say some good and helpful things, but they forfeit the one thing that is given to them alone to speak: the hope granted by God's coming victory over sin and death, revealed proleptically in Jesus Christ, a hope that transcends the possibilities contained in the present. They may speak sagely about such matters as codependency, handling personal finances wisely, being an effective parent, getting on the right side of some political issue, stress management, or coping with grief, but whatever power such wisdom holds resides fully in the present tense. As theologian James Smart puts it:

> Biblical eschatology has an interest only for [those] who at least have discovered that no future worth having can be of their own making and who have become willing not only to hear what the Scriptures have to tell them about their future but also to receive their future . . . from God. . . . Eschatology is the vision of the future that gives direction to the present and confidence to take the next necessary step toward a future goal.[6]

The Loss of Eschatology in the Contemporary Pulpit

Despite its central importance for Christian theology and gospel proclamation, the fact remains that eschatology has become a corrupt and neglected category. Three basic types of distortions can be observed.

1. In fundamentalist circles, eschatology has been turned into a parody of "Bible prophecy," mechanical and mathematical speculation about the end time. Every tremor in Israel, every leadership change in Russia, every currency crisis in the Common Market, every war rumor in the Middle East lets loose a riptide of Armageddon anxiety. Among the fundamentalist preachers are those who specialize in apocalyptic texts (especially the prophets, Daniel, and Revelation). They have their charts and their formulas and their calculations, but their main message is some literalistic variation of "Jesus is coming to end world history very, very soon."

This claim betrays both the historical naïveté and the essentially narcissistic assumptions that lie behind fundamentalist eschatology—namely, that the whole of God's hidden plan for the world, the magnificent span of God's redemptive activity, and the sum of all biblical

---

6. James Smart, *The Old Testament in Dialogue with Modern Man* (Philadelphia: Westminster Press, 1964), 106.

prophecy have to do with me and my generation. It is as though Isaiah, Jeremiah, Amos, and the whole sweep of the great prophetic tradition, not to mention the dazzling visions of Daniel and John, are all really about stuff that appeared in last week's issue of *U.S. News and World Report*. The conceit of such a view of eschatology indicates that fundamentalism is but an exotic strain of the same virus that infects notions of eschatology in popular piety.

2. In popular piety, eschatology has been reduced to what George Caird has called "eschatology of the individual."[7] Here, eschatology has less to do with the end of the world and everything to do with the end of me. The future triumph of God is not so much about the establishing of peace and justice as it is about the furnishing of my mansion in paradise.

It has been the particular gift and mission of biblical scholar and theologian Krister Stendahl to puncture this self-serving view of eschatology. "The question of eschatology," he writes:

> is not what is going to happen to little me—that is a Western preoccupation. Augustine, I am sorry to say . . . is one of the most intelligent chief sinners in turning man in on himself. As we say, he is the first one who wrote an autobiography. And narcissism has not gone out of our Western system ever since. . . . Even so, it is important to note that biblical eschatology is not answering the question of the future of the individual, but has its searchlight, its laser beam, on the question of God's victory.[8]

3. The mainline moderate to liberal pulpit has been so embarrassed by the eyeball-rolling fanatics on the fundamentalist fringe and still so captivated by a present-tense, let's-get-real, demythologized gospel that eschatological language has either ceased altogether or become hopelessly vague. In his book *Paul's Apocalyptic Gospel*, New Testament scholar J. C. Beker records the following revealing and amusing correspondence from an official mainline denominational magazine. The exchange discloses the mainline discomfort with eschatological language. A reader had submitted a question to the "Question and Answer" column, which was answered by one of the editors:

> Q. Why are there so few sermons in our churches on the Second Coming? Is this part of our belief or not?

---

7. George B. Caird, *The Language and Imagery of the Bible* (London: Duckworth, 1980), 243.

8. Krister Stendahl, as quoted in Joseph Papin, *The Eschaton: A Community of Love* (Villanova, Pa.: Villanova University Press, 1971), 59.

A. Not all Christians think alike on matters of theology, but it would be hard for someone to feel at home in our tradition who did not understand God as the One who has come, who is present (Christ is risen) in our lives today, and who is yet to come in whatever form the future winds up taking. To literalize the Second Coming is to ruin both its beauty and its significance. To ignore it is to avoid what may be the most important part of the Gospel we know about since the past and present, relatively speaking, are brief, while tomorrow borders on forever.

In a later issue of the magazine, another reader responded to this answer:

I compliment the Rev. ＿＿＿ for his illusive non-answer to what I am sure was a serious question concerning the Second Coming of Jesus Christ. If I understood his answer, he said, in effect, "We don't all agree. But if you want to be comfortable in the [United Church of Christ and Presbyterian Church], you will need to agree that Jesus is coming again, but not really— for if you actually believe in the Second Coming you will ruin both its beauty and its significance. Yet you can't ignore it because it's in the future." Why not a simple answer? Why not admit that those who cannot receive the Bible literally must spiritualize the Second Coming because it is too large a segment of the New Testament to be ignored?[9]

What is needed is a recovery of the authentic, strong, ethically bracing, hope-giving eschatological vision of the Scripture. The biblical writers were persuaded that the future was not to be found in an extrapolation of the present set of human possibilities but, rather, was to be discerned in the saving character of God. In other words, if one wishes to know what the future holds, one does not look to the potential that can be seen in the available circumstances; one looks to the promises made by God in Jesus Christ.

The future, then, is not emerging developmentally from current trends; it is coming as a gift from the grace of God. God's future will surprise and disrupt human expectations. This does not mean that faithful people sit passively and numbly through history's veil of tears, waiting for God's consummation. To the contrary, the community of faith lives by the promises, serving today as citizens of God's future. Eschatology, far from lifting the church out of the world, guides the church to passionate and prophetic service toward the world, confident that, despite appearances, such gracious action really counts. In the battle between the eye and the ear, the promises of God, spoken to the ear, are to be trusted every time. As Aukerman maintains:

9. This exchange is recorded in J. Christiaan Beker, *Paul's Apocalyptic Gospel* (Philadelphia: Fortress Press, 1982), 12-13.

To live in hope of the glorious Appearing of Jesus should not at all lead to giving up on the present world, filled as it is with illness, starvation, pollution, violence, armaments, repression, and official lying. The One who will vanquish the powers of darkness at the End is moving in might against them now. The Pentagon, the White House, the Capitol, all their counterparts, and the death dances within them are relatively insubstantial and are about to shrink away before the manifest reality of the coming One. The Servant, who will bring "justice to victory" (Matt. 12:20) in the consummation, is doing that proleptically in these days. Under the Servant Lord, Christians have stronger reasons than others to live for humaneness of life and against the powers of death.[10]

Eschatological Preaching

The recovery of authentic biblical eschatology and the restoration of the eschatological context of Christian preaching would mean much more than an occasional sermon about the doctrine of hope or an Advent series on the coming victory of God. Indeed, a truly eschatological perspective on preaching would refresh the whole act of proclamation—content, method, and vision.

There are, then, many implications of such an approach to preaching. I can suggest here only a few:

1. An eschatological understanding of preaching would clarify our vision of the breadth of the church to whom we preach. Most preachers stand in pulpits and look at congregations made up of more or less similar folks. Even the rare multiracial or multiclass congregation does not come close to embracing what an eschatological perspective reveals: We preach to the whole communion of saints, to the gathering of Christians of all times, places, races, and circumstances. Eschatologically, preachers in Beverly Hills, whether they know it or not, are preaching also to the saints in Watts and South Los Angeles. Preachers in contemporary America are proclaiming the gospel to those Christians who gave their lives in the persecutions of ancient Rome. Such an understanding increases the stakes, makes us careful about our words, more diligent in our fidelity to the gospel.

Part of the purpose of the Pentecost narrative in Acts 2 is to disclose this eschatological character of congregations gathered in the Spirit for worship. Look, for example, at that list of ethnic types assembled in Jerusalem on that first Pentecost: Parthians, Medes, Elamites, residents of Mesopotamia, and so on (Acts 2:9-11). Many commentators note that this

10. Aukerman, *Reckoning with Apocalypse*, 216.

lengthy list conveys the truth that Jews were in Jerusalem that day from all over the world—east and west, north and south.

That's true, as far as it goes, but it doesn't go nearly far enough. This conglomeration of peoples is not only a diverse and pluralistic gathering of tourists, but it is also a historically impossible collection of folks, save in an eschatological event. Consider the Medes, for instance. They must have had a rather difficult journey to Jerusalem since they would not only have had to travel several hundred miles, but several hundred years as well, Medes having already disappeared from the canvas of history. The same is true evidently of Elamites, who seemed to have wandered over to this Pentecost story not from the Tigris River, where Elamites once lived, but rather from the annals of history and particularly the pages of the Old Testament (see especially Ezra 2:7).

Eschatologically, the congregation at Pentecost is a representative collection of every kind of person who ever lived, anywhere and at any time. Luke's list of nations present at Pentecost is the equivalent of the statement, "You should have been in church Pentecost Sunday. We had a huge number of visitors, some from Montana, others from Arizona and Michigan, not to mention the vanload of Assyrians and the nice little Hittite couple who signed the friendship pad."[11] The same is true of every preaching event.

2. The eschatological character of preaching enables us to take on one of the central false doctrines of our culture: progress. Corporate America may proclaim that "progress is our most important product," but the Christian faith does not believe in progress. It believes in hope. Progress is a product of the "eye," of the potentialities of the present maximized by human effort. Hope is trust in what we cannot produce ourselves. Progress looks for signs of growth; hope looks to the promise of the resurrection. Progress begins to wither under adversity; hope endures even in the face of persecution. As Christopher Lasch has claimed:

> If we distinguish hopefulness from . . . optimism, we can see why [hope] serves us better . . . than a belief in progress. . . . The worst is always what the hopeful are prepared for. . . . Believers in progress . . . though they like to think of themselves as a party of hope, actually have little need of hope, since they have history on their side. [They have] a blind faith that things will somehow work out for the best, [which] furnishes a poor substitute for the disposition to see things through even when they don't.[12]

---

11. Much of this description of Pentecost is drawn from my article "A Night at the Burlesque: Wanderings Through the Pentecost Narrative," *Journal for Preachers* XIV, 4 (Pentecost 1991): 25-31.

12. Christopher Lasch, *The True and Only Heaven: Progress and Its Critics* (New York: Norton, 1991), 81.

---

3. An eschatological perspective allows us to preach the prophetic call for justice not on the basis of guilt, moralism, or some misguided obedience to a principal of political correctness, but on the same basis that the prophets themselves did: a joyful, even festive response to God's inbreaking future. Justice is a dance that people are free to do when they hear the music of God's future being played in the present.

Christian preachers call for the hungry to be fed, for the spirit of peace to prevail over hostility, for justice to be done in the land, for the natural environment to be protected. They do so not just because hunger, warfare, injustice, and environmental disregard are bad, but because they are obsolete. The gospel has promised a world where justice rolls down like the waters and righteousness like an ever-flowing stream. These words are not rhetorical prods to get human society to behave as nobly as it can; they are promises backed up by the trustworthiness of God's character; they are descriptions of what the community of faith genuinely believes will come to be.

A faculty colleague of mine, having arrived at the airport early for a flight to a conference, sat down in one of the waiting areas and passed the time by grading some papers. His seat was directly opposite one of the airport restaurants, and, as he worked, he noticed that the restaurant was empty except for one man, who was sitting idly at one of the tables, his head resting on the tabletop. It was clear from his dress that he was one of the homeless folk who have taken up residence in the airport, and it was clear from his manner that he was not in the restaurant as a paying customer.

A few minutes later, a man who appeared to be the restaurant manager walked firmly and swiftly toward the homeless man. Observing this, my colleague feared that a scene was about to develop as the manager was surely going to toss this street person out of the restaurant. He was surprised, however, to see the manager walk rapidly by the homeless man's table, pausing only long enough to put a hot dog in front of the man. On the way back across the dining area, the manager placed a cup of coffee beside the hot dog.

From one angle of vision, this was a simple act of kindness, giving food to a hungry person. From another perspective, however, an eschatological point of view, it was a radical and joyful act of prophetic civil disobedience. The manager refused to obey the laws of custom, the prevailing rules of the present tense. When he gave the man some food and drink, not stopping to receive praise or to make the man feel like a debtor, he said in essence, "Friend, in a few minutes I am probably going to have to pretend that my main identity is as the manager of a restaurant and that your main identity is as a homeless trespasser, but, at least for a moment, you and I will act now out of the identities that we will surely have in the future of God. Here, brother, welcome to the feast."

In essence, then, it is the duty and the delight of the eschatological preacher to announce the future, to say to the ears of those who will hear what the eye has not yet seen. The Christian preacher calls people to deeper trust in God and more faithful service to the neighbor, not on the basis of human potential and intrinsic good will, but on the basis of God's future, which can be heard already stirring in the present.

Just prior to its 1994 elections, I was doing research in South Africa, just as that complex nation was making its fearful and wonderful turn toward a multiracial democracy. One Sunday evening, I was driving on the freeway into Pretoria. Pretoria is the administrative capital of South Africa, and it is an impressive city of tall office towers, imposing government buildings, and modern universities. As I drew closer to the downtown area, I was astonished to see a small congregation of black Christians, what is called an "indigenous church," worshiping in the little green circle of grass formed by the circular expressway exit ramp.

The contrast could not have been more stark. Here against the skyline of the great governmental city of Pretoria, strong symbol for many of the bitter years of apartheid, was a tiny group of those who had been denied standing in the society. Here, in the shadow of the capital of a nation built on gold and diamonds and ivory, was a poor band of Christians with no building, no pews, no paid clergy, no musical instruments save tambourines. The buildings of Pretoria were glistening glass and bright steel; the worshipers all wore handmade robes of many colors, decorated with cloth crosses sewn across the front. Pretoria stood majestically, the embodiment of the present power. The little flock danced and sang and praised the God of Jesus Christ in the power of the Holy Spirit.

To the eye, it was no contest. The little church held no power and could easily have been crushed by those in control. As I drove by, however, I could hear the chants of praise and the great mirth of those who worshiped in the Spirit. You just had to say that the future belongs to them.

AN INTERVIEW WITH JAMES EARL MASSEY: VETERAN INHABITANT OF THE WORLD WE HOPE FOR[1]

Henry H. Mitchell

Mitchell: James Earl, as you have long known from some of my earlier writings, I have always wondered how on earth you have managed to move so smoothly and effectively in the multicultured worlds of both scholarship and churchmanship. There are probably a lot more people who wonder the same thing. I am delighted that you have consented to let us all have a look. May I start with your roots? Knowing that there have been several ministers in your family tree, may I ask how many, and who?

Massey: Six, actually. My grandfather Collins Townsend; my father, George W. Massey, Sr.; my three older brothers, George, Jr., Raymond, Melvin, and myself.

Mitchell: That fascinates me, of course, because both of my grandfathers were pastors.

Massey: Interestingly, I was the first of the sons to announce my call from God to be a preacher.

Mitchell: Is preaching the specific ministry to which you felt called originally?

Massey: Yes, it was, and so it remains.

Mitchell: What was your age at the time you experienced your call, and what was the setting within which that call happened?

Massey: I was sixteen years old, a student at Cass Technical High School in Detroit, Michigan, at the time of my call. I was in a college prepara-

---

1. This interview was conducted in August 1994, especially for inclusion in this volume.

ory course, majoring in music, with plans to become a classical pianist. I was also taking piano classes at the same time at the Detroit Conservatory of Music.

The call "happened" within me one Sunday morning as I was sitting in church during worship. With my deep love for music, it was my custom to have a musical score with me at all times, so that I could use every spare moment to feed my memory bank and advance my repertoire. That morning I had an album of Chopin preludes and was busy reading through one of them. As the service moved forward, my mind left the score and became engrossed in the depth of the worship. In an almost transfixed state of mind, I heard a Voice insinuating itself in my consciousness, saying, "I want you to preach!" The Voice was strange but settling. The meaning was so forceful, and the bidding was so insistent, that I knew what I would have to do. The Voice was so clear that I have never afterward had reason to question or reinterpret that moment of high insight![2]

I knew that I had been called, but I did wonder how my natural bent toward music making would fit into the new demand God had pressed upon my life. The period of wonderment continued across a year, or longer, but as I yielded myself to be "obedient to the heavenly vision," as Paul once put it, I discovered that music was a creative outlet for my spirit. There are times now when I play Bach chorale preludes in prayer to God. I did know a time, during that first year after being called, when I hungered more for the piano than I was eager for the pulpit. But that hunger was finally disciplined, and my interest in the pulpit became keener than my retreat into music.

Mitchell: I can understand what you are saying about your great love for music. I studied voice and violin, and still sing in choirs whenever I can. But tell me, has your music background influenced your pulpit work? If so, how?

Massey: Indeed it has![3] I have found so much that has been of transfer value from my years as a music student. For one thing, there is the ability to focus attention on a given text, and to search its structure and the flow of meaning it seeks to give. In addition, the discipline of

2. For an earlier published report of Massey's "call story," see "Called While Reading a Score of Chopin," an interview reported in *The Irresistible Urge to Preach: A Collection of African American "Call" Stories,* ed. William H. Myers (Atlanta: Aaron Press, 1992), 230-32. For an interpretation of this call story, see also William Myers, *God's Yes Was Louder Than My No: Rethinking the African-American Call to Ministry* (Grand Rapids: Eerdmans, 1994), esp. 30-31, 49. 3. This circumstance helped to inspire the title of this volume.

3. This circumstance helped to inspire the title of this volume.

memorizing has benefited from a background in music. I used to practice at the piano from five to seven hours a day; I had learned how to "stay put" at the instrument until the score was not only in my mind but in my fingers as well. I afterward used that time in Scripture study, in memorizing passages, so that I gained a firm grasp of the contents of the book from which I would be teaching and preaching. My study of the biblical languages, all three of them, came later, of course, but becoming familiar with the whole Bible at that early stage allowed me to focus attention later on interpreting and applying Scripture wisdom.

There is yet another carryover from my musical past: the importance of taking the text seriously, of being servant to the text and not manipulating it. Just as I honored the musical score as a pianist, taking the composer's work as a proper guide, so also I view the biblical text as central for receiving God's message.

Mitchell: You have referred to your study of the biblical languages. Where did you do your seminary work?

Massey: I received my seminary training and degree from Oberlin Graduate School of Theology, with a concentration in biblical studies, but I went there after graduating with a rich background as a Bible-theology major at Detroit Bible College (later renamed William Tyndale College). With two years of Hebrew as an undergraduate, plus intensive study of New Testament Greek at Wheaton College Graduate School during the summer after I graduated, I was ready for advanced Hebrew and Aramaic and the exegetical course work that filled my schedule when I was admitted at Oberlin.

Mitchell: When and where did your studies begin in communicating that Word in preaching? Who were some of your models?

Massey: I began the serious study of speech and communicating during my last year as a student at Cass Tech, since I then knew that the ministry was to be my future. I did the same while in college, and later, after graduating from Oberlin, while in the pastorate, I did postgraduate courses in communication arts at the University of Michigan.

As for my models, there were four of them. The first was my preacher-father. He impressed me by his ready knowledge and handling of the scriptures when he was preaching. In fact, it was his masterful memorizing of the Bible that challenged me to begin my quest to know "The Book." The second pulpit model who influenced me was Raymond S. Jackson, the pastor who nurtured me during my teenage years. I learned the power and source of pulpit courage by what he modeled. The third model was Howard Thurman, whom I met in 1949 while in college. From Howard Thurman I gained insight into the importance of depth for pulpit work, especially spiritual depth as a witness for God. All three persons just named, my father, Raymond S. Jackson, and Howard Thurman, were African Americans. The fourth preacher whose life and work greatly influenced me differed from them in that he was white. That preacher was George Arthur Buttrick. He impressed me by his skills in sermon development, his provocative handling of a text.

Mitchell: You have mentioned an interesting mix of persons and a rather wide array of reasons why you were impressed by them all. All of this moves me to ask just what were the cultural and socioeconomic characteristics of the home and church environment in which you were reared. Did you start out in white culture as a black person, or did you start out in a black culture and become bicultural on the way?

Massey: I was born into and grew up in a bicultural setting. Our family was lower middle class. Both my father and my mother were devout Christians, and so were my grandparents. Our family life was influenced by two churches, both from the same denominational background and doctrinal emphases. The one congregation met just four blocks from our house, while the other was located in downtown Detroit. It was the "Mother Church" to all the other African American congregations of our group in the metropolitan area. My grandparents, the Reverend Collins Townsend and Amanda Townsend, were two of the "pillars" in the downtown Detroit church, where he had served across many years as the associate pastor to all four distinguished preachers who had filled that pulpit. The "Mother Church," as most people called it, was now predominantly black in membership, a separate group after racial friction blighted the unity a previously interracial congregation had enjoyed in another sector of the city.

The congregation that met in our community was still interracial, however, and it was a rather intimate circle of members. I grew up in its life as one who sensed a God-given tie with all the other members, black and white. Belonging to that fellowship helped me to understand the meaning and application of the unity theme that was so often treated from the pulpit, a theme that was explained as one of the cardinal teachings of the Reformation Movement, of which our church sought to be fully representative. From an early age I was taught, and embraced, the biblical ideal of the unity of believers, on the one hand. On the other, because the majority of our members were black, I knew the impacting quality of black spiritual vitality. There were three white families in our church in those years, and the interaction and intimacy seemed altogether natural. Early on, I saw that what is African American can be in essential working agreement with what is Anglo-Saxon, when both traditions are informed by agape love. I learned that what is best in both traditions always provides a creative context for spiritual vision and social learning.

I took such vision and learning with me as I went to school every day. It lasted with me through my grade school years and companioned me on into high school. In both settings I was in daily touch with whites, always aware of my distinctive differences as a black person. But I was still secure within, because of a sense of worth instilled within me through informed, caring, and patient parents, teachers, neighbors, pastors, and church members.

The principal at our grade school—located just across the street from our house—was white, but he was sensible about being so, which did not make us sensitive to the fact that he was white. In addition, most of the teachers I had for classes were black, which kept a black leadership presence steadily visible.

I am thinking now of one of my grade school teachers, Mr. Coit Cook Ford. He was an able, industrious, concerned and dapper figure. He had the ease of someone at home in his work, and he gave his students a steadying assurance that we mattered to him. I shall never forget the walls of Mr. Ford's classroom, each with a wall-length blackboard. Just above the border line, he had placed photographs of important black leaders for our recognition and emulation. At strategic times during the semester, Mr. Ford called attention to one or more of those pictured leaders, in order to supplement the class lesson. In this way he gave us further insight into American history by treating the life and work of blacks whose stories had not been included in the textbooks we had to use.

As I think back on it all, I see that his treatments of black success stories held me in awe, like what I knew in church or in devotionals at home when listening to passages about Bible characters. In this way I came to know about black heroes and heroines, some of whom Mr. Ford knew or had known personally. With each mention he made concerning them, the hero or heroine stood out from the photoframe a little more, life-sized and legendary, grand models for us younger Negroes (as you well know, we were not calling ourselves "Black" or "African American" in those days).

There is one additional detail I must report about Mr. Ford. He kept us sensible about how achievement happens. Quoting what I later learned were lines from Longfellow's "The Ladder of Saint Augustine," Mr. Ford cautioned us with this wisdom:

The heights by great men reached and kept
Were not attained by sudden flight;
But they, while their companions slept,
Were toiling upward in the night.

These lines still inspire me. They stir my spirit and prod the diligence to which they point. Small wonder, then, that the spirit to strive and the strength to endure is so strong within me. The need to toil "goes with the territory" of being a preacher and living, like Paul, in readiness to preach. This was the conditioning that I underwent through the providence of God, buttressed by such grand human models, some white, some black.

Mitchell: I am impressed with what you recount about your own church group. Your story differs greatly from so many others, who point to denominational failure as a cause for their disillusionment where religion and race are concerned. Tell me more about the Church of God.

Massey: Gladly! As you know, the Church of God (Anderson, Indiana)—we always add that parenthesis to distinguish our group from the many others who use this biblical designation—is a religious communion that is predominantly white in membership. Its origins lie in the late nineteenth century, and it is one of the holiness groups that have continued the tradition of honoring experiential religion, doctrinal purity, evangelistic outreach, and the quest to unify fellow believers. It is also one of the holiness groups from which blacks have not broken away. A part of the reason for this might well lie in the fact that black members of the Church of God (Anderson, Indiana) continue to find the unity emphasis in the church's message so appealing and life within the group sufficiently open and promising.

In 1974 there were nearly 20,000 blacks among a total North American church membership of just above 160,000. By 1980 that number had increased to almost 30,000 black members among a total membership in North America of 179,000 plus. I mention these round figures because they show a steady relationship between blacks and the larger body of Church of God members in the United States. But the figures also show an instructive growth pattern.

Unlike some other church groups whose doctrinal positions accent nonrelational themes, the central theme of our communion is an openly relational one: the unity of believers. Although the social relations within our church group have witnessed the same problems and strains faced by other church bodies, as I admitted in part while reporting what happened to one of our Detroit churches back in 1915, the challenge of our unity ideal, coupled with the demand for experiential religion, has always been present as a factor to prod us toward correction and reform.

Mitchell: So the two worlds of race have been a part of your church story as well. But I am aware of some significant strides your group's story evidences. I speak now about your appointment some years ago, and your subsequent service for several years, as preacher for your denomination's international radio ministry. And there is also your present role as dean of your denomination's graduate School of Theology (Anderson University). How long was your tenure as radio preacher? What was the response of the church to your ministry in that post?

Massey: I am going to answer these questions, but let me first say that my appointments, while significant, were not as signal, racially, within our group as was the election in 1988 of Edward L. Foggs, another black leader among us, to serve as our communion's general secretary, the highest elective office within our church body. He has since been reelected after serving his first five-year term.

I must also point out that another significant appointment preceded the radio ministry to which I was elected by the General Assembly of our church body. During the last seven years of my pastorate at Metropolitan Church of God in Detroit, Michigan, I also served concurrently as campus minister at Anderson University in Anderson, Indiana. I was the university's first campus minister. I was on campus Monday through Friday, and returned to my Detroit pulpit each weekend. A steady, trustworthy staff of local ministers handled the day-to-day needs of the church across the week. I had been pastor of that church for eighteen years before I took on the responsibilities of the campus ministry assignment. So I was blessed by a strong pastoral relationship with the people—nearly a thousand members—when I was invited by Robert H. Reardon, the university president, to join the faculty and administrative staff at Anderson.[4]

I was still serving both the campus and the congregation when the invitation was issued in 1976 for me to become the denomination's radio voice. In accepting that appointment, I resigned from both Metropolitan Church and my campus ministry post. At my leaving, after twenty-four progressive years, there was a unanimous vote by the

---

4. For numerous references to the ministry of Dr. Massey at Anderson University, see the published history of the university, *Guide of Soul and Mind*, by Barry L. Callen (Anderson, Ind.: Anderson University and Warner Press, 1992).

church in response to a resolution from the church council that I be made Pastor-at-Large. This encouraged me greatly. The university also asked me to continue teaching as my new schedule would allow.

The appointment as preacher on our international radio broadcast meant that I was the radio spokesperson for our communion. The fact that a black man would thus represent a majority-white religious fellowship was not a problem to the Mass Communications Board, which presented my name for ratification to the General Assembly. However, there were a few whites to whom that board's plan for the future was sufficiently strange and unsettling that they reacted with obvious reticence or cold regard initially. The climate surrounding the vote taken on me during the assembly meeting in 1976 was carefully democratic, and some whites who were from regions where blacks were not accorded equal opportunities in relation to whites had to yield their questions, fears, and preferences when the majority of delegates approved me.

Although I had the majority backing me, I also knew that there were some pockets of people among us within which I would need to move, helping them to adjust to the realities that Christian unity makes possible. My service as speaker for the church, and as a guest within churches across the land, proved effective, and I continued in that post across six years. It was a fruitful and productive period for the broadcast ministry. Early in my fourth year, I decided that I would not accept another term because I wanted to go back into the classroom, and I was longing for more time to do the research and writing to which I had been accustomed as a senior pastor responsible for preaching, and as a teaching professor. Later, after I announced that I would not be available to serve another term as our communion's radio speaker, President Reardon asked me to return full-time to the university's School of Theology as professor of New Testament and Preaching. I did.

Mitchell: When, and why, did you leave to go to Tuskegee? Did your acceptance of a post at that predominantly black university have anything to do with race concerns?

Massey: I left Anderson and went to Tuskegee University in July 1984. No, my leaving was not in response to any problems at Anderson of a racial nature. My move to Tuskegee was the result of a call from the president there, inviting me to become Dean of the Chapel and University Professor of Religion and Society. I had been a guest preacher there in 1983. At that time President Payton and I had talked at length about his vision and concerns for the famed University Chapel and its historic ministry. The incumbent chaplain was about to retire, and President Payton was eager to enhance the religious tradition at the school by instituting a newly structured arrangement for campus ministry that would match the growing needs of an ever-expanding school.

I was not surprised, then, when in February 1984, he telephoned to inform me that the search committee had voted unanimously that I be asked to become dean at the retirement of the incumbent chaplain. Dr. Payton then stated his own desire that I take it. You know that I did, and that period of service was one of the most pleasurable and meaningful in my entire span of ministry.

When the news broke that I was leaving Anderson to go to Tuskegee, many ministers across the Church of God voiced their surprise. Some black pastors thought I was leaving because of some disappointment or mistreatment on the Anderson campus. I informed those who asked me that such was not the case. In all my dealings with President Robert A. Nicholson, and with former President Robert H. Reardon, I could not have had a better relationship nor had I suffered at all in my relationships with other faculty members. Interestingly, when Reardon learned about my call to Tuskegee, he came to me, and with a gleam of pride in his eyes, he commented, "Now that is a premier institution!" Our subsequent conversation about how I would be missed on the Anderson campus did not blunt his concern to show his admiration for where I would be going to serve.

Neither Reardon nor Nicholson (then college dean) asked why I was leaving. Both of them knew that I had always followed an inner guidance. That guidance had brought me to Anderson University in 1969, when I began service as the school's first campus minister; in 1984 that guidance was taking me in another direction. I was grateful for their trust in my walk with the Lord.

Having said all that, I readily admit that in going to serve at Tuskegee University I knew I was being privileged to minister at a strategic educational center among historically black colleges and universities. In going there, I moved with purpose into a major center of black education and into the African American heritage in a deeper way. More important, Gwendolyn, my wife, and I felt assured that God was being honored in our going there to serve. The years that·followed strongly confirmed the wisdom and timeliness of our choice.

From the start I gave myself with intensity to the campus ministry there. I focused all my energies on the new role, and once fully into the new pattern I felt quite fulfilled, especially in my work as preacher to the university. I felt that I had made my final vocational move.

Interestingly, my work at Tuskegee brought me into closer relations with white members in churches of the South! Never had I enjoyed such widened windows of opportunity among white Southerners. I was especially gladdened when many of my former students at Anderson School of Theology, now settled into their work as pastors in that region, sought me out for counsel. They opened themselves to my interest and assistance, and they opened the pulpits of their churches to me. Busy each Sunday morning in the chapel pulpit, I could not accept all of the many invitations to preach in the pulpits opened to me, but I was grateful that ties established earlier in Anderson were still being honored, and for deeper reasons.

When I went to Tuskegee in 1984, at least ten percent of the student body was international, representing over forty different countries. I liked the international flavor that was present in nearly every worship service. In the act of delivering a sermon, I was, in a sense, "going into all the world, preaching the gospel" every Sunday morning. I felt a stronger sense of mission as a preacher who, by my message, was touching so much of the known world. Situated as I was at the center of campus life as the university minister, it was my joyful responsibility and privilege to think through and share the message and implications of the Christian faith not only for "the Chapel family," as we referred to ourselves as regular worshipers, but with the larger community of churches and community leaders as well.

The area pastors and ministers looked to me as their resident theologian; some of them came to the early morning chapel service to hear me preach, before rushing out to fill their own pulpits at the traditional eleven o'clock hour. I did not take my post and privilege lightly. Never have I so enjoyed preparing to preach, and then standing up to preach! It was stimulating and encouraging to watch the students, staff personnel, and faculty members experience rational, moral, and spiritual change through sound religious teaching and vital fellowship. I had the added pleasure of providing counsel for several students who experienced a call to ministry through my preaching and presence. I helped some of them in their choice of a seminary and later saw some of them graduate and enter upon their own fields of service.

Mitchell: With all of that taking place under your leadership at the Tuskegee Chapel, why on earth did you break that pace and return to Anderson?

Massey: Your question is fair, and timely. Many persons at Tuskegee asked me that when the news broke that I would be leaving, and even since I have been gone some have asked that when I have returned to be guest preacher at the chapel there.

To put it plainly and quickly, my answer again involves "sensed guidance." I returned to Anderson because, after praying steadily and seriously about the request from the president and the search committee for my services at the seminary as its dean, I finally sensed a "tug" upon my heart to accept that duty. I had been so sure that I was already where I needed to be—and wanted to be—until time to retire. But, as someone once put it, if you talk to God, be willing to change your mind and your plans.

The decision to return to Anderson School of Theology as its dean was perhaps the hardest decision I have ever made during my ministry, but then and now the assurance has been mine that the move was in obedience to a higher will. Even so, in leaving the Tuskegee University Chapel scene, Gwendolyn and I both "died a little." Our sense of loss was somewhat relieved when, in June 1989, during the General Assembly vote on the seminary deanship, I was duly and strongly ratified by a ninety-five percent majority of the delegates.

Mitchell: Having myself served as dean at Virginia Union University's School of Theology, I am tempted to ask what your full and informed opinion is of the vocation of a dean. But I am going to leave that out.

Massey: You don't have to do that. Actually, I view administrative responsibilities as a necessary work, and I feel privileged to assist faculty in their work of readying students for ministry. As you well know, Paul included "forms of leadership" (1 Cor. 12:28), or administration, in his listing of the spiritual gifts.

Mitchell: Yes, I know, but so often being an administrator places one in a vulnerable position, with little opportunity for being thanked or duly appreciated for what one does.

James Earl, your pulpit prowess and exemplary teaching have made you an acknowledged, well-received leader in the field, and leading seminaries have had you do major lectureships on preaching. I marvel that Yale has never sought you to do the Lyman Beecher Lectures on Preaching at the Divinity School. Or have you been asked?

Massey: No, I have not been invited to serve that lectureship at Yale, but I am pleased that two of our mutual friends, who followed you in giving those lectures, did quote from my written work about preaching while treating their themes. Kelly Miller Smith quoted from my *Designing the Sermon* during his Beecher Lectures in 1983.[5] In 1986, James A. Forbes, Jr., commented at length in one of his Beecher Lec-

---

5. See Kelly Miller Smith, *Social Crisis Preaching: The Lyman Beecher Lectures, 1983* (Macon: Mercer University Press, 1984), esp. 82ff.

tures about my concept of "anointing," on which I wrote in the last chapter of my book *The Sermon in Perspective*.[6] How well I remember the evening I was in New York and sat with Jim in the kitchen of his apartment on campus, talking on that subject. He was still homiletics professor at Union then, and we discussed the concept of anointing in great detail. I don't know if Forbes had been scheduled as yet as a future Beecher Lecturer, but at the time we talked he did share his joy in having found what I had written on the subject of anointing as applied to the preaching task. I am glad that my treatment was of help as he shaped the substance and scope of his lectures. I understand that his lectures were well received.

Incidentally, I am quite familiar with the course of the lectureship, and am most fortunate in that I possess a near-complete set of the published lectures. I am missing only five from the set, and I am constantly on the lookout, seeking to locate those five. Having studied the lectureship across so many years—and having personally known many of those who have been the lecturers during the last twenty years, I know where some of the gaps are that need to be filled by future lecturers. I hope this does not appear to be presumptuous on my part, but if invited to give the Beecher Lectures, I would not lack a point of interest or need toward which the lectures should be focused.

Mitchell: Dare I ask what some of those gaps are?

Massey: This is not the time to volunteer a list, but I will share with you the fact that a publisher has asked me to prepare a new, updated assessment of that lectureship. As you well know, the survey and appreciation Edgar DeWitt Jones wrote and published under the title *The Royalty of the Pulpit* came out in 1951, and so much about preaching has changed since the eighty-year period treated in his illuminating survey. The request has come to me, and I want to honor it, but present administrative duties have dictated that even such a worthy project must wait.

Mitchell: I do hope that you will set apart the time for this. A fresh survey and assessment of the Beecher Lectureship is certainly necessary and timely.

Let me ask another question with respect to homiletics. As a competent practitioner of the African American approach to preaching, how do you draw from that tradition while teaching homiletics to the white students who fill your classes? What do you hold forth as the major emphases within that tradition?

---

6. See James A. Forbes, Jr., *The Holy Spirit and Preaching: The Lyman Beecher Lectures, 1986* (Nashville: Abingdon Press, 1989), 53-55.

Massey: I am glad that you asked this question, because it allows me to point out how I seek to apply my principle of a bicultural approach as I teach seminarians about our preaching task. In addition to course work on the general history of preaching, together with acknowledgment of styles of delivery, I always expand the range of lectures and assigned readings to include the abundant data from the strongest preaching traditions, including the black pulpit. The inclusion of such additional data has been made standard within the discipline wherever I have taught. This has also demanded the gathering of substantial resources for use in daily classroom instruction, as well as supportive library holdings of rich materials on noted African American preachers (i.e., autobiographical and biographical works, taped and printed sermons, and other instructive memorabilia).

As for the emphases drawn from within the black preaching tradition, I tend to stress five as essential for effectiveness in any setting, bicultural or otherwise. (1) The first emphasis is on the functionality of the sermon—an emphasis on the end or purpose of the sermon. (2) The second emphasis is the encouragement of festivity, celebration in the worship of God. Festivity allows the sermon to be spirited instead of stilted; this emphasis, so germane to the African American church pulpit experience, can help white students as well, because it offers a positive clue about being one's full self—with emotions included—as a spokesperson for God. (3) A third emphasis within our black preaching tradition upon which I draw in teaching is the promotion of community through the sermon. I explain to all my students that preaching must unify the gathered congregation; it must affirm and undergird each worshiper, generating vision, yes, but also sharing. (4) A fourth element that I emphasize is the necessity for radical proclamation—the imperative for a free and authoritative stance in the sermon as God's messenger. (5) And fifth, I stress the importance of the sermon's producing a climax of impression from being heard. It is the climax of impression that helps the hearer feel the touch of the Beyond.

Drawing thus upon the black preaching tradition, I seek to flavor my teaching of homiletics. In teaching, I am committed to a bicultural approach, always seeking a two-way acculturation as most germane for classrooms filled with persons whose horizons need to be expanded, and whose understandings need to include a wider range of facts, methods, approaches, and groups.

As I see it, the homiletics professor must be concerned to inculcate the principles of preaching, as one aim, and to unlock the personal gifts of the preacher as the other. Unlocking the potential of any preacher, whether white, black, or otherwise, demands that attention be given to that student's process, expectations, and abilities, not in strict relation to the ideals of the majority culture and its settings, but without failing to take these into account. The best of "both worlds," both preaching cultures, should be held to view. The stress should be placed not upon what preaching style or tradition is the best, but upon how to capture the best of what is offered in other traditions in the quest to be more effective both within and beyond one's own.

Our beloved Gardner C. Taylor is a grand example of a biculturally conditioned preacher. So were the late Howard Thurman and Kelly Miller Smith, Sr. Because of their bicultural approach in preaching, each one of these pulpit masters was equally at home in any pulpit, whether witnessing from a black pulpit or standing before a white or mixed congregation. All three excelled because within their pulpit work they wedded the best from more than one preaching tradition. This is what I seek to help my homiletics students achieve.

Mitchell: I applaud that, as my own teaching approach attests, and I can see how your bicultural background has played such a role in shaping your approach and point of view. I must confess, however, that when I read your first books about preaching, I wondered whether you started out in a white cultural setting, or if you started in a black setting and became bicultural.

Massey: I recall that sense of wonderment showing itself in a review you kindly prepared of two of my preaching books for our guild's *Homiletic* journal. I believe it was the first volume.[7] I recall that while you commended each of the two books being reviewed, *The Responsible Pulpit* (1974) and *The Sermon in Perspective* (1976), for which I remain grateful, you did clearly state your hope that in any future treatments of the subject I would deal more in depth with the black preaching tradition, "with which he is unashamedly familiar." You would have little reason to remember that review, but I do. Many of us hold you in high regard and deeply appreciate your pioneering work in the study of black preaching. Given your own detailed treatment of the subject, I have felt no compelling need to plow ground you have ably covered. Instead, my concern has been to share with the wider church the homiletical emphases we both love and teach. This approach has been vital and valuable.

Mitchell: Now, at last, I understand your motivation. So, it was a conscious decision on your part not to major in black homiletics?

---

7. See *Homiletic: A Review of Publications in Religious Communication*, I (1976), listings 9 and 10.

Massey: Yes, it was. I also remember a published comment that appeared about me in a survey of recent studies on black preaching, which you prepared for a later issue of *Homiletic*. After making mention of one of my books, you paid me a kind of "back-handed" compliment when you suggested that my book showed "how literate and creative a Black preacher can be within the bounds of the White tradition, since he has very little to say about the black church tradition."[8]

Working as I have done "within the white tradition," as you put it, I consciously chose an approach by which our black preaching particularity could be taught, modeled, assessed, and, hopefully, adopted. To this end it was wiser to treat our pulpit particularities within the wider context of preaching approaches. With me it has never been a matter of living at the extreme of no recognition of my black heritage or the opposite extreme of emphasizing only the black heritage. My concern has been, rather, to honor and live out of my heritage while engaged, as teacher, with others who bring into the circle of life and learning the best from their own heritage. In this way, all of us remain challenged and called into a larger frame of reference. As I look back on my efforts and their results across these years, I remain convinced that my bicultural approach has helped me to be reasonable, realistic, relational, and effective.

Mitchell: Listening to you, after watching your life and career, I am convinced that your home background and religious ideals have been something fundamental to your being.

Massey: Indeed, they have. The insights and emphases of the Church of God (Anderson, Indiana), my "denominational home," to use your expression, have been of inestimable value to me in my heart concern to be genuinely related in the problematic social settings that make up America. I have dared to trust the creative power and possibilities of agape love, and I have found that it is possible to commit to heart and mind a way of relating that promotes unity and trust rather than hate and divisiveness. This is one of several reasons why I have continued in ministry as a member of the Church of God movement.

I recall reading a statement Elton Trueblood wrote about how he, a Quaker, settled the question of what church group would be his denominational home base. Once out of divinity school, Trueblood received several invitations to engage in pastoral work. Bishop Charles Slattery, of the Episcopal Church, volunteered to welcome him into that church body, assuring the young Trueblood that he would be

---

8. See *Homiletic IV* (1979), 9.

warmly welcomed into the group if he were to turn in that direction. Trueblood reported the bishop's suggestion to his wife, who expressed rather firmly her conviction that he should remain a Quaker, not especially because Quakers had a monopoly on any truth, but because with that background and relation he could be more effective in the world.

It was Trueblood's testimony after many years that he never regretted remaining a Quaker, because for him it opened more doors than it closed.[9] As for me, it is my testimony that, given its emphasis on unity and holiness, remaining with the Church of God movement has granted me the freedom to enter more doors than would have been possible for me as an African American otherwise. The relational imperative found in the teachings of Jesus and heralded in the unity theme on which I was reared kept me open to relate and share, despite all the costs and periodic disappointments involved in doing so.

Mitchell: Well, James Earl, I certainly want to thank you for this candid, fascinating sharing of yourself. And I am sure that I am already speaking for those who will read these words. In very truth, you have demonstrated that an African American with rare gifts and under rare circumstances and in the providence of God can live a relatively color-blind existence. Few if any of our ethnic brothers and sisters have transcended as many boundaries as you have, and with such grace. Or, to use another metaphor, few have walked with such grace through a minefield of so many subtle discriminations.

What you have illustrated, across the board, places in the concrete worlds of church, denomination, and the theological academy an ideal otherwise only abstract for all too many. You have mastered Euro-American culture and made so rich a contribution that your white colleagues were made at ease and forgot to consider your race. Thus you have lived all your days in an almost raceless world that most of us have talked about and hoped for, but never have seen. An awareness of your rare experience is essential to any comprehensive understanding of race and culture in the Christian churches of the United States.

I wish I could leave it at this point, but I am convinced that I dare not. African Americans especially must know that what you have accomplished is not to be thought of as able to be replicated by human effort. Nor should anyone even try to walk the same path without comparable providential preparations. The odds against such are too great; the kingdom hasn't come yet, not even in the Church of

---

9. See Elton Trueblood, *While It Is Day: An Autobiography* (New York: Harper & Row, 1974), 38.

God (Anderson, Indiana). They still have an all African American conference ground in Pennsylvania, about which I have heard, and lots of black members have had less than comparable experiences to yours at the membership base, as opposed to the top leadership. Nevertheless, it has been a marvelous experience to walk with you through these years, and all of us will be enriched and inspired by your gift of yourself. May God bless and continue to use you in your retirement years.

AN APPRECIATION OF
JAMES EARL MASSEY

Michael Duduit

A s editor of *Preaching* magazine, I have the wonderful opportunity to hear many of the finest preachers of our day. Frequently I am asked to provide a list of the "best" preachers in America. The list varies from year to year, but one name appears every time: James Earl Massey.

Massey is not the best-known preacher among the general public, although his gifts are equal to or greater than most of those who have become widely known through television, radio, or other media. Many preachers know him through his several books, but I have advised him to use his retirement years to write even more so that future generations can benefit from his gifts and insight.[1]

But when it comes time to stand in the pulpit, James Earl Massey is in his element, a man upon whom the Holy Spirit rests and through whom the gospel of Jesus Christ is proclaimed with boldness and power.

Massey has been blessed by God with a remarkable combination of gifts. He is an accomplished pianist, having had plans for a career on the concert stage until God intervened and gave him a new and higher platform from which to work. He is a talented educator who brings to the classroom both knowledge of his subjects (New Testament and homi-

---

1. A bibliography of James Earl Massey's published works is found at the back of this book. In the most recent years, because of his love of teaching and of nurturing young pastors, he has given himself to the deanship of the School of Theology of Anderson University. This has slowed the pace of his writing ministry. However, at least two other books of his are coming soon, including a much-anticipated autobiography.

letics) and a concern for students. He is an able administrator whose leadership of the School of Theology at Anderson University has brought renewed energy and achievement to that institution.

Beyond all of these, however, Massey is first and foremost a preacher of the Word. As he steps into the pulpit and begins to unfold the Scripture, his listeners sense that they are in the presence of one who has not only studied the Word, but also has made it a part of his life. There is in Massey a tenderness, a graciousness, and a sincerity that give evidence of his walk with Christ.

Massey is not only an able practitioner of the preaching craft, but he also is a student and scholar of homiletics. He is widely respected by his peers in the academy. They recognize his unique gifts and presence.

As a teacher, Massey's talents are not limited to the classroom. He has shared his time and attention with countless young pastors who have been blessed to consider him both friend and mentor. He has a generous spirit and has given of himself freely to help new generations of preachers. He has made a significant impact on the lives of thousands upon thousands of Christian believers through his influence on the life and ministry of their pastors.

Perhaps nothing expresses my own admiration for James Earl Massey so much as his frequent participation as a featured speaker for the National Conference on Preaching, which I direct. When he has been available, I have scheduled him to present the opening keynote address for the conference, knowing that he will set the proper tone and level of quality for the entire event. I also arrange for him to preach the final sermon, which closes the conference, knowing that he will exalt Christ, honor the Word, and offer a note of encouragement to his fellow pastors.

Like so many others whom he has assisted and encouraged, I am blessed to call James Earl Massey a friend and brother. For all that he has contributed to the church and its ministry, we owe him a debt of gratitude.

AN APPRECIATION OF JAMES EARL MASSEY

Calvin S. Morris

J ames Earl Massey was a significant presence in my life before we ever met. The year was 1967. Reverend Mrs. Willie Taplin Barrow spoke to me about James, her close brother in the faith. Her words about him were ones of deep affection, admiration, and nearly awe. She explained, in her powerfully direct and unabashed fashion, that Massey is an individual of the highest intellect, a preacher of rare ability, a prolific author, a renowned teacher, a college chaplain, a successful urban pastor, yea, a veritable prince of their movement, the Church of God (Anderson, Indiana).

Many have been the highly successful African American pastors in the Church of God (Anderson, Indiana), such as Willie's pastors and mine at the time, the Reverends Mr. Claude and Mrs. Addie Wyatt of the Vernon Park Church of God in Chicago. But few, if any, were said to combine, as did James Earl Massey, the shepherding acumen and scholarly prowess. He was said to model in his person the combination of head and heart about which Howard Thurman would write near the end of his distinguished and profoundly inspiring life. Since I had a particularly intellectual bent, according to Willie, she surmised that I would benefit from, and find amenable in my spirit, meeting and getting to know Dr. Massey. She was absolutely correct!

Massey came to preach at Vernon Park for a special day in 1968. I remember observing a man of medium height, slight of build, comfortably handsome, elegant in appearance and presence, velvet of voice and articulation, and brilliant in his crafting of sermonic discourse. His sermon theme on that occasion, so artfully designed, was Christian obedience. At a meal later that day in the Wyatt home, I had the temerity to take issue with him on some aspects of his message. What, for instance, about the servile implications of the word *obedience* for a people whose forebears had not too long ago been slaves admonished by their captors to obey their masters? Massey listened quietly, not defensively, but penetratingly.

My somewhat sophomoric question was honored with caring, clarity, and grace. Said Massey, in part, as I now recall: "True obedience to God in Christ surely would have undermined any believer's assumption that one group of human beings could legitimately hold another in bondage. True obedience sees God alone as sovereign and humankind as related creatures."

I recall that, during the broad-ranging discussion that followed, Massey's eyes sparkled and danced. Humor and joy lurked behind his ecclesiastical and intellectual demeanor. One only has to be a recipient of his laughter, a sound that seems to erupt from some inner volcanic chamber of heart and soul, to recognize a man who loves life and people.

For more than twenty-five years now, during his many travels, James Earl Massey has called me from many airports in the United States to check on the condition of my soul, my vocational challenges, and my children. He also has accompanied me in the sorrowing of my days. During my divorce many years ago; after the death of Clyde and Willie's son, Keith, in 1983; and following the recent death of my youngest daughter, Rachel, James has been a source of loving and faithful support. He has been present in our lives in season and out of season, sorrowing and rejoicing with us.

Some of my most wondrously sublime moments of sharing with Massey have occurred during our periodic opportunities to break bread together. Over good food and warm fellowship, we have discussed many subjects of theology, history, preaching, biblical scholarship, pastoral theology, the writings of Howard Thurman, higher education, music, art, and poetry. James Earl Massey is truly a renaissance man in every way. Often I have wondered how an individual so catholic in his living, so open to the world, could have survived, yes, even flourished in cultural and church environments that are sometimes narrow and provincial in outlook. This is one of the mysteries of the man!

I suspect that the signal place of James Earl Massey in the academy and in the church has been maintained through the integrity of his being and living. He has sought to live the life about which he has taught, preached, and written. This he has done, leaning on the Lord, with elegance, eloquence, and grace.

AN APPRECIATION OF JAMES EARL MASSEY

Robert H. Reardon

I t is a pleasure and honor to write a few words about my friend Dr. James Earl Massey and to reflect on the remarkable impact of his life across many years. Although we both sat at the feet of Clarence Tucker Craig, Walter Marshall Horton, and Herbert May at Oberlin's Graduate School of Theology, we did not come to know each other until he came from his post at the great Metropolitan Church of God in Detroit to speak in chapel at Anderson College in the 1950s.

My introduction of Massey to the 1,200 college students was a source of amusement to them and an embarrassment to me. Instead of presenting James Earl Massey, I presented Raymond Massey, the star of stage and films. This occasioned quite a rumble in the audience. Massey began his sermon by saying, "I observe that your president is much more conversant with the world of the theater than with the world of the church." He got a big laugh at my expense and, of course, endeared himself to the students.

I shall not forget, however, the twenty minutes that followed as his message began to grip the audience. Slowly students accustomed to studying during chapel began to put down their books and look up attentively. They found themselves being carried along by this intense young expositor of the Word. *Here,* I said to myself, *is a man who could make a profound impact on the campus if we could entice him to come.*

I shall forever be grateful to the members of the Metropolitan Church for releasing him with their blessing and grace to join the faculty of Anderson College (now University) and become our campus minister in 1969. Massey arrived at Anderson when the storms of campus unrest were nearing their worst. It was a time of rancor and rebellion against the government, the police, the draft, the church, education, and traditional values.

Late one night I, as campus president, was sitting on the floor of the student lounge in Smith Hall doing my best to discuss what students had on their minds. One young man, deeply moved, spoke up. "Do you know what would help me?" he asked. "I need some adults I can really believe in." During Massey's years as campus minister, college teacher, and then seminary dean, such students found someone unafraid to speak the word of truth, superbly prepared in pulpit and classroom, compassionate and tender hearted with the troubled student, warm, approachable, affirming. What a gift to us all. He was and still is someone to believe in.

Among Massey's many gifts is his ability at the piano. Many encouraged him early on to prepare for the concert stage and follow his idol Claudio Arrau, whose records he often brought to my office or house. But music was not his first love. The great Arthur Rubinstein was once asked in an interview what his interests were. He replied, "I don't have interests; I only have passions."

Preaching has been Massey's passion—to study it, write about it, teach it, but most of all to do it. And he has done it superbly well in churches large and small, in chapels, on the mission field, and on radio and television. In an age when preaching has become marginalized in the eyes of many seminary faculties, and often contemptible or at least irrelevant in the public eye, Massey has stood as a giant among us. He has, by example, shown several generations what excellence in preaching can be. Along with biblical context and exposition, empowered by the Holy Spirit, he has shown us what God can do through preaching to herald the gospel of Jesus Christ and to build up the church. This is not lost on young people considering their call to the ministry.

In our Lord Jesus Christ we find two unusual characteristics combined. They are strength and sweetness. I find both of these in James Earl Massey, and also in Gwendolyn, his wonderful wife of many years. May God continue to use them as they now move on to a different stage, always sharing heaven's music.

SELECT BIBLIOGRAPHY: PUBLISHED WORKS OF JAMES EARL MASSEY*

I. Books

1955. *The Growth of the Soul: Meditations on Spiritual Meaning and Behavior.* Printed privately. 36 pages.

1957. *An Introduction to the Negro Churches in the Church of God Reformation Movement.* New York: Shining Light Survey Press. 70 pages.

1960. *When Thou Prayest: An Interpretation of Christian Prayer According to the Teachings of Jesus.* Anderson, Ind.: Warner Press. 64 pages. Second edition, 1978.

1961. *The Worshiping Church: A Guide to the Experience of Worship.* Anderson, Ind.: Warner Press. 106 pages.

1967. *Raymond S. Jackson: A Portrait.* Anderson, Ind.: Church Service Printing/Warner Press. 96 pages.

1970. *The Soul Under Siege: A Fresh Look at Christian Experience.* Anderson, Ind.: Warner Press. 110 pages. Second edition, Francis Asbury Press/Zondervan, 1987.

1972. *The Hidden Disciplines.* Anderson, Ind.: Warner Press. 120 pages. Revised edition, *Spiritual Disciplines,* Francis Asbury Press/Zondervan, 1985.

1974. *The Responsible Pulpit.* Anderson, Ind.: Warner Press. 115 pages.

1976. *The Sermon in Perspective: A Study of Communication and Charisma.* Grand Rapids: Baker Book House. 116 pages.

1979. *Concerning Christian Unity: A Study of the Relational Imperative of Agape Love.* Anderson, Ind.: Warner Press. 140 pages.

---

*Compiled by Daniel Williams, University Archivist, Tuskegee University, and Barry L. Callen.

1979. *Christian Brotherhood Hour Study Bible.* Editor. Nashville: Thomas Nelson Publishers.

1980. *Designing the Sermon: Order and Movement in Preaching.* Nashville: Abingdon Press. 127 pages.

1982. *Interpreting God's Word for Today: An Inquiry into Hermeneutics from a Biblical-Theological Perspective.* Co-editor with Wayne McCown. Wesleyan Theological Perspectives Series, Vol. 2. Anderson, Ind.: Warner Press. 270 pages.

1984. *Educating for Service: Essays in Honor of Robert H. Reardon.* Editor. Anderson, Ind.: Warner Press. 244 pages.

1988. *The Bridge Between: A Centennial History of Campus Ministry at Tuskegee University, 1888–1988.* Tuskegee: Tuskegee University Press. 120 pages.

Forthcoming. *Preaching from Hebrews: Hermeneutic and Homiletic Insights.* Grand Rapids: Zondervan. 288 pages.

Forthcoming. *African-Americans and the Church of God: Aspects of a Social History.* Anderson, Ind.: Warner Press.

Forthcoming. *Aspects of My Pilgrimage: An Autobiography.*

II. Selections from Contributions to Composite Works

1970. "The Face of Jesus." In *The Church of God in Black Perspective: Proceedings of the Caucus of Black Churchmen in the Church of God.* Edited by Ronald Fowler. New York: Shining Light Survey Press. Pages 115-122.

1977. "Teaching Homiletics to Black Seminarians: Some Essential Methods." In *The Teaching of Preaching.* American Academy of Homiletics, for annual meeting at Princeton Theological Seminary.

1982. "The Preacher's Rhetoric." In *A Celebration of Ministry: Essays in Honor of Frank Bateman Stanger.* Edited by Kenneth Cain Kinghorn. Wilmore, Ky.: Francis Asbury Publishing Company. Pages 88-99.

1982. "Hermeneutics and Pulpit Work." In *Interpreting God's Word for Today: An Inquiry into Hermeneutics from a Biblical Theological Perspective.* Wesleyan Theological Perspectives series, Vol. II. Edited by Wayne C. McCown and James Earl Massey. Anderson, Ind.: Warner Press. Pages 249-64.

1983. "Thurman's Preaching: Substance and Style." In *God and Human Freedom: A Festschrift in Honor of Howard Thurman.* Edited by Henry J. Young. Richmond, Ind.: Friends United Press. Pages 110-21.

1983. "Temples of the Spirit." In *Shalom: Essays in Honor of Charles G. Shaw.* Edited by Eugene J. Mayhew. Farmington Hills, Mich.: William Tyndale College. Pages 73-84.

1983. "Preaching from Hebrews and the General Epistles." In *Biblical Preaching: An Expositor's Treasury.* Edited by James W. Cox. Philadelphia: Westminster Press. Pages 327-51.

1984. "On Being a Preacher." In *Educating for Service: Essays in Honor of Robert H. Reardon.* Edited by James Earl Massey. Anderson, Ind.: Warner Press. Pages 187-99.

1986. "The Coloring of America." In *Into the Next Century: Trends Facing the*

Church. Edited by Terry Muck. A Christianity Today Institute Supplement. Pages 10-11.

1987. "The Black Contribution to Evangelicalism." In *Evangelicalism: Surviving Its Success.* Edited by David A. Fraser. Princeton: Princeton University Press. Pages 50-58.

1988. "Culture but Without Color." In *Evangelizing Blacks.* Edited by Glenn C. Smith. Wheaton: Tyndale House Publishers. Pages 187-95. Published for the Paulist National Catholic Evangelization Association, Washington, D.C.

1990. "Ministerial Authority in Biblical Perspective." In *Listening to the Word of God: A Tribute to Dr. Boyce W. Blackwelder.* Edited by Barry L. Callen. Anderson, Ind.: Anderson University and Warner Press. Pages 153-62.

1992. "An African-American Model." In *Hermeneutics for Preaching: Approaches to Contemporary Interpretations of Scripture.* Edited by Raymond Bailey. Nashville: Broadman Press. Pages 135-59.

1992. "Application in the Sermon." In *A Handbook of Contemporary Preaching.* Edited by Michael Duduit. Nashville: Broadman Press. Pages 209-14.

1994. "Reading the Bible from Particular Social Locations: An Introduction." In *The New Interpreter's Bible,* Vol. 1. Nashville: Abingdon Press. Pages 150-53.

1994. "Reading the Bible as African Americans." In *The New Interpreter's Bible,* Vol. 1. Nashville: Abingdon Press. Pages 154-60.

1994. "Preaching Truth in an Age of Doubt." In *The Abingdon Preaching Annual 1995.* Compiled and edited by Michael Duduit. Nashville: Abingdon Press. Pages 25-30.

III. Selections from Articles in Scholarly Journals

1969. "Christian Theology and Social Experience," *The Covenant Quarterly* (August): 26-36.

1971. "Christian Theology and the Social Experience of Being Black," *Christian Scholar's Review* 1:3 (Spring): 207-16.

1972. "Howard Thurman and Rufus M. Jones, Two Mystics," *Journal of Negro History* LVII:2 (April): 190-95.

1975. "Semantics and Holiness: A Study in Holiness Texts' Functions," *Wesleyan Theological Journal* 10 (Spring): 60-69.

1977-78. "Howard Thurman and Olive Schreiner on the Unity of All Life: A Bibliographical Essay," *The Journal of Religious Thought* XXXIV:2 (Fall-Winter): 29-33.

1988. "On Being a Preacher," *Covenant Quarterly* (February): 3-11.

1988. "Planning for Worship at The Tuskegee Chapel," *Review and Expositor* (Winter): 71-78.

1988. "The Dream of Community," *The Princeton Seminary Bulletin* IX:3, 211-12.

1993. "Hermeneutics for Preaching," *Review and Expositor* 90:3 (Summer): 359-69.

IV. General Writings

More than five hundred articles, sermons, and book reviews by Dr. James Earl Massey have been published in various church and parachurch magazines.

V. Editorships

1960–77, 1984–93. Contributing Editor, *Vital Christianity,* published by Warner Press.

1968–69. Editorial Advisor, Tyndale House Publishers.

1973–77. Editorial Board Member, *Christian Scholar's Review.*

1980–present. Charter Member, Editorial Advisory Board, *Leadership* magazine (publication of *Christianity Today*).

1987–present. Contributing Editor, *Preaching* magazine.

1988. Contributing Editor, *Best Sermons I.* Edited by James W. Cox. San Francisco: Harper & Row.

1988. Member, Board of Reference, *Religious Book Journal,* Minister's Personal Library.

1990. Contributing Editor and Member, Board of Judges, *Best Sermons III.* Edited by James W. Cox. San Francisco: Harper & Row.

1990–present. Member, Editorial Board, *The New Interpreter's Bible* series. Nashville: Abingdon Press.

1993–94. Corresponding Editor, *Christianity Today.*

1994–present. Senior Editor, *Christianity Today.*